P9-CCS-877

The Supreme Court Yearbook

1990-1991

KF
8742
.S95
1990-
1991

The Supreme Court Yearbook
1990-1991

Joan Biskupic

Congressional Quarterly Inc.
Washington, D.C.

JAN 28 1992

Congressional Quarterly Inc.

Congressional Quarterly Inc., an editorial research service and publishing company, serves clients in the fields of news, education, business, and government. It combines specific coverage of Congress, government, and politics by Congressional Quarterly with the more general subject range of an affiliated publication, *CQ Researcher.*

Congressional Quarterly publishes the *Congressional Quarterly Weekly Report* and a variety of books, including college political science textbooks under the CQ Press imprint and public affairs paperbacks on developing issues and events. CQ also publishes information directories and reference books on the federal government, national elections, and politics, including the *Guide to the Presidency,* the *Guide to Congress,* the *Guide to the U.S. Supreme Court,* the *Guide to U.S. Elections, Politics in America,* and *Congress A to Z: CQ's Ready Reference Encyclopedia.* The *CQ Almanac,* a compendium of legislation for one session of Congress, is published each year. *Congress and the Nation,* a record of government for a presidential term, is published every four years.

CQ publishes the *Congressional Monitor,* a daily report on current and future activities of congressional committees, and several newsletters including *Congressional Insight,* a weekly analysis of congressional action.

An electronic online information system, Washington Alert, provides immediate access to CQ's databases of legislative action, votes, schedules, profiles, and analyses.

Cover design: Julie Booth

Photo credits: cover, pp. 3, 19, 24, 196, 227, 229 - R. Michael Jenkins; p. 11 - Supreme Court Historical Society/National Geographic Society; p. 29 - Art Stein; pp. 43, 48, 65 - Library of Congress; pp. 57, 75, 85 - Ken Heinen; p. 193 - AP/Wide World Photos; pp. 217, 219, 220, 221, 223, 224 - Supreme Court of the United States.

Copyright © 1992 Congressional Quarterly Inc.
1414 22nd St. N.W.
Washington, D.C. 20037

All rights reserved. No part of this publication may be reproduced or transmitted in any form or by any means, electronic or mechanical, including photocopy, recording, or any information storage and retrieval system, without permission in writing from the publisher.

Printed in the United States of America

ISBN 0-87187-637-X
ISBN 0-87187-638-8 (pbk.)
ISSN 1054-2701

WITHDRAWN

Contents

Preface

As the 1990-1991 volume of *The Supreme Court Yearbook* was nearing publication, it appeared President Bush's second nominee to the Court, Clarence Thomas, might not win confirmation. The nomination had taken an unprecedented turn as allegations of sexual harassment surfaced and prompted the Senate to reconvene hearings on the nominee. Although Thomas eventually was sworn in and the Senate moved on to other controversies, many Americans no doubt will remember the televised confirmation turmoil for years.

This edition of the *Yearbook* chronicles the Thomas nomination as well as provides an in-depth look at the 1990-1991 Court term. Like the inaugural 1989-1990 edition, this book is written for people who are interested in the Court and the impact of the justices' decisions on public issues, but who are not experts in the law.

Although the books in this series are intended to stand alone, with thorough coverage provided of the Court's decisions during a given term, they are used best with CQ's *Guide to the U.S. Supreme Court, Second Edition*, which captures 200 years of Supreme Court history.

The *Yearbook* begins with an account of the nomination of Thomas, who was chosen to replace Thurgood Marshall and who took his judicial oath October 23, 1991. Chapter 2 presents an overview of the 1990-1991 term and details its major cases. Chapter 3 contains summaries of all the Court's signed opinions for the term, arranged alphabetically by subject. Excerpts from the major cases of the 1990-1991 term are in Chapter 4. It is followed by a preview of the 1991-1992 term and a listing of the major cases docketed as the new term began October 7, 1991. Rulings in those cases and all other decisions from the 1991-1992 term will be the subject of the third volume of the *Yearbook*. The inner workings of the Court, a staple of all editions in the series, are detailed in Chapter 6.

Aside from having a more provocative story to tell, because of the Thomas nomination, this *Yearbook* is better than the first in several other regards. New type treatments make finding and reading the case excerpts easier, and pictures have been added to supplement case information and Court history.

I am indebted to CQ Book Department director David R. Tarr and his colleagues for their continued guidance in this annual endeavor. I owe particular appreciation to Colleen McGuiness, whose scrupulous editing improved this year's volume and whose good humor never waned when the twists of the confirmation process threatened to delay publication.

1 Trials for a New Justice

Clarence Thomas, President George Bush's choice to succeed Thurgood Marshall on the Supreme Court, was poised to win confirmation in early October 1991. But two days before the Senate vote was scheduled to take place, University of Oklahoma law professor Anita F. Hill made public her accusation that Thomas sexually harassed her while she worked for him at the Department of Education and at the Equal Employment Opportunity Commission (EEOC). An outpouring of anger and protest from women throughout the United States forced the Senate to delay its vote and order an investigation of the charges. What followed were hearings that marked one of the wildest spectacles in modern congressional history, a subject for satire and scorn that rocked the Senate.

The drama, played out before the Senate Judiciary Committee, was larger than Thomas and Hill themselves. At stake was a lifetime appointment to the highest court in the country. In doubt was how the president and Senate screen candidates for the bench. At issue during the nationally televised hearings were sexual harassment and how men and women treat each other on the job.

When it was all over, the Senate on October 15 voted 52-48 to confirm Thomas. It was the closest Supreme Court confirmation vote in more than a century.

Marshall, whose six-decade legal career shaped the country's civil rights struggle and liberal activism, was the Court's first black justice. His retirement and the elevation of Thomas, a conservative federal appeals court judge, were emblematic of the conservative shift of the Court, which had become increasingly activist since the conservative majority solidified in the late 1980s. Between 1981 and 1991, like-minded presidents Ronald Reagan and George Bush named six jurists, including the 1986 elevation of William H. Rehnquist to chief justice. No Democrat had nominated a justice in twenty-four years. That disparity raised the stakes on the Thomas nomination and in many ways contributed to the nasty confirmation battle that ensued.

Thomas, forty-three at the time of his nomination, brought powerful symbolism as the second black chosen to be an associate justice of the Supreme Court. But a greater reaction came as a result of what he represented as a conservative who worked for Reagan and Bush for eight years and how he was expected to be another vote favoring government interest over individual rights, particularly on abortion.

□□□

When an October 8, 1991, Senate vote on Thomas was scheduled, he already had survived a series of threats to his nomination. First, he overcame protests that Bush chose him because his race would divide potential opponents. Then, liberal groups attacked him for opposing affirmative action and suggesting he would vote to overturn legalized abortion. He weathered five days of tense confirmation hearings, during which he refused to be pinned down on questions about his judicial philosophy, and, finally, a split 7-7 vote by the Judiciary Committee.

On October 6 Anita Hill went public with her allegations of sexual harassment. Revealed also was that the members of the Senate Judiciary Committee were aware of the allegations when they cast their votes September 27. Majority Leader George J. Mitchell, D-Maine, and Minority Leader Bob Dole, R-Kan., had known of the charges, too. Sexual harassment, illegal under federal law, is "unwelcome sexual advances, requests for sexual favors, and other verbal or physical conduct of a sexual nature" when acceptance or rejection of this conduct affects a person's employment.

After a public outcry over the seriousness of sexual harassment and whether the Judiciary Committee was right to keep the allegations secret from the full Senate, the scheduled vote was postponed. The committee reconvened October 11 in televised hearings that turned into three days of sensational and prurient drama for the Senate and millions of Americans.

The first day began in the Senate Caucus Room with a declaration of innocence by Thomas. For the next seven hours Hill meticulously recounted her story of how Thomas humiliated her with lewd comments. Hill was an attorney-adviser to Thomas from 1981 to 1982, when he was assistant secretary of education in the civil rights division. She was a special assistant, from 1982 to 1983, to Thomas as EEOC chairman. Hill said that, early on, Thomas asked her out socially. She said she declined because she believed it would corrupt their professional dealings. Under questioning from senators, she detailed the nature of the alleged sexual harassment, which she said occurred mostly in his office and when the two were alone. She said she believed he wanted to have sexual intercourse with her. And she provided embarrassing details of what she said were Thomas's comments to her on the job: talk of women's breasts, the size of penises, accounts of movies of group sex and bestiality. Hill also spoke of the anguish she felt over speaking of the incidents publicly.

Senators asked Hill to explain why, if she was so offended by harassment at the Education Department, she then would move with Thomas to EEOC. "I needed the job," she said, noting that she was twenty-five at the time and perhaps had not made the best judgment. "There was a period prior to the time we went to the EEOC, there was a

Supreme Court nominee Clarence Thomas testified for five days before the Senate Judiciary Committee in September 1991, then was recalled in October when allegations of sexual harassment arose.

period where the incidents had ceased," she said. "And so after some consideration of the job opportunities in the [civil rights] area, as well as the fact that I was not assured that my job at Education was going to be protected, I made a decision to move to the EEOC."

After nightfall, an angry Thomas was back with his own accusations. "This is a circus, it's a national disgrace, and from my standpoint as a black American," Thomas said, "it's a high-tech lynching for an uppity black who in any way deigns to think for himself." Thomas said the message was "that unless you kowtow to an old order, this is what will happen to you. You will be lynched, destroyed—caricatured by a committee of the U.S. Senate rather than hung from a tree." He categorically denied Hill's claim of sexual impropriety, although he also said he did not listen to any of her testimony. Thomas said he always treated Hill professionally and cordially. He said he never asked her out and never talked in such pornographic terms.

Thomas drew a picture of a man wrongly accused, his reputation in shreds and his family destroyed. "In my 43 years on this Earth, I have been able with the help of others to defy poverty, avoid prison, overcome segregation, bigotry, racism and obtain one of the finest educations available in this country. But I have not been able to overcome this process." Nevertheless, the next day he said he "would rather die" than withdraw from consideration. Witnesses in support of Hill and Thomas testified on the final day of the hearings.

Hill's poised and unwavering testimony rang true with many who heard it, polls showed, until Thomas returned to testify. Republican senators and the White House then attacked Hill's credibility, portraying her as a deluded, scorned woman. Underneath it all, and despite the fact that Hill also is black, were Republican intimations that Thomas was being attacked out of racism. Thomas was first to introduce the race issue into the hearings, with his charge of a "high-tech lynching," but this was pounded away by committee Republicans during their questioning of subsequent witnesses.

Ironically, Hill's charges raised fundamental questions about Thomas's character—the one attribute that the White House and his Republican Senate supporters had played up. Democrats who opposed Thomas, however, were never able to capitalize on the character issue. Throughout the entire process they lacked a strategy, stymied in part because the nomination of a conservative black split their liberal constituency.

In the end, most senators said Hill's charges and Thomas's defense were inconclusive, while more of the American public believed Thomas over Hill. Senators fell back on their previous positions based on Thomas's judicial philosophy or his determined rise from poverty in rural Georgia. Both sides estimated that Thomas lost about ten votes that he might have had before the allegations emerged—narrowing an outcome that still would have been one of the closest in history.

Hill's charges not only upset Thomas's confirmation but also put under siege the judicial screening process and the Senate as an institution. Senators were barraged with accusations from constituents and the media that they were insensitive to women and out of touch with America. Angry women asked whether the male-dominated institution recognized the seriousness of Hill's charge and why the full Senate had been left in the dark. "What disturbs me as much as the allegations themselves," said Sen. Barbara A. Mikulski, D-Md., "is that the Senate appears not to take the charge of sexual harassment seriously." Senate leaders said that Hill originally sought confidentiality and that they acted properly by keeping her charges within the committee's purview. Hill subsequently went public in an interview with a National Public Radio reporter who obtained a leaked copy of her complaint to the committee.

□□□

The first round of hearings also were controversial, although hardly as sensational. Thomas testified September 10-13 and on September 16, then outside witnesses appeared September 18-20. Senators were frustrated over how little Thomas would reveal about his judicial philosophy, and the committee deadlocked on whether to favorably recommend Thomas to the full Senate. (Thomas's successful confirmation marked the first time since the 1950s that a nominee was approved by the full Senate without an endorsement from the Judiciary Committee.) The committee voted to send Thomas's name to the Senate without a recommendation.

Thomas brought a contentious record to the hearings. In numerous writings and speeches, he seemed to endorse going beyond the Constitution to "natural law" to resolve cases. He previously hinted that he opposed abortion. And the former head of the EEOC disparaged affirmative action as prejudicial to both blacks and whites, faulted Congress as meddlesome, and criticized a law setting up a special prosecutor of executive branch wrongdoing, suggesting that it violated the constitutional separation of powers doctrine.

But through his five days of testimony, Thomas tempered or divorced himself from those views. He said he adopted some of his positions as an administration advocate. Since becoming a federal appeals court judge in 1990, Thomas said, he purged himself of many opinions so that he could look at any dispute clearly. Instead of elaborating on his record, he copiously recalled his boyhood poverty in Georgia and his struggle to learn to read and write English. His black heritage, which had sown ambivalence among the liberal-leaning groups inclined to oppose him, made for a captivating portrait. His supporters echoed that theme, depicting him as a decent, well-qualified jurist.

To senators concerned that there no longer is a majority on the Court that believes a woman has a fundamental right to end a pregnancy, Thomas tried to explain why he would not talk about abortion: "I have indicated and I think it is important to indicate that the area of *Roe v. Wade* is a difficult, it is a controversial area. Cases are coming before the Court in many different postures. I think it would undermine my ability to impartially address that very difficult issue—if I am confirmed, to go further than I have gone." While Thomas deflected abortion questions and said he did not even discuss *Roe v. Wade* with anyone since the decision was issued in 1973, he said he believed that the Due Process Clause of the Fourteenth Amendment embodied a privacy right for married and single people on procreation.

During senators' questioning, the most prevalent subject besides abortion was natural law, a theory that an individual is endowed with certain inherent rights that cannot be restricted by written law. Thomas distanced himself from his previous writings on natural law and said, contrary to the impression left by some of his statements on the theory, he would not use it to adjudicate a dispute.

Senators also wanted to know whether he would extend his idea of natural law to rights for unborn children or to protections for business against governmental regulation. He answered generally about his view of the philosophy: "My point has been that the framers [of the Constitution] . . . reduced to positive law in the Constitution aspects of life principles that they believed in; for example, liberty. But when it is in the Constitution, it is not a natural right; it is a constitutional right. And that is the important point."

Thomas was fond of saying "all blacks don't think alike," and probably the greatest chasm between him and black activists was in the area of affirmative action. "The notion that blacks must be given preferences in order to succeed and should not be judged by the same standards as other people is founded upon the racist assumption that blacks are inherently inferior," Thomas had written.

Just as Thomas's professional record thwarted predictions, it was difficult to say how Thomas's early hardships affected him or would influence his rulings. Thomas recounted with gratitude how, after his parents broke up, he was taken in by grandparents and raised to believe in hard work and independence, and how he was educated in segregated Georgia schools by white nuns. But he also said no matter what a black person accomplishes, people will always judge him by his skin color first. In speeches, Thomas cited a white classmate's note in his high school yearbook: "Keep on trying, Clarence, one day you will be as good as us."

The witnesses who appeared for and against Thomas in the September hearings were by turns predictable and compelling. Supporters described Thomas as a competent, caring person who would offer skill and a deep understanding of the rights of the individual. Opponents said Thomas is not in touch with his roots and that his attitudes would lead him to undermine the Constitution and reject congressional intent in ruling on statutes.

Kate Michelman, executive director of the National Abortion Rights Action League, urged the committee to defeat Thomas on the grounds that he would vote on the Court to make abortion illegal. "No issue—none—has a greater impact on the lives and futures of American women and their families," she said after recounting the trauma of her own abortion. Benjamin Hooks, executive director of the National Association for the Advancement of Colored People, also testified against Thomas: "He talks about his experiences, that his grandfather was called 'boy,' but those experiences did not leave him with the lesson" of overcoming bias.

But Edward Hayes, Jr., who appeared for Thomas on behalf of the Council of 100, a national organization of black Republicans, said that Thomas's disagreement with national organizations' quest for affirmative action demonstrates independent thinking. "Judge Thomas' independence of mind has not come without a great deal of personal cost to him and to his family," Hayes said, referring to Thomas as well-qualified and possessing great character. Police officers, testifying for Thomas, said that as a federal appeals court judge he had struck the right balance between defendants' rights and law enforcement's efforts to catch wrongdoers.

Senators said they were puzzled by the conflicting assessment, as well as Thomas's discrepancies in his own statements. Howell Heflin, D-Ala., who ended up voting against Thomas, asked, "What is the real Clarence Thomas like? What would the real Clarence Thomas do on the Supreme Court?" Thomas responded, "I am the real Clarence Thomas, and I have attempted to bring that person here. . . . I am simply different from what people painted me to be."

□□□

Overall, the anguished Senate debate focused on sex, character, and the confirmation process. But beneath the storm—and in many ways leading to it—was the conservative bent of the Court.

Not since Franklin D. Roosevelt (FDR), who completed an unprecedented three full terms, had a president, or a pair of succeeding like-minded presidents, had such sweeping influence over the makeup of the third branch of government and used appointments to further a political agenda. The Court always has been a prize for the White House, and presidents often have attempted to use the Court to execute their priorities. But the politics has been tempered, given that the philosophy of successive presidents shifts, that most presidents name an average of three justices, and that, with a few exceptions, presidents do not campaign on changing the Court.

Sen. Bill Bradley, D-N.J., said, "The composition of the Supreme Court is always extremely relevant to the ability of the executive and the legislative to shape the future of America. FDR wasn't disturbed by a very conservative court for nothing." But unlike Roosevelt, who was paired with a Congress led by his own Democratic party, Republican Bush constantly faced off on domestic policy with a Democratic Congress.

Factions in Congress had been struggling with legislation to undo various recent Court rulings—including those involving abortion counseling at publicly financed clinics, defendants' challenges to the death penalty, and the admissibility at trial of coerced confessions—but the needed two-thirds votes to ensure overrides of threatened vetoes proved elusive. Indeed, by late October 1991, Congress had failed to override any of Bush's vetoes. The congressional Democratic leadership was foundering, and many members felt that the balance of powers was two against one.

Against this backdrop, the process of confirming justices "has taken on the trappings of a political campaign," said Senate majority leader Mitchell. Reagan and Bush ran on platforms advocating conservative justices, particularly those who oppose abortion, Mitchell observed before the final vote on Thomas. "In the eyes of many Americans, the [confirmation] process has become confused with electoral politics."

But Texas Republican Phil Gramm said, "I submit to my colleagues that the people who voted for George Bush in 1988 had every reason to expect that, if he were elected, he would appoint conservative justices to the Supreme Court. Now what has happened is that the people who lost that election are using the advice-and-consent clause to try to win what they could not win at the ballot box."

Democrats countered by noting that past presidents at times named justices from the other party. William J. Brennan, Jr., one of the Court's most liberal activists, was chosen by Republican Dwight D. Eisenhower. "In addition," said Sen. Paul Simon, D-Ill., "presidents have appointed people who have differed very substantially in terms of philosophy. . . . I have suggested that balance is needed."

In the end, the lesson of Thomas's confirmation was that while the Senate Judiciary Committee aspired to be a forum for constitutional debate, it was in reality a political obstacle course for the nominee and the White House to negotiate. Thomas's effective cry of racism against the Hill charges aside, his testimony on judicial issues in the early testimony mirrored the winning strategy of evasion used by David H. Souter, Bush's 1990 nominee to fill the seat vacated by Brennan. Since the bitterly divisive fight over the 1987 nomination of Robert H. Bork, the White House carefully controlled its nominees' performances before the panel, and senators were hard pressed to wrest many direct answers from them.

To be sure, politics has been in the shadows since 1955, when nominees began regularly appearing before the committee. Senators continually have argued over what questions should be asked and answered. They complain that constitutional issues get short shrift, when, as in the Thomas case, a nominee refuses to talk about politically volatile matters—even those he has written about—using as a shield a judge's need to stay impartial.

The conflict mirrors a larger question: Should the Senate defer to the president once a nominee has been shown to meet minimal qualifications for ability and integrity or should it more independently scrutinize a lifetime appointment to the highest court? Some Democrats remarked that it is almost as if people have come to believe that justices, nominated by the president and owing their confirmation to his political network, serve the executive instead of their separate branch of government.

Senate Judiciary Committee chairman Joseph R. Biden, Jr., D-Del., placed the blame on Bush for the turn the confirmation process had taken: "A fervent minority within the president's party is engaging in an open campaign . . . to shift the court dramatically to the right. And the president has not been willing to engage in the kind of consultation with the Senate that would give this body [the Senate] more assurance that his nominees are not participants in that campaign."

2 The 1990-1991 Term

During the 1990-1991 Supreme Court term, justices appointed by Republican presidents Ronald Reagan and George Bush formed a solid majority that moved with new boldness to carry out a conservative agenda. Strengthened by David H. Souter, who was appointed in 1990, this majority led by Chief Justice William H. Rehnquist shifted into an activist gear that was unknown in the late 1980s when the majority first coalesced.

Conservatives used to excoriate judicial activism, which most commonly has been associated with the tenures of Chief Justices Earl Warren and Warren E. Burger. In the Warren era (1953-1969), for example, the concept of equal protection for minorities was augmented, notably in *Brown v. Board of Education* (1954), and criminal defendants' rights were strengthened. Under Burger (1969-1986), affirmative action was sanctioned and abortion became legal nationwide.

Generally speaking, "conservative" in the judicial context means that the courts will not decide issues that are the province of legislators and, in a contest between government interest and individual rights, will enhance government power. That approach was the hallmark of the Supreme Court in the 1988-1989 and 1989-1990 terms with all the Reagan appointees in place. The Court basically said it was up to Congress and the states to make policy. Unlike the Warren and Burger Courts, the Rehnquist Court declined to write law that would address social dilemmas.

A hint of activism, however, emerged in the 1988-1989 term when the majority rewrote longstanding interpretations of federal laws barring job discrimination. The Court's ruling in *Wards Cove v. Atonio Packing Co.*, for example, reversed a 1971 decision and made it harder for workers to bring cases of indirect discrimination, stemming from, for example, hiring tests or academic requirements. In the 1989-1990 term, precedent was abandoned in a key religious liberty case, *Employment Division, Department of Human Resources of Oregon v. Smith*. The Court said that states no longer had to prove they had a "compelling interest" in enforcing a general statute that infringed on religious freedom.

With Bush's first appointee on the bench, the majority began reaching out more assertively toward politically conservative goals. In the 1990-1991 term, the conservative majority clearly had policy objectives in nind. Overruled were five criminal law precedents, which resulted in a tronger hand for police and prosecutors. The Court in other cases went beyond the questions directly before it and addressed constitutional issues that dissenting justices said did not have to be considered.

At the close of the 1990-1991 term, legal scholars predicted that, with yet another conservative on the way to replace retiring justice Thurgood Marshall, decisions shattering the Warren and Burger legacies were possible in the areas of abortion, separation of church and state, affirmative action, and free speech.

The politically conservative slant of the majority's rulings distressed some members of Congress. Senate Judiciary Committee chairman Joseph R. Biden, Jr., D-Del., said the Rehnquist Court "in too many cases" took "a pro-active stand in changing the laws." He and other members of the committee, which chooses whether to recommend a nominee to the full Senate for confirmation to the Court, asserted that a lopsided conservatism had begun to mark the Court. Republican committee member Arlen Specter, Pa., termed the majority "revisionist" and said it went beyond the traditional idea of judicial conservatism.

Chief Justice Rehnquist defended the Court's departure from precedent in one case, saying, "Stare decisis [the principle of adherence to settled cases] is not an inexorable command." He said the Court during the past twenty terms overruled in whole or in part thirty-three of its earlier constitutional decisions.

Securely ensconced in the conservative camp during the 1990-1991 term were Rehnquist, Antonin Scalia, Anthony M. Kennedy, and Souter. Byron R. White and Sandra Day O'Connor also voted with them most of the time. All were named by Reagan or Bush, except White, who was appointed by President John F. Kennedy, and Rehnquist, who was selected by President Richard Nixon. Reagan elevated Rehnquist to chief justice.

On the liberal side were Marshall, Harry A. Blackmun, and, usually, John Paul Stevens. They were appointed by Presidents Lyndon B. Johnson, Nixon, and Gerald R. Ford, respectively.

The Court issued 112 signed opinions in its 1990-1991 term, down from the 129 opinions announced in the previous term and its lowest total in twenty years. A number of factors accounted for the low number, including the dominance in lower courts of Reagan and Bush appointees who were in step with the high Court's views and the Court liberals' votes not to hear certain cases, and thus not risk overturning precedents. (It takes four justices to vote to accept a case for review.)

In many of its most controversial decisions, the Court took its lead from the Bush administration, particularly in the criminal law area. A majority of justices decided that coerced confessions used at trial do not automatically taint a verdict (abandoning a 1967 decision). Rehnquist, writing for the majority in *Arizona v. Fulminante*, said if other evidence was overwhelmingly against the defendant, a compelled confession may be

The 1990-1991 Court: (seated, from left to right) Harry A. Blackmun, Byron R. White, Chief Justice William H. Rehnquist, Thurgood Marshall, John Paul Stevens, (standing, from left to right) Anthony M. Kennedy, Sandra Day O'Connor, Antonin Scalia, and David H. Souter.

"harmless error"—and not require a new trial.

In another major case, *McCleskey v. Zant*, involving habeas corpus petitions (by which death row inmates challenge their sentences), the Court adopted policies similar to those that President Bush and Chief Justice Rehnquist, in vain, had been urging Congress to pass. The Court ruled in *McCleskey v. Zant* that a death row prisoner may file only one habeas corpus petition in federal court unless a good reason existed for why any new constitutional claim was not raised on the first round. In another habeas corpus case, *Coleman v. Thompson*, a majority found that a prisoner may not bring such a petition in federal court if he failed to meet state court procedural rules.

Both of those rulings were attacked by three-justice minorities (Marshall, Blackmun, and Stevens) as infringements on congressional prerogative. Marshall in *McCleskey v. Zant* said the majority was serving as a "backup legislature." But Marshall reserved his fiercest criticism for a dissent in another criminal law case on the last day of the term. It was then that the six-justice majority ruled in *Payne v. Tennessee*, reversing 1987 and 1989 decisions, that evidence of a victim's character and the effect of a crime on her family could be used against a defendant at a sentencing hearing.

"The implications of this radical new exception to the doctrine of stare decisis are staggering," Marshall said in a dissent issued just hours before he announced his retirement. "The majority today sends a clear signal that scores of established constitutional liberties are now ripe for reconsideration."

Aside from the criminal law decisions, the most noticed ruling was *Rust v. Sullivan*. In that case, the majority went beyond the straightforward question at issue to decide the constitutionality of administration regulations barring abortion counseling in publicly funded clinics. By a 5-4 vote, the majority held that a Department of Health and Human Services directive prohibiting workers at publicly funded clinics from counseling pregnant women on abortion was constitutional. The Court's message was that if government was going to pay for a program, it can attach conditions, even if the conditions infringe on constitutional rights.

The ruling prompted Justice O'Connor, typically with the conservatives, to chide the Rehnquist majority in a dissent for violating "a fundamental rule of judicial restraint that this Court will not reach constitutional questions in advance of the necessity of deciding them." She said the Court could have ruled on the abortion counseling regulations by confining itself to the statute, which she found had been misapplied by the administration. The ruling also provoked abortion rights advocates in Congress to begin pushing a bill that would bar enforcement of the gag order on abortion counseling.

Two other First Amendment cases, *Barnes v. Glen Theatre* (holding that nude dancing can be outlawed by a state indecency statute) and *Cohen v. Cowles Media* (ruling that newspapers can be held liable when they break promises of confidentiality), showed that the Court was less inclined than past majorities to give special attention, or restriction, to the media.

In an extension of the new conservatism, the Court increasingly turned away from legislative history to interpret a statute, opting instead for a more literal approach. This has been prompted by Justice Scalia, who some members of Congress regard as the strongest "conservative activist." Reliance on an agency's interpretation of a statute, in lieu of an explanation in legislative history—such as congressional committee reports and floor statements by members of Congress—gives virtual lawmaking power to the executive branch. *Rust v. Sullivan* was an example of this.

In another opinion, *West Virginia University Hospitals v. Casey*, the six-justice conservative majority said that Congress did not intend to allow winning civil rights plaintiffs to get compensation for expert witness fees when it wrote a 1976 statute allowing winning plaintiffs "reasonable attorneys' fees." Dissenting justices Marshall, Blackmun, and Stevens said that the statute's legislative history undermined that conclusion. "We needlessly ignore persuasive evidence of Congress' actual purpose," Stevens wrote of the majority's literalism.

Justice Souter's first year on the bench cast little light on his judicial temperament, except that he could be counted on in most cases to sign on with Chief Justice Rehnquist. Souter wrote eight opinions, the fewest of any justice, and the majority of the cases had been decided by unanimous votes.

Although Souter remained the mystery he was when he emerged from the Senate confirmation hearings in fall 1990, his vote changed the Court. Last term, one-third of the Court's decisions were 5-4 rulings. This term, only one-fifth were so narrowly decided, and many pivotal cases were settled by 6-3 votes. More freedom exists in wording and in the breadth of an opinion when six justices sign on than when the author is struggling to hold together a slim five-member majority.

Souter provided Rehnquist with a majority when the more centrist conservatives, O'Connor and White, opposed the chief. Without Souter, Rehnquist would not have been able to uphold the abortion counseling ban in *Rust v. Sullivan*, nor is it likely the Court would have ruled that states may outlaw nude dancing in adult clubs in the 5-4 *Barnes v. Glen Theatre* decision.

Souter, however, also provided a fifth vote for liberal-leaning Blackmun's decision on fetal protection policies in *United Automobile Workers v. Johnson Controls Inc.* The Court ruled unanimously that companies cannot exclude women from jobs that might harm a developing fetus. It divided, however, over standards in federal antidiscrimination law. Blackmun's majority said that Congress intended to forbid all hiring practices based on a worker's ability to have children. Four justices (White, Rehnquist, Kennedy, and Scalia) said situations could arise in which a company, because of personal injury liability and workplace costs, could exclude women based on hazards to unborn children.

□□□

Following are ten major cases, listed chronologically as they were announced, from the 1990-1991 Supreme Court term:

Pacific Mutual Life Insurance Co. v. Haslip, decided by a 7-1 vote, March 4, 1991; Blackmun wrote the opinion; O'Connor dissented; Souter took no part in the case.

The Court held that juries have broad discretion to decide punitive damages even when the awards are greatly disproportionate to the actual injury suffered. Ruling in an Alabama insurance fraud case, the Court said Alabama trial procedure offered adequate safeguards, in the jury instructions and post-verdict review, to ensure that an award was not arbitrary. The decision was a blow to efforts by business interests to curb large jury awards in civil liability cases.

The seven-justice majority noted that punitive damages are an ancient part of tort law and declined to draw a line between constitutional and unconstitutional awards. The only dissent was Justice O'Connor, who argued that the Alabama jury instructions were so vague that they violated due process of law.

Punitive damages are awarded in civil cases to punish defendants or to deter future illegal conduct. The Court in a 1989 case had rejected a challenge to a punitive damages award based on the Eighth Amendment's Excessive Fines Clause. But the Court at that time hinted that a test based on the Fourteenth Amendment's Due Process Clause might succeed, and businesses were hoping for some restrictions on punitive damages in this case.

Pacific Mutual, which had been found liable for the fraud of one of its insurance agents, said in its appeal to the high Court that the punitive damages awarded by an Alabama jury stemmed from unbridled discretion that breached the company's due process rights. Its case arose from an award for Cleopatra Haslip and other municipal workers in Roosevelt City, Alabama, who were cheated out of their insurance coverage when an agent pocketed their premiums. Haslip's case involved a $1 million-plus verdict.

Haslip did not realize the premiums she was paying to the agent were not being forwarded to the insurance company until she was hospitalized. The hospital, unable to confirm her coverage and with her bill unpaid, turned over her account to a collection agency. Haslip sued the agent and Pacific Mutual, for whom he worked, seeking damages for fraud.

Of the jury's $1.04 million award for Haslip, the punitive damages component was an estimated $840,000, more than four times the amount of compensatory damages that Haslip had claimed. The Alabama Supreme Court affirmed the award.

Upholding that ruling, the Supreme Court first acknowledged that in earlier cases it had raised doubts about the constitutionality of certain punitive damages awards. The most recent instance came in the 1989 case of *Browning-Ferris Industries of Vermont v. Kelco Disposal*, in which the majority held that the Excessive Fines Clause of the Eighth Amendment did not apply to a punitive damages award in a civil case between private parties. In *Browning-Ferris*, a claim of excessiveness under the Due Process Clause of the Fourteenth Amendment was rejected because it had not been raised in the lower courts.

Justice Blackmun, writing for the majority in *Pacific Mutual v. Haslip*, closed the door left open in *Browning-Ferris*. He noted that the trial judge instructed the jury that punitive damages were "not to compensate the plaintiff for any injury" but "to punish the defendant" and "for the added purpose of protecting the public by [deterring] the defendant and others from doing such wrong in the future." He said that instruction sufficiently limited the jury's discretion to deterrence and retribution. He wrote, "The discretion allowed under Alabama law in determining punitive damages is not greater than that pursued in many familiar areas of the law as, for example, deciding 'the best interests of the child,' or 'reasonable care,' or 'due diligence,' or appropriate compensation for pain and suffering or mental anguish."

Blackmun said that adequate checks by the trial judge on the amount of the award also protected against any arbitrariness that would have breached the fundamental fairness of due process. He was joined in the opinion by Rehnquist, White, Marshall, and Souter.

Alabama's common law rule holds that a corporation is liable for both compensatory and punitive damages for the fraud of an employee, and the Court found that the agent clearly was acting on behalf of Pacific Mutual. Justices said that the agent used Pacific Mutual letterhead, which he was authorized to use, and that, before the fraud in this case occurred, Pacific Mutual had been warned that the agent was engaged in a similar pattern of wrongdoing.

Concluding, Blackmun said, "We are aware that the punitive damages award in this case is more than four times the amount of compensatory damages, is more than 200 times the out-of-pocket expenses of respondent Haslip . . . and, of course, is much in excess of the fine that could be imposed for insurance fraud under [Alabama law]. . . . While the monetary comparisons are wide and, indeed, may be close to the line, the award here did not lack objective criteria."

Scalia concurred in the judgment, writing separately on the historical roots of punitive damages and declaring more broadly that such awards are constitutional. He said no procedure so firmly rooted could be so "fundamentally unfair" as to deny due process of law. Kennedy also wrote separately, saying that Scalia's "historical approach to questions of procedural due process has much to commend it," but adding that "I cannot say with the confidence maintained by Justice Scalia, however, that widespread adherence to a historical practice always forecloses further inquiry when a party challenges an ancient institution or procedure as violative of due process. But I agree that the judgment of history should govern the outcome of the case before us."

Dissenting, Justice O'Connor argued that due process of law requires clearer standards than those used in Alabama for jury awards of punitive damages. She said the jury instructions were "so fraught with uncertainty that they defy implementation. Instead they encourage inconsistent and unpredictable results by inviting juries to rely on private beliefs and personal predilections."

She termed the instructions unconstitutionally vague. "While I do not question the general legitimacy of punitive damages," she wrote, "I see a strong need to provide juries with standards to constrain their discretion so that they may exercise their power wisely, not capriciously or maliciously." O'Connor predicted the majority's decision would "substantially impede punitive damages reforms."

□□□

International Union, United Automobile, Aerospace & Agricultural Implement Workers of America, UAW v. Johnson Controls, Inc., decided by 9-0 and 5-4 votes, March 20, 1991; Blackmun wrote the opinion; White, Rehnquist, Kennedy, and Scalia dissented from a portion of the opinion.

Companies may not exclude women from jobs that might harm a developing fetus, the Court ruled unanimously in its first look at "fetal protection" policies. The justices, however, divided over standards in federal antidiscrimination law. Five justices said that Congress had intended to forbid all hiring practices based on a worker's ability to have children. Justice Blackmun said for the majority that "Congress has left this choice to the woman as hers to make." He was joined by Justices Marshall, Stevens, O'Connor, and Souter.

Four justices (White, Rehnquist, Kennedy, and Scalia) said situations could arise in which a company, because of personal injury liability and workplace costs, could exclude women based on hazards to the unborn. White said that Title VII of the Civil Rights Act of 1964 could be satisfied if an employer showed that excluding women from certain jobs was reasonably necessary to avoid major lawsuits.

Overall, the rulings were applauded by unions and working women. And the majority's broad interpretation of federal antibias law gratified members of Congress who were considering legislation that would forbid a firm from making sterilization a condition of employment or promotion, as had Johnson Controls, a Milwaukee battery manufacturer, which was sued because it excluded women of childbearing age from hazardous jobs. Some proponents of such legislation argued that fetal protection policies often were used as an excuse to deny women good jobs or to infringe on their right to privacy.

As many of 20 million jobs in the United States leave workers open to reproductive or fetal health hazards, according to a 1990 report by the House Education and Labor Committee's majority staff.

Business groups voiced disappointment at the pronouncement. Employers said the decision increases their liability for workers who have babies with birth defects. But Blackmun discounted the likelihood of a rash of lawsuits. While more than forty states recognize a right to recover for a prenatal injury based on negligence or wrongful death, Blackmun noted that without negligence it would be difficult for a court to hold an employer liable.

"Our holding today that Title VII, as so amended [by a pregnancy antidiscrimination law], forbids sex-specific fetal-protection policies is neither remarkable nor unprecedented," Blackmun wrote. "Concern for a woman's existing or potential offspring historically has been the excuse for denying women equal employment opportunities."

The decision broke from a series of Court rulings in 1989 that narrowed the breadth of federal discrimination statutes and has since been the subject of efforts in Congress to reverse the Court.

The case began when, in 1982, Johnson Controls started barring women of childbearing age from jobs that exposed them to lead. The policy applied to all women except those who could prove they were sterile. The main ingredient in some batteries, lead has been shown to cause birth defects. Workers sued, saying that the company violated Title VII of the Civil Rights Act, which bars sex discrimination, and the 1978 Pregnancy Discrimination amendments.

A federal district court upheld the policy as being required by business necessity, and the U.S. Court of Appeals for the Seventh Circuit affirmed. But the Supreme Court, in reversing the appeals court, held that because the Johnson Controls policy requires only women, not men, to prove that they cannot reproduce, it is overt discrimination. As such, simply being justified by business necessity will not cure it of any discrimination.

Such a practice is illegal, the Court said, unless a company can show that sex is a "bona fide occupational qualification," or essential, under the Pregnancy Discrimination Act. All nine justices agreed that was the test to be used and that Johnson Controls had failed the test, with both its assertion that the risk of lead poisoning is higher for women, compared with men, and its desire to avoid civil liability. In this case, Blackmun relied on evidence that men exposed to lead also could hurt their future children and added that "[t]he safety exception [in federal law] is limited to instances in which sex or pregnancy actually interferes with the employee's ability to perform the job."

The justices split on how readily the test could be met. Blackmun said that Congress had set a high level of antidiscrimination protection for women in Title VII and its amendments that neither safety concerns nor exposure to lawsuits could override: "Decisions about the welfare of future children must be left to parents who conceive, bear, support and raise them rather than to the employers who hire those parents." He was joined by Marshall, Stevens, O'Connor, and Souter.

But White said federal law could be satisfied if an employer showed that excluding women from certain jobs was reasonably necessary to avoid major lawsuits. White wrote that the Court's "narrow interpretation" of the law meant that an employer could not exclude even pregnant women from jobs involving materials that are highly toxic to their fetuses. "It is foolish to think that Congress intended such a result," White wrote, joined by Rehnquist and Kennedy.

Scalia wrote separately that a company should be able to turn away pregnant women if keeping them on the job would be "inordinately expensive."

□□□

Arizona v. Fulminante, decided by separate 5-4 decisions, March 26, 1991; White first wrote an opinion for five justices saying that a defendant's confession, based on the proper standard of totality of the circumstances, was coerced (Rehnquist, O'Connor, Kennedy, and Souter dissented); Rehnquist then wrote for five justices that a coerced confession used at trial does not necessarily taint a conviction (White, Marshall, Blackmun, and Stevens dissented); finally, White wrote for a new coalition of five justices that in this case the confession was not "harmless error" (Rehnquist, O'Connor, and Scalia dissented; Souter did not sign on to either side for this part of the opinion).

In a complex opinion written by shifting majorities, the Court held that a coerced confession does not automatically taint a conviction. That part of the ruling reversed a 1967 decision establishing the rule that due process is denied when a forced confession is used against a defendant, regardless of other evidence.

The 1967 case, *Chapman v. California*, stood for the proposition that a coerced confession would never be "harmless error" and must result in reversal of the conviction. The justices specified that in that case, in addition to a coerced confession, denial of counsel and a biased judge are grounds for a new trial.

Writing for five justices on this critical part of *Arizona v. Fulminante*, Chief Justice Rehnquist said, if other evidence were enough to convict the defendant, a compelled confession may be harmless error—and thus not dictate a new trial. Justice White, dissenting in this part of the opinion, said the Court had overruled a "vast body of precedent." He said, "Permitting a coerced confession to be part of the evidence ... is inconsistent with the thesis that ours is not an inquisitorial system" of justice.

The case arose from Oreste Fulminante's prison confession to another inmate, who happened to be serving—unbeknownst to Fulminante—as an FBI informant, about the murder of Fulminante's eleven-year-old stepdaughter. Fulminante was in prison on a firearms conviction at the time. The disclosure about the stepdaughter's murder followed Fulminante's apparent concerns about a prison rumor of the

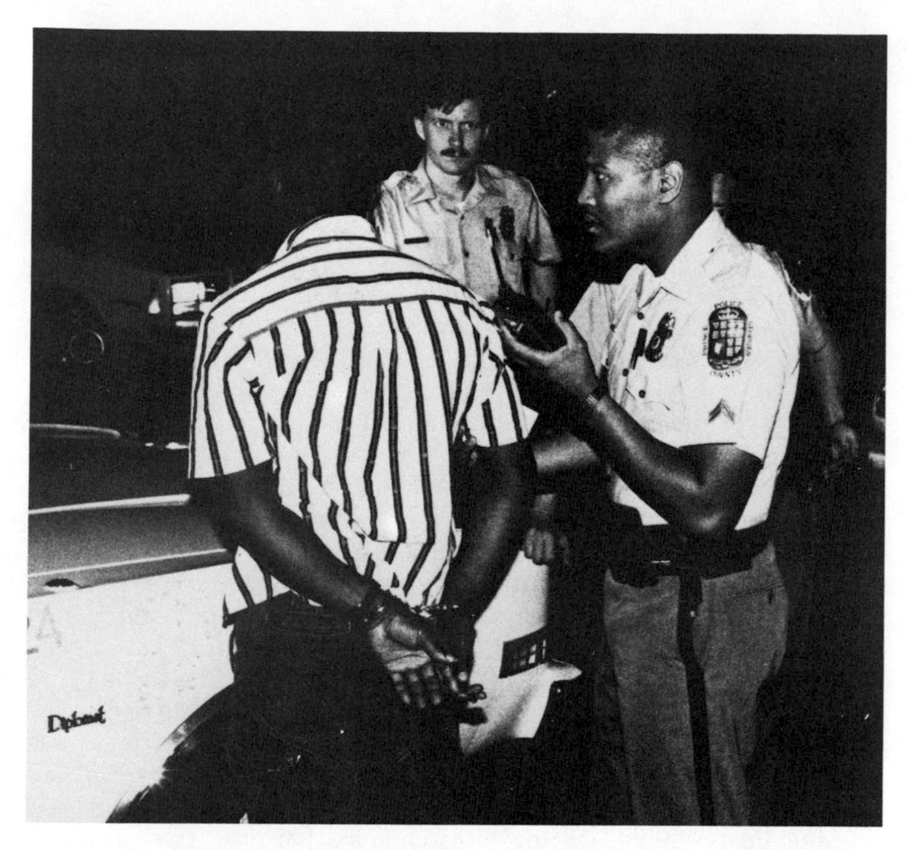

During its 1990-1991 term, the Court reversed five criminal law precedents, strengthening the hand of law enforcement.

murder and his fears of abuse by other inmates. The inmate offered to protect Fulminante but told him, "You have to tell me about it." Fulminante then admitted that he had driven his stepdaughter to the desert, where he choked her, sexually assaulted her, and made her beg for her life before shooting her twice in the head.

After Fulminante was released from prison on the firearms charge, he was indicted in Arizona for the murder of the girl. He moved to suppress the statement he had given to the inmate-informant and then to the inmate's wife. Fulminante asserted that the original confession was coerced by an agent of the government and that the second confession was the "fruit" of the first. A trial court denied the motion, finding that both confessions were voluntary. The confessions were used at trial, and Fulminante was convicted of the murder and sentenced to death.

The Arizona Supreme Court, however, on appeal held that the first confession was coerced because Fulminante thought his life was in danger.

It found that, based on Supreme Court precedent at the time, a coerced confession could never be ruled harmless error.

The Supreme Court's opinion began with White writing for the majority that the confession was coerced. He was joined on this part of the opinion by Marshall, Blackmun, Stevens, and Scalia.

Rehnquist won the majority for the next part of the opinion: that once a confession was found to be coerced, it could be subjected to harmless error analysis. He said the harmless error doctrine stems from the idea that "the central purpose of a criminal trial is to decide the factual question of the defendant's guilt or innocence . . . by focusing on the underlying fairness of the trial rather than on the virtually inevitable presence of immaterial error."

He called the admission of an involuntary confession a "trial error," comparable to the erroneous admission of other types of evidence. Referring to *Chapman*'s list of errors that could not be considered harmless, Rehnquist said a coerced confession is unlike denial of counsel and trial before a biased judge, terming those "structural defects in the constitution of the trial mechanism." He said the error here was just in the process itself. Rehnquist was joined by O'Connor, Scalia, Kennedy, and Souter.

White, who wrote for the dissent on this point, accused the majority of abandoning a long-held proposition that a defendant is deprived of due process of law if his conviction is founded on an involuntary confession. He said a defendant's confession is probably the most damaging evidence that can be used against him.

But then White, applying the Rehnquist harmless error analysis, regained a majority to find that the state of Arizona had not demonstrated beyond a reasonable doubt that the admission of the confession did not contribute to Fulminante's conviction. White was joined by Marshall, Blackmun, Stevens, and, for this part only, Kennedy.

Rehnquist, who disagreed with White about whether, ultimately, Fulminante should get a new trial and who was joined by O'Connor and Scalia, noted that at a hearing on whether to suppress the confession, Fulminante had accepted the prosecutor's statement that "[a]t no time did the defendant indicate he was in fear of other inmates nor did he ever seek [the informant's] protection."

Kennedy, in a concurring opinion, agreed with Rehnquist that the confession was not coerced and that harmless error analysis could be applied to the case. But, in explaining why he joined White in the end, Kennedy said, given that five justices had found the confession coerced (in the first part of the opinion), an appeals court "must appreciate the indelible impact a full confession may have on the trier of fact." He said it would be hard to find evidence more incriminating. Kennedy, however, was not one of the justices who believed Fulminante's confession was coerced.

□□□

McCleskey v. Zant, Superintendent, Georgia Diagnostic and Classification Center, decided by a 6-3 vote, April 16, 1991; Kennedy wrote the opinion; Marshall, Blackmun, and Stevens dissented.

Barring extraordinary circumstances, death row prisoners may undergo only one round of federal court review through petitions for habeas corpus. The Court's ruling pleased state prosecutors who believe that condemned inmates are beating the system by dragging out the appeals process and indefinitely postponing their execution dates. But civil libertarians and other defendants' rights advocates said the decision could lead to the executions of innocent people.

McCleskey v. Zant involved a murder defendant who had been appealing his case for more than a decade.

Latin for "you have the body," a habeas corpus writ is used to determine whether a person is lawfully imprisoned. Defendants who have exhausted direct appeals apply for a writ of habeas corpus on the ground that the conviction under which they are held is unconstitutional.

The Court's opinion refined the doctrine known as "abuse of the writ," which governs the circumstances in which federal courts decline to hear a prisoner's claim presented for the first time in a second or subsequent petition for a writ of habeas corpus. It was written by Kennedy and joined by Chief Justice Rehnquist and Justices White, O'Connor, Scalia, and Souter.

The majority said that a prisoner may file only one habeas corpus petition in federal court unless good reason exists for why any new constitutional error was not raised on the first round. The standard for a second petition is difficult, and the prisoner also must show that he suffered "actual prejudice" from the error he claims.

Under earlier Court rulings, second and subsequent habeas corpus petitions were dismissed out of hand only if a prisoner deliberately withheld grounds for appeal in bad faith (possibly to raise the arguments in later petitions). Dissenting justices asserted that the majority "exercises legislative power" by providing a tougher standard, a reference to Chief Justice Rehnquist's longtime effort to persuade Congress to streamline the habeas corpus process. The highly controversial and political legislation repeatedly died without final action.

Two years earlier, the Court similarly made it harder for death row prisoners to file habeas corpus petitions when it restricted, in *Teague v. Lane*, the situations under which a prisoner could establish an appeal based on a favorable court ruling issued in another case after his own conviction became final.

In the new decision, Warren McCleskey, convicted of murder in 1978, raised in a second federal habeas petition a claim that he had not presented in his first federal habeas corpus petition. The new claim challenged prosecutors' use during McCleskey's trial of a conversation he had with a jail cellmate who was an informant for state officials. McCleskey supposedly told the cellmate that he indeed had robbed a Georgia furniture store and shot and killed an off-duty police officer who had entered the store.

McCleskey argued to the district court that heard the habeas petition that his rights were breached by the state's use of an informer to obtain the incriminating statements. The court agreed, granting McCleskey relief based on a violation of *Massiah v. United States* (1964), in which the Supreme Court held that a right-to-counsel applied as much to an undercover use of police tactics as it did to a jailhouse interrogation.

But the U.S. Court of Appeals for the Eleventh Circuit reversed, holding that the district court exceeded its discretion by failing to dismiss McCleskey's *Massiah* claim as an abuse of writ. The appeals court said that, because McCleskey included the complaint in a state petition, dropped it in his first federal petition, and then reasserted it in his second federal petition, he "made a knowing choice not to pursue the claim after having raised it previously."

The Supreme Court, affirming the appeals court decision, ruled that subsequent habeas consideration of claims not raised on the first round, and thus defaulted, should be prohibited unless a prisoner can show cause and prejudice. That standard requires a defendant to prove that "some objective factor" beyond the defense's control frustrated its efforts to raise the claim in an earlier petition. The defendant would have to demonstrate, for example, that the state interfered or that the factual or legal basis for a claim was not available to his lawyer during the earlier appeal. Once the defendant has established cause, he then would have to show actual prejudice to his case.

"The cause and prejudice standard should curtail the abusive petitions that in recent years have threatened to undermine the integrity of the habeas corpus process," Justice Kennedy wrote for the majority. In McCleskey's case, Kennedy found no cause for his failing to raise the complaint about the informant at the outset. Kennedy said allowing successive petitions may give defendants incentives to withhold claims for manipulative purposes. "Neither innocence nor just punishment can be vindicated until the final judgment is known," Kennedy said, adding that continued litigation through habeas review "places a heavy burden on scarce federal judicial resources, and threatens the capacity of the system to resolve primary disputes."

Justice Marshall, in a dissent joined by Justices Blackmun and Stevens, said the majority's "decision departs drastically from the norms that inform the proper judicial function." He asserted that refinements in habeas corpus procedure are up to Congress, which "has affirmatively ratified the [formerly used] good-faith standard in the governing and procedural rules, thereby insulating that standard from judicial repeal."

"Confirmation that the majority today exercises legislative power not properly belonging to this Court is supplied by Congress' own recent consideration [in 1990] and rejection" of legislation that would restrict habeas corpus review. Marshall added, "It is axiomatic that this Court does not function as a backup legislature for the reconsideration of failed attempts to amend existing statutes."

Dissenting justices also said a consequence of the new standard would be that defendants raise in their first federal habeas corpus petition all conceivable claims, whether they have merit.

□□□

Rust v. Sullivan, decided by a 5-4 vote, May 23, 1991; Rehnquist wrote the opinion; Blackmun, Marshall, Stevens, and O'Connor dissented.

The issue was abortion counseling, but the Court's ruling carried a broader message: If the government is going to pay for a program, it can attach conditions—even if they infringe on free speech. A five-justice majority said the Bush administration may forbid workers at publicly funded clinics to counsel pregnant women on abortion. The Court said Title X of the Public Health Service Act of 1970 may be read to bar not only abortions but also abortion counseling.

The Court in the past has given Congress broad leeway to define the limits of a program when it appropriates public funds. But the decision in this case, which went a step further, said Congress may regulate the content of speech it funds.

The decision could have implications for arts funding and other areas of government-subsidized speech. The decision also served notice that if Congress wants to dictate how the administration carries out a law, it had better do so explicitly.

Chief Justice Rehnquist wrote the opinion. He was joined by Justices White, Scalia, Kennedy, and Souter.

In Title X of the Public Health Service Act, written before the Court's 1973 *Roe v. Wade* ruling that legalized abortion nationwide, Congress stipulated that no federal funds could be used in "programs where abortion is a method of family planning." In the 1980s, the Reagan administration, consistent with its effort to stem abortions, used the language to try to stop abortion counseling at federally funded clinics. The Bush administration continued the practice.

Planned Parenthood and the state and city of New York sued, saying the statute only meant no money for abortions. They also said the regulations infringed on doctors' First Amendment rights and interfered with a woman's privacy right to abortion and ability to hear competent medical advice. Federal appeals courts split on whether the regulations violated the Constitution, and the U.S. Court of Appeals for the Second Circuit, which heard this case, ruled that the regulations followed from Title X and that no constitutional infringement had occurred.

Affirming the circuit court ruling, the Supreme Court rejected both the statutory interpretation and the constitutional challenge. On the First Amendment question, it said, "The employees' freedom of expression is limited during the time that they actually work for the project; but this limitation is a consequence of their decision to accept employment in a project" the government financed.

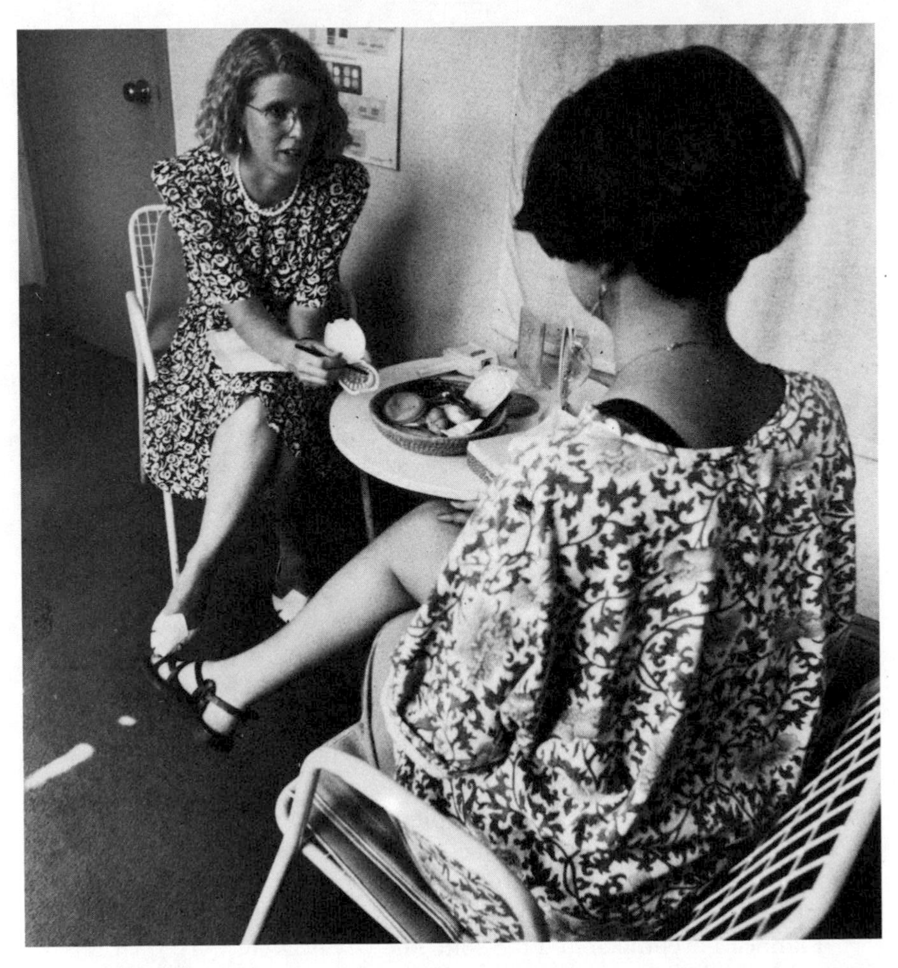

In May 1991, the Court upheld a Bush administration prohibition on abortion counseling at publicly financed clinics.

This was new justice Souter's first abortion-related case. While the ruling did not reveal his position on abortion rights—an issue on which the Court is divided—it could indicate sympathy with the anti-abortion position. The majority included an assertion that the Reagan administration's rules were "supported by a shift in attitude against the elimination of unborn children by abortion."

Dissenting were Blackmun, Marshall, Stevens, and O'Connor. Blackmun, author of *Roe*, said the ruling allows the government to interfere with a woman's abortion choice. On the First Amendment question, Blackmun said, "The Court, for the first time, upholds viewpoint-based suppression of speech solely because it is imposed on those dependent upon the government" for funds.

The abortion implications drew the most reaction from Capitol Hill and the public. But while there no longer is a majority on the Court willing to find a fundamental right to abortion in the Constitution, the ruling did not suggest the Court was ready to overturn *Roe v. Wade.*

In his majority opinion, Rehnquist first found that Congress did not clearly exempt counseling in its prohibition on abortion in Title X. His ruling said precedent dictates that, unless the administration's interpretation of a statute is not "plausible," it must be upheld. In this case, the Court said, the Department of Health and Human Services' (HHS) regulations were more consistent with the statute than regulations between 1981 and 1988 requiring federally funded family planning clinics to tell pregnant women about abortion. The Court called the legislative history "ambiguous and unenlightening."

Rehnquist then turned to the regulations' constitutionality. He cited rulings allowing government to forbid abortions in publicly financed programs. "The government may make a value judgment favoring childbirth over abortion . . . and . . . implement that judgment by the allocation of public funds," he reiterated. The bottom line, Rehnquist said, is that the government has no constitutional duty to subsidize an activity because it is constitutionally protected, be it free speech or privacy. He rejected arguments that government cannot condition funds on a waiver of constitutional rights.

The HHS regulations, the chief justice said, "do not force the recipients to give up abortion-related speech; they merely require that the grantee keep such activities separate and distinct" from the funded programs. He asserted that the Title X program is limited to care of a patient before conception and that, as a result, a doctor's silence on abortion "cannot reasonably be thought to mislead a client into thinking that the doctor does not consider abortion an appropriate option for her."

In his dissent, Blackmun said, "By refusing to fund those family-planning projects that advocate abortion because they advocate abortion, the government plainly has targeted a particular viewpoint." He said the government's interest in forbidding money for abortion counseling was not sufficient to justify restricting truthful information and the free flow of medical opinions.

Stevens dissented separately, suggesting that the regulations amounted to censorship: "Not a word in the statute . . . authorizes the [HHS] Secretary to impose any restrictions on the dissemination of truthful information or professional advice by grant recipients." O'Connor, who wavers on abortion and whose vote has been carefully watched by people on both sides of the abortion question, also wrote separately that she did not believe the majority should have addressed constitutional issues. She said the case could have been decided on the basis of the statute. O'Connor wrote, "It is enough in this case to conclude that neither the language nor the history of [Title X] compels the secretary's interpretation, and that the interpretation raises serious First Amendment concerns."

□□□

Edmonson v. Leesville Concrete Co., decided by a 6-3 vote, June 3, 1991; Kennedy wrote the opinion; O'Connor, Rehnquist, and Scalia dissented.

Potential jurors in civil cases cannot be rejected because of race, the Court ruled in a decision that broadened a landmark opinion barring discrimination in criminal case jury selection. The Court extended to a negligence trial a criminal law rule from the 1986 case *Batson v. Kentucky* that prevents prosecutors from using peremptory strikes to exclude jurors solely because they are of the same race as the criminal defendant.

During criminal and civil trials, both parties are allowed a certain number of peremptory jury challenges, which permit potential jurors to be dismissed without reason.

Justice Kennedy wrote for the Court that the conduct of private parties usually is outside the scope of the Constitution. But he said race-based peremptory challenges in civil action constitute "state action" for protection under the Equal Protection Clause of the Fourteenth Amendment. "Racial bias mars the integrity of the judicial system and prevents the idea of democratic government from becoming a reality," Kennedy said, joined by Justices White, Marshall, Blackmun, Stevens, and Souter.

Dissenting, Justice O'Connor said race discrimination in peremptory challenges was "abhorrent" but the guarantee of equal protection in jury selection did not extend to disputes between private parties. "The government is not responsible for everything that occurs in a courtroom," she said. "The government is not responsible for a peremptory challenge by a private litigant."

The ruling was one of two significant cases involving jury selection in the 1990-1991 term. In *Powers v. Ohio*, the Court by a 7-2 vote said a criminal defendant may object to race-based exclusions of jurors through peremptory challenges whether or not the defendant and the excluded jurors share the same race.

Edmonson v. Leesville arose after a construction worker, Thaddeus Donald Edmonson, was injured in a job-site accident in Fort Polk, Louisiana, and sued Leesville Concrete Co. for negligence. During jury selection, Leesville used two of its three peremptory challenges authorized by statute to strike black persons from the prospective jury. Edmonson, who is black, asked the district court judge to demand that Leesville give an explanation for striking the two jurors. The judge denied the request, saying that *Batson* does not apply in civil proceedings. The U.S. Court of Appeals for the Fifth Circuit similarly held that a private party in a civil case need not be accountable for striking people on the basis of race.

Reversing, the Supreme Court majority said that jury selection in a private lawsuit is subject to the Constitution's guarantee of equal protection of the laws because the government participated significantly in peremptory challenges and civil litigation generally.

The only purpose of peremptory strikes, Kennedy wrote, "is to permit litigants to assist the government in the selection of an impartial trier of fact. . . . Peremptory challenges are permitted only when the government, by statute or decisional law, deems it appropriate to allow parties to exclude a given number of persons who otherwise would satisfy the requirements for service on the petit jury."

Kennedy applied an analytical approach taken in *Lugar v. Edmondson* (1982) to determine whether a private party could be considered a government actor in the use of peremptory challenges. "Although private use of state-sanctioned private remedies or procedures does not rise, by itself, to the level of state action, our cases have found state action when private parties make extensive use of state procedures with 'the overt, significant assistance of state officials,' " he said, quoting *Lugar*.

Kennedy continued, "If peremptory challenges based on race were permitted, persons could be required by summons to be put at risk of open and public discrimination as a condition of their participation in the justice system. The injury to excluded jurors would be the direct result of governmental delegation and participation."

Justice O'Connor dissented, joined by Rehnquist and Scalia. She said that jury selection by private litigants should be a matter of private choice: "The decision to strike a juror is entirely up to the litigant, and the reasons for doing so are of no consequence to the judge. . . . In point of fact, the government has virtually no role in the use of peremptory challenges."

Justice Scalia dissented separately to complain about the majority's interpretation of state action doctrine and its conferral of additional responsibility on judges overseeing jury selection. "[Y]et another complexity is added to an increasingly Byzantine system of justice that devotes more and more of its energy to sideshows and less and less to the merits of the case."

□□□

Chisom v. Roemer, Governor of Louisiana; United States v. Roemer, Governor of Louisiana, decided by a 6-3 vote, June 20, 1991; Stevens wrote the opinion; Scalia, Rehnquist, and Kennedy dissented.

Houston Lawyers' Association v. Attorney General of Texas; League of United Latin American Citizens et al. v. Attorney General of Texas et al., decided by 6-3 votes on June 20, 1991; Stevens wrote the opinion; Scalia, Rehnquist, and Kennedy dissented.

In two separate opinions on related controversies, the Court said the Voting Rights Act of 1965, as amended in 1982, applies to elections for judges. The rulings paved the way for major changes in how many states, particularly in the South, elect judges. An estimated forty states use ballots to select some or all of their judges.

The cases stemmed from discrimination challenges to at-large judicial districts in Louisiana and Texas. Such voting schemes usually minimize the voting strength of minorities by allowing the majority to elect all representatives of the district. In both cases, the suing parties argued that the power of blacks and other minorities was diluted because of the way judicial districts were drawn. The Voting Rights Act, as amended in 1982, prohibits any voting practice that "results in a denial or abridgement of the right . . . to vote on account of race or color." It states that the test for determining the legality of a practice is whether "based on the totality of circumstances" minority voters "have less opportunity than other members of the electorate to participate in the political process and to elect representatives of their choice." Before the 1965 voting act, blacks were denied access to the polls through literacy tests, whites-only primaries, and poll taxes.

The primary purpose of Congress's enacting the 1982 amendment was to institute the "results test" to overturn the Supreme Court's 1980 ruling in *Mobile v. Alabama* that proof of intentional discrimination was necessary for a violation of the Voting Rights Act. But in trying to ensure that unintentional biases in voting processes would be remedied, Congress introduced a new problem. By using the term "representatives" in the amendment, Congress raised questions about whether judges still were covered by the act, as they indisputably were in 1965. No overt evidence in the legislative history revealed that Congress was trying to either retain or exclude judges.

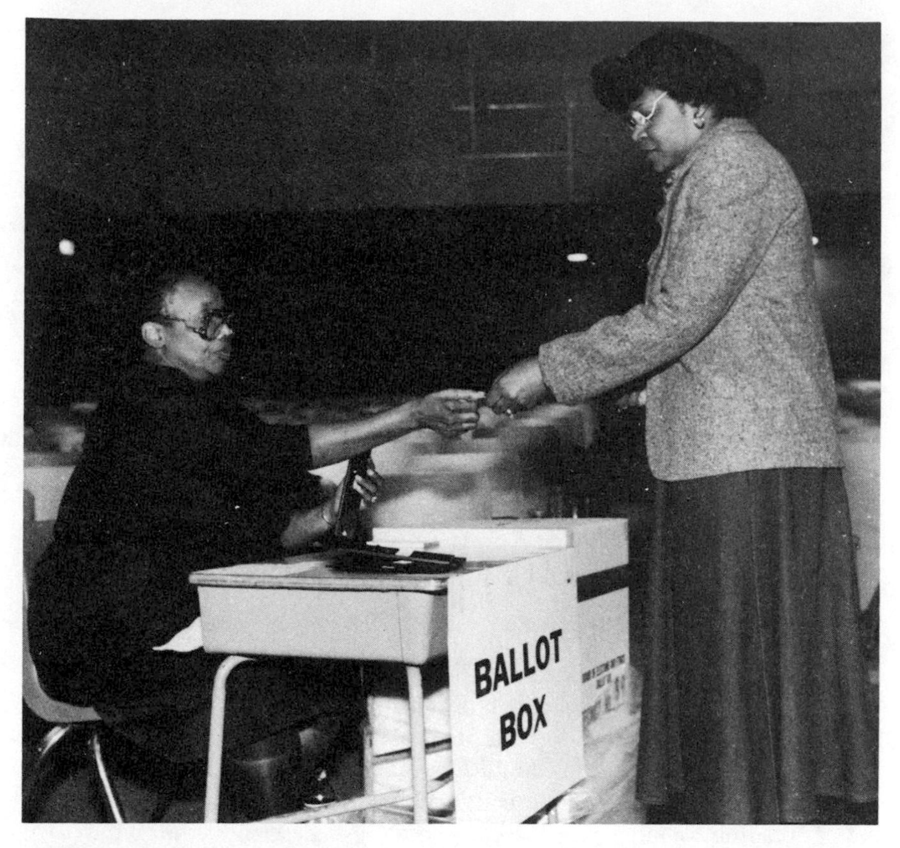

The Court ruled that state elections for judges are covered by the antidiscrimination provisions of the Federal Voting Rights Act.

Both Louisiana and Texas argued that judicial elections were not protected by the law because judges are not "representatives." Federal district courts agreed and dismissed the cases. The U.S. Court of Appeals for the Fifth Circuit affirmed.

But the Supreme Court, in reversing the rulings, said that, because the act clearly applied to judicial elections before the 1982 amendments and that those amendments were chiefly aimed at removing a requirement of proof of intentional discrimination, no reason existed to believe that Congress intended to remove judges from coverage of the act.

Stevens, writing for the majority in *Chisom v. Roemer*, said, "It is difficult to believe that Congress, in an express effort to broaden the protection afforded by the Voting Rights Act, withdrew, without comment, an important category of elections from that protection." Justices White, Marshall, Blackmun, O'Connor, and Souter signed onto the opinion.

Dissenting were Justices Scalia, Rehnquist, and Kennedy. Scalia, writing for the trio, accused the majority of interpreting the words of the statute to meet its own expectations.

In the leading case, *Chisom v. Roemer*, black voters contested Louisiana's system for electing its Supreme Court justices, contending that the at-large elections for the New Orleans area weakened minority voting strength. More than one-half of the registered voters of Orleans Parish were black at the time and more than three-fourths of the registered voters in the other parishes in the area were white. No black person ever had been elected to the Louisiana Supreme Court, either from the New Orleans-area First Supreme Court District or from any one of the other five judicial districts.

In *Houston Lawyers' Association*, black and Hispanic voters challenged the at-large, countywide election procedures for state trial judges, also saying they diluted minority votes. The voters cited the example of Harris County, which has a population that is 20 percent black but has elected only three black judges out of a total fifty-nine judgeships in the district.

Both cases, which had been dismissed, were reinstated because of the ruling.

In the Court's opinion in *Chisom v. Roemer*, Stevens said that when the Voting Rights Act was enacted in 1965, it unquestionably applied to judicial elections. The 1965 text had not used the term "representatives." He said if Congress, in adopting such a term in 1982, had intended to exclude judicial elections, it would have been explicit, or at least referred to such a major change in the legislative history. "We think . . . that the better reading of the word 'representatives' describes the winner of representative, popular elections. If executive officers, such as prosecutors, sheriffs, state attorneys general and state treasurers, can be considered 'representatives' simply because they are chosen by popular elections, then the same reasoning should apply to elected judges."

Stevens reiterated the point in *Houston Lawyers' Association*.

Scalia's dissent criticized the majority's interpretation of the 1982 amendment, saying it "is not some all-purpose weapon for well-intentioned judges to wield as they please in the battle against discrimination." He said the plain meaning of the term "representative" does not include judges. "We are here to apply the statute, not legislative history, and certainly not the absence of legislative history," he said, referring to a remark by Stevens construing Congress's lack of a reference to the possible elimination of judges from the act. "There is little doubt that the ordinary meaning of 'representatives' does not include judges," Scalia wrote. "The Court's feeble argument to the contrary is that 'representatives' means those who 'are chosen by popular election.' On that hypothesis, the fan-elected members of the baseball All-Star teams are 'representatives'—hardly a common, if even a permissible, usage."

□□□

Barnes, Prosecuting Attorney of St. Joseph County, Indiana v. Glen Theatre, Inc., decided by a 5-4 vote, June 21, 1991; Rehnquist wrote the opinion; White, Marshall, Blackmun, and Stevens dissented.

In a case that required justices to ponder the message behind nude dancing at adults-only bars, a majority ruled that an Indiana public indecency statute outlawing totally nude dancing does not violate the First Amendment's guarantee of freedom of expression. The justices split on their reasoning, but basically all in the majority said that, even if nude dancing is subject to some First Amendment protection, other community interests of safety and morality present overriding concerns. Only Justice Scalia said nude dancing was entitled to no First Amendment protection.

Dissenting justices said the Indiana law violated the First Amendment because it was targeting an "expressive activity." The effect of the law, the dissent asserted, was to say that nudity in a dance is a crime because of the erotic message it communicates.

The dispute began when individual dancers, a go-go bar, and an adult bookstore that offered nude performances sued the Indiana County of St. Joseph to stop enforcement of Indiana's public indecency law, which required dancers to wear pasties and a G-string. A federal district court ruled that nude dancing, at least in this case, was not expressive conduct and therefore not impinged by the statute. The U.S. Court of Appeals for the Seventh Circuit reversed, ruling that nude dancing performed for entertainment—and not obscene—is protected expression. The court said the Indiana statute improperly encroached on the dancing, which was intended to convey an erotic and sexual message.

But the Supreme Court, in reversing the appeals court, said the statute is justified "despite its incidental limitations on some expressive activity" because it fulfills a greater societal purpose of morality and public order. Chief Justice Rehnquist wrote for the five-justice majority: "The requirement that the dancers don pasties and a G-string does not deprive the dance of whatever erotic message it conveys; it simply makes the message slightly less graphic. The perceived evil that Indiana seeks to address is not erotic dancing, but public nudity."

Rehnquist said that the statute's purpose of protecting society is clear from its text and history. He added that such public indecency statutes are of ancient origin and exist in at least forty-seven states. Rehnquist said, "The traditional police power of the states is defined as the authority to provide for the public health, safety, and morals, and we have upheld such a basis for legislation." He said the state's interest in protecting order and morality is unrelated to the suppression of free expression.

The chief justice evaluated the statute using a legal analysis from the

1968 case of *United States v. O'Brien*, in which a Vietnam War protester who burned his draft card on the steps of a South Boston courthouse was convicted of violating a statute that prohibited the destruction or mutilation of a draft card. The protester argued that his conviction was contrary to the First Amendment because his act was "symbolic speech"—expressive conduct. Creating a test for deciding the legality of conduct that has both speech and nonspeech elements, the Court said the governmental interest in preserving draft cards overrode the speech interests. Although the protester's action was a form of expression, it could be outlawed because the government's reason for doing so was "substantial" and "unrelated to the suppression of free expression."

In the Indiana case, Rehnquist said the nude dancing statute met the *O'Brien* test for a substantial governmental interest over a "modest" restriction on conduct. He was joined by Justices O'Connor and Kennedy.

Justice Scalia, writing separately in a concurrence, agreed with the judgment but differed with the plurality's reasoning, saying that the First Amendment issue did not need to be addressed. "Moral opposition to nudity supplies a rational basis for its prohibition," Scalia asserted, saying that should be the end of the Court's consideration.

The approach Scalia adopted was similar to one he used in his 1990 majority opinion in *Employment Division, Oregon Department of Human Resources v. Smith*, in which he wrote that, when a general law regulating conduct is not specifically directed at expression, it is not subject to First Amendment scrutiny. In that case, the majority held that a general law prohibiting the use of peyote and other drugs did not require heightened First Amendment scrutiny even though it diminished some people's ability to practice their religion. The state of Indiana in *Barnes v. Glen Theatre* sought to extend *Smith* to the free speech context. (The *Smith* decision has drawn criticism in Congress, where some lawmakers were pressing legislation to reinstate the tougher standard for laws that incidentally breach the First Amendment.)

Scalia referred to the language of the Indiana statute outlawing anyone "engaging [in public] in sexual intercourse, deviate sexual conduct, appearing in a state of nudity or fondling the genitals of himself or another person." He said where, as here, suppression of expression is "merely the incidental effect of forbidding the conduct for other reasons," the Court has allowed the regulation to stand without First Amendment analysis. Justice Souter also wrote separately, saying that nudity per se was not expression: "It is a condition, not an activity, and the voluntary assumption of that condition, without more, apparently expresses nothing beyond the view that the condition is somehow appropriate to the circumstances."

Souter, like Rehnquist, said that nude dancing is subject to a degree of First Amendment protection, but that the state has a "substantial interest" in trying to fight the deleterious effects of adult entertainment, such as, he said, prostitution, sexual assault, and other criminal activity. "Because the state's interest in banning nude dancing results from a simple correlation of such dancing with other evils, rather than from a relationship between the other evils and the expressive component of the dancing, the interest is unrelated to the suppression of free expression," Souter concluded.

Dissenting were Justices White, Marshall, Blackmun, and Stevens. They argued that justices in the majority were trying to apply principles from other cases that involved general proscriptions on individual conduct, which the dissent said was not the case here. The dissenting justices said the Indiana statute should have been subject to higher judicial scrutiny, requiring a "compelling state interest." They said the statute does not meet that standard.

"That the performances in the Kitty Kat Lounge may not be high art, to say the least, and may not appeal to the Court, is hardly an excuse for distorting and ignoring settled doctrine," White wrote.

"The Indiana law, as applied to nude dancing, targets the expressive activity itself; in Indiana nudity in a dancing performance is a crime because of the message such dancing communicates," White continued. Referring to the 1990 peyote case, he said, "In *Smith*, the use of drugs was not criminal because the use was part of or occurred within the course of an otherwise protected religious ceremony, but because a general law made it so and was supported by the same interest in the religious context as in others."

But, here, White said, no general interest is served in preventing nude dancing in theaters and barrooms "since the viewers are exclusively consenting adults who pay money to see these dances. The purpose of the proscription in these contexts is to protect the viewers from what the state believes is the harmful message that nude dancing communicates."

Nudity was an essential part of the dance in question, he said: "[T]he emotional or erotic impact of the dance is intensified by the nudity of the performers. . . . The sight of a fully clothed, or even partially clothed, dancer generally will have a far different impact on a spectator than that of a nude dancer, even if the same dance is performed."

If crime control were the purpose of the statute, White said, the state could have imposed alternative, narrower restrictions.

□□□

Cohen v. Cowles Media Co., dba Minneapolis Star & Tribune Co., decided by a 5-4 vote, June 24, 1991; White wrote the opinion; Souter, Marshall, Blackmun, and O'Connor dissented.

The First Amendment does not shield the news media from lawsuits if reporters break promises of confidentiality to their sources, the Court ruled in a case in which reporters pledged anonymity in exchange for a tip about a political candidate. The Court said a state doctrine of promissory estoppel, which protects people who rely to their detriment on promises from others, applies to all citizens' daily transactions without targeting or singling out the press.

The majority used a legal analysis that provided no extra protection for the media based on the First Amendment. The message was in keeping with a trend in Court decisions that the media should not be singled out for special attention or restriction.

Dissenting justices argued that First Amendment guarantees for the reporting of truthful information should supersede a state's interest in enforcing a newspaper's promise of confidentiality.

The dispute at the heart of this case arose from the 1982 Minnesota gubernatorial race, in which Dan Cohen, a Republican political consultant, offered to turn over to reporters damaging information, stemming from two minor criminal charges, about the Democratic lieutenant governor candidate. After being assured anonymity, Cohen gave the information to reporters from the *St. Paul Pioneer Press Dispatch* and the *Minneapolis Star & Tribune*. Despite the reporters' promises, the two newspapers printed Cohen's name, believing he was part of a smear campaign. Cohen was immediately fired from his advertising agency job. He sued the newspapers, alleging fraudulent misrepresentation and breach of contract.

A state jury awarded him $200,000 in compensatory damages and $500,000 in punitive damages. The state court of appeals affirmed, but the Minnesota Supreme Court reversed, holding that a contract cause of action was inappropriate and that the enforcement of confidentiality under promissory estoppel would violate the newspapers' First Amendment rights.

The Supreme Court disagreed. In ruling that the First Amendment does not bar action for a broken contract, the Court said any resulting constraint on truthful reporting "is no more than the incidental, and constitutionally insignificant, consequence of applying to the press a generally applicable law that requires those who make certain kinds of promises to keep them." Justice White, writing for the majority, dismissed arguments that the ruling would cause the media not to disclose a confidential source's identity—even when it is newsworthy—to avoid lawsuit.

"Minnesota law simply requires those making promises to keep them. The parties themselves, as in this case, determine the scope of their legal obligations and any restrictions which may be placed on the publication of truthful information are self-imposed," White said. Underlying his ruling is the assumption that newspapers have no special immunity from the application of general laws.

Dissenting were Justices Blackmun, Marshall, O'Connor, and Souter.

Blackmun, joined by Marshall and Souter, said that the Court should have applied the standard used in *Hustler Magazine, Inc. v. Falwell* (1988), which said the use of a claim of intentional infliction of emotional distress for the publication of a parody violated the First Amendment. As in that case, Blackmun said, a generally applied law that would suppress speech must meet a strict test. "To the extent that truthful speech may ever be sanctioned consistent with the First Amendment," Blackmun wrote, "it must be in furtherance of a state interest 'of the highest order.' Because the Minnesota Supreme Court's opinion makes clear that the State's interest in enforcing its promissory estoppel doctrine in this case was far from compelling, I would affirm that court's decision."

Justice Souter wrote a dissent, joined by Marshall, Blackmun, and O'Connor. He argued that a law of general applicability affecting free speech rights must be balanced with an interest in a free press and an informed public. He said the state's interest in enforcing a newspaper's promise of confidentiality does not sufficiently outweigh an interest in unrestricted publication of campaign information.

"There can be no doubt that the fact of Cohen's identity expanded the universe of information relevant to the choice faced by Minnesota voters in that state's 1982 gubernatorial election," Souter said. "The propriety of his leak to respondents could be taken to reflect on his character, which in turn could be taken to reflect on the character of the candidate who had retained him as an advisor. An election could turn on just such a factor; if it should, I am ready to assume that it would be to the greater public good, at least over the long run."

□□□

Payne v. Tennessee, decided by a 6-3 vote, June 27, 1991; Rehnquist wrote the opinion; Marshall, Blackmun, and Stevens dissented.

Evidence of a victim's character and the impact of a crime on the victim's family may be used against a murder defendant in a sentencing hearing for capital punishment, the Court ruled in a departure from its precedent. The majority said the Eighth Amendment, which bans cruel and unusual punishment, does not bar a capital sentencing jury from considering such factors.

In allowing such "victim impact statements," the Court overruled two earlier cases (*Booth v. Maryland* (1987) and *South Carolina v. Gathers* (1989)) that prohibited such evidence from being introduced. The Court's premise had been that the information would call too much attention to the victim's character, instead of the defendant's blameworthiness, and would be difficult for the defendant to rebut.

Writing for the majority, Chief Justice Rehnquist said, "We are now of the view that a state may properly conclude that for the jury to assess meaningfully the defendant's moral culpability and blameworthiness, it should have before it at the sentencing phase evidence of the specific harm caused by the defendant." He said adherence to a precedent is usually the "best policy" but is "not an inexorable command."

The abandonment of recent rulings prompted six separate opinions and provoked an outraged dissent. Marshall wrote, "Power, not reason, is the new currency of this Court's decisionmaking. . . . Neither the law nor the facts supporting *Booth* and *Gathers* underwent any change in the last four years. Only the personnel of this Court did."

This case involved Pervis Tyrone Payne, who was convicted by a Tennessee jury of the murders of a woman and her two-year-old daughter and of assault with intent to murder her three year-old son. During his sentencing hearing, the victim's mother testified that the boy missed his mother and baby sister and the prosecutor commented on the continuing effects on the son of his experience and the effects of the crimes on the victims' family.

Payne was sentenced to death. The Tennessee Supreme Court affirmed the conviction and sentence, rejecting the defendant's contention that the grandmother's testimony and the state's closing argument constituted prejudicial violations of his rights under the Eighth Amendment.

In his appeal to the Court, Payne revived concerns from *Booth* and *Gathers* that the admission of victim impact evidence allows a jury to find that defendants whose victims were assets to their community should be more severely punished than victims not as praiseworthy. But Rehnquist wrote, "[V]ictim impact evidence is not offered to encourage comparative judgments of this kind—for instance, that the killer of a hardworking, devoted parent deserves the death penalty, but that the murderer of a reprobate does not. It is designed to show instead each victim's 'uniqueness as an individual human being,' whatever the jury might think the loss to the community resulting from his death might be."

Rehnquist, who was joined by Justices White, O'Connor, Scalia, Kennedy, and Souter, said such evidence is merely another way of generally informing the court about the specific harm caused by a crime. The chief justice also said an inherent unfairness existed in allowing testimony about the defendant's character and not about the victim's.

Payne had argued that, despite any problems with the rules of *Booth* and *Gathers*, the Court should follow the doctrine of stare decisis and leave those decisions alone. Rehnquist first responded that stare decisis "promotes the evenhanded, predictable and consistent development of legal principles, fosters reliance on judicial decisions and contributes to the actual and perceived integrity of the judicial process." But then he added,

"Stare decisis is not an inexorable command; rather, it is a principle of policy and not a mechanical formula of adherence to the latest decision. This is particularly true in constitutional cases, because in such cases correction through legislative action is practically impossible."

Rehnquist said the Court during the past twenty terms has overruled in whole or in part thirty-three of its previous constitutional decisions. He noted that *Booth* and *Gathers* were decided by narrow margins, over dissents challenging the underpinnings of those decisions.

Justice O'Connor wrote a concurring opinion, joined by Justices White and Kennedy, that played up state authority to determine capital sentencing proceedings. She also detailed the brutality of the killings and questioned how the testimony from the grandmother possibly could have inflamed the jury more than the information that the victims died after repeated thrusts from a butcher knife.

In another concurrence, Justice Scalia, joined by O'Connor and Kennedy, criticized Justice Marshall for his dissent lashing out at the Court for turning its back on stare decisis. Scalia said, "It seems to me difficult for those who were in the majority in *Booth* to hold themselves forth as ardent apostles of stare decisis. . . . It was, I suggest, *Booth*, and not today's decision, that compromised the fundamental values underlying the doctrine of stare decisis."

Finally, the Court's newest justice, Souter, joined by Kennedy, offered a concurrence that "*Booth* promises more than it can deliver, given the unresolved tension between common evidentiary standards at the guilt phase and *Booth*'s promise of a sentencing determination free from the consideration of facts unknown to the defendant and irrelevant to his decision to kill."

Marshall was joined by Blackmun in his dissent. "The implications of this radical new exception to the doctrine of stare decisis are staggering," Marshall wrote. "The majority today sends a clear signal that scores of established constitutional liberties are now ripe for reconsideration, thereby inviting the very type of open defiance of our precedents that the majority rewards in this case." He said the value of victim impact evidence is always outweighed by its prejudicial effect because of its inherent power to divert the jury from the character of the defendant.

In another dissent, Stevens, with whom Blackmun joined, argued that the majority's ruling would encourage jurors to decide in favor of death instead of life imprisonment on the basis of emotions, not reason. Noting the current popularity of capital punishment in a crime-ridden society and the victims' rights movement, Stevens said it was a "great tragedy" that the Court bowed to public opinion: "Today is a sad day for a great institution."

3 Case Summaries

The Supreme Court issued 112 signed opinions during the 1990-1991 term, the lowest number in twenty years. One hundred twenty-nine opinions were handed down in the 1989-1990 term; 133, in the term before that. In recent years, the Court has been choosing to hear fewer cases. Justices do not give a reason when they do not accept a dispute. But the decreasing number of cases has been attributed to the dominance in lower courts of appointees of Ronald Reagan and George Bush who are in step with the Court's views, to comparatively fewer requests since the mid-1980s by the U.S. solicitor general that certain cases be reviewed, and to the liberal justices' votes not to hear controversial disputes and thus not risk overturning precedents.

Following are the case summaries for all signed opinions from the 1990-1991 term:

Business Law

Antitrust

City of Columbia v. Omni Outdoor Advertising, Inc., decided by a 6-3 vote, April 1, 1991; Scalia wrote the opinion; Stevens, White, and Marshall dissented.

Cities are protected from antitrust liability, even when they have conspired with private business to enact regulations favoring one company over another. The Court ruled that the city of Columbia, South Carolina, which had imposed a restriction on billboard construction partial to a single company, was exempt from federal antitrust liability under the Court's long-established state-action immunity doctrine. The six-justice majority said that there is no "conspiracy" exception to state-action immunity, as some federal appeals courts previously ruled. The decision reversed a Fourth Circuit ruling.

In this case, one billboard company controlled more than 95 percent of the market in Columbia and had successfully lobbied city officials to pass ordinances favoring its business and limiting the construction of billboards by other outdoor advertising companies. Upholding the city's actions, the Court said localities have wide latitude for regulating domestic commerce. Scalia, writing for the majority, said a conspiracy exception would be impractical: "This would require the sort of deconstruction of the governmental process and probing of the official 'intent' that we have consistently sought to avoid."

Stevens, writing for dissenting justices, said "a private party's agreement with selfishly motivated public officials" should be "sufficient to remove the antitrust immunity."

Norfolk & Western Railway Co. v. American Train Dispatchers Association; CSX Transportation, Inc. v. Brotherhood of Railway Carmen, decided by a 7-2 vote, March 19, 1991; Kennedy wrote the opinion; Stevens and Marshall dissented.

Once the Interstate Commerce Commission approves a rail carrier's merger plan, exempting the railway from antitrust and other laws that might hinder the merger, the railway may be released from its legal obligations under a collective bargaining agreement. A lower federal court held that the statute governing railway consolidations did not authorize the commission to relieve a carrier of collective bargaining responsibility.

Reversing that decision, the Supreme Court said a federal law stipulating that an approved carrier "is exempt from the antitrust laws and from all other law, including state and municipal law, as necessary to let [it] carry out the transaction" encompasses any obstacle to a merger. The statute does not exempt carriers from all law, the Court said, but from all laws necessary to carry out the approved consolidation.

Summit Health, Ltd. v. Pinhas, decided by a 5-4 vote, May 28, 1991; Stevens wrote the opinion; Scalia, O'Connor, Kennedy, and Souter dissented.

An eye surgeon who was denied staff privileges at a Los Angeles hospital and claimed he was the target of a conspiracy to drive him out of business may sue under federal antitrust law. The Court said there is a sufficient connection, or "nexus," between the anticompetitive activity alleged and interstate commerce for the surgeon to invoke the Sherman Act. The surgeon asserted that the hospital retaliated against him in a congressionally regulated peer review process because he refused to follow unnecessarily costly surgical procedures. The surgeon said he had been hurt in California and the medical market generally.

Stevens, who wrote for the majority, said the physician need not argue that the conspiracy had an actual effect on interstate commerce to support federal jurisdiction. "[His] claim that members of the [hospital] peer-review committee conspired with others to abuse that process and thereby deny [him] access to the market for ophthalmological services provided by general hospitals in Los Angeles has a sufficient nexus with interstate commerce to support federal jurisdiction," he said.

Dissenting justices said the Sherman Act should be used only for those conspiracies that restrain trade among several states. Scalia said the ruling would allow routine lawsuits against business to become federal cases and eligible for triple damages, "contributing to the trivialization of the federal courts."

Attorneys' Fees

Chambers v. NASCO, Inc., decided by a 5-4 vote, June 6, 1991; White wrote the opinion; Scalia, Kennedy, Rehnquist, and Souter dissented.

A district court judge may require one party to pay the other party's attorneys' fees and expenses as a sanction for the first party's bad faith conduct. A judge found that a Louisiana television station owner violated court orders and engaged in meritless filings and delaying actions to avoid fulfilling a contract to sell the station.

The Supreme Court said that federal courts have inherent power to manage their own proceedings and to control the conduct of those who appear before them. The Court noted that the "American Rule" generally prohibits the shifting of attorneys' fees, but an exception is allowed when one side has abused the court system.

The Court also said that nothing in the Federal Rules of Civil Procedure, including Rule 11 governing lawyers' behavior and allowing sanctions, precludes a court from imposing attorneys' fees as punishment for bad faith.

Dissenting justices said that, while the behavior deserved sanction, the majority was broadening a federal judge's inherent authority beyond statutory and case law.

Kay v. Ehrler, decided by a 9-0 vote, April 16, 1991; Stevens wrote the opinion.

An attorney who successfully represents himself in a civil rights lawsuit may not be awarded attorneys' fees under Section 1988 of Title 42 of the U.S. Code. The Court said neither the attorneys' fees statute nor its legislative history clearly provides for whether a lawyer who represents himself should be treated like a client who has an independent attorney.

But the unanimous Court said Section 1988's overriding goal is to ensure that victims of civil rights violations are able to hire lawyers for the effective prosecution of their claims. The Court said that policy is served best by a rule that "creates an incentive to retain counsel in every case," instead of a disincentive to hire a lawyer whenever a party believes himself competent to represent himself.

West Virginia University Hospitals, Inc. v. Casey, Governor of Pennsylvania, decided by a 6-3 vote, March 19, 1991; Scalia wrote the opinion; Marshall, Stevens, and Blackmun dissented.

Winning parties in civil rights litigation cannot recover expert witness fees as part of reasonable attorneys' fees under a 1976 federal law.

Section 1988 of Title 42 allows "a reasonable attorney's fee" to be imposed on the losing party in civil rights cases.

The Court said the phrase "attorney's fee" means only that and was not written by Congress to include fees for experts' services.

Dissenting justices said the Court should take a broader reading of the statute. Stevens said, "[W]e do the country a disservice when we needlessly ignore persuasive evidence of Congress' actual purpose and require it to take the time" to rewrite a statute. He said the majority's holding would hurt persons trying to vindicate civil rights.

Bankruptcy

Farrey v. Sanderfoot, decided by a 9-0 vote, May 23, 1991; White wrote the opinion.

Federal bankruptcy law cannot be used by a former spouse to avoid the other spouse's lien on what had been the couple's home. In this case, the husband was given the house in a divorce judgment, subject to the wife's lien for half of the estate, estimated at $30,000. Instead of paying off the lien, the husband declared bankruptcy, claimed a homestead exemption, and tried to avoid the wife's lien.

White, writing for the unanimous Court, said a debtor must have an interest in the property before the lien attaches if he wants to avoid the lien through a bankruptcy action. White said the husband had no interest in the property covered by the lien before it attached, because the husband's half-interest was ended in the divorce decree.

Grogan v. Garner, decided by a 9-0 vote, January 15, 1991; Stevens wrote the opinion.

Under federal bankruptcy law, a defrauded creditor may prove his claim with a "preponderance of the evidence" to make sure the claim is not discharged in a bankruptcy proceeding. The section of the Bankruptcy Code at issue barred the discharge of debts for money obtained fraudulently.

The case was brought by a creditor who won a civil fraud judgment against an individual who then filed for bankruptcy. The fraud judgment was based on a preponderance of the evidence standard, and the creditor argued that he should not have to relitigate to prevent discharge of the debtor's obligation to him. But a federal appeals court held that a higher "clear and convincing" standard of proof should be the test, because that standard traditionally was applied in common law fraud and dischargeability cases.

The unanimous Court sided with the creditor, saying the preponderance standard, not the clear and convincing standard, is presumed to apply in civil actions between private parties unless particularly important individual interests or rights are at stake.

The Supreme Court first met on February 1, 1790, in the Royal Exchange building at the intersection of Broad and Water streets in what now is Manhattan's financial district.

Johnson v. Home State Bank, decided by a 9-0 vote, June 10, 1991; Marshall wrote the opinion.

A debtor may include a mortgage lien in an approved reorganization plan under Chapter 13 of the Bankruptcy Code even after his personal liability in the mortgage has been discharged in a Chapter 7 liquidation. The Court said a mortgage lien securing an obligation for which a debtor's personal liability has been discharged in a Chapter 7 liquidation still is a "claim" under a necessarily broad reading of the Chapter 13 provisions.

Chapter 13 allows reorganization for consumer debtors and business owners with small debts. In this case, a farmer who defaulted on promissory notes secured with a mortgage on his farm was discharged from personal liability on the notes after filing under Chapter 7 of the Bankruptcy Code. He then filed under Chapter 13 to protect his farm from foreclosure, raising the question whether his surviving mortgage interest should be considered a claim included in a Chapter 13 reorganization.

The unanimous Court said the surviving interest is an "enforceable obligation" for the debtor. Even after his personal obligations have ended, justices said, the bank-creditor still retains a "right to payment" from proceeds from the sale of the property.

Owen v. Owen, decided by an 8-1 vote, May 23, 1991; Scalia wrote the opinion; Stevens dissented.

A Florida law that exempted homestead property from liens does not supplant a federal Bankruptcy Code provision that presumes the attachment of liens, allowing the liens later to be eliminated when an individual files for bankruptcy. In this case a wife had obtained a $160,000 judgment against her former husband. He did not own any property at the time, but, under the law, the judgment would attach to any later-acquired property. When he bought a condominium in 1984, the lien effectively attached to that. A year later, Florida amended its homestead law allowing the ex-husband's condominium to qualify as a homestead and thereby be exempt from liens. However, Florida specifically disallowed the homestead exemption if there was a preexisting lien.

In 1986, the ex-husband filed for bankruptcy, claimed a homestead exemption, and tried to discharge the lien.

The Court said the Bankruptcy Code allows states to exempt property from an estate that will be distributed among the debtor's creditors. But the code also provides that judicial liens encumbering exempt property can be eliminated. The question, Scalia said, is whether the lien destroys an exemption to which the debtor would have been entitled but for the lien itself. The Court sent the case back to the appeals court for resolution.

Toibb v. Radloff, decided by an 8-1 vote, June 13, 1991; Blackmun wrote the opinion; Stevens dissented.

The Bankruptcy Code permits individual debtors not engaged in business to file for relief under Chapter 11, which allows reorganization instead of liquidation of assets. In a ruling favoring bankruptcy consumers, the Court said that, although the structure and legislative history of Chapter 11 demonstrate that it was intended primarily for the use of business debtors, no "ongoing business" requirement exists for Chapter 11 reorganization.

In this case, the debtor originally filed under Chapter 7, but, after he discovered that stock he owned in an electric power company had substantial value, he tried to avoid its liquidation by seeking to convert the

Chapter 7 case to one under Chapter 11. The Supreme Court reversed a lower court ruling that said he did not qualify for relief under Chapter 11 because he was not engaged in an ongoing business.

Copyright

Feist Publications, Inc. v. Rural Telephone Service Co., Inc., decided by a 9-0 vote, March 27, 1991; O'Connor wrote the opinion.

Telephone white pages generally are not entitled to protection under federal copyright law, because they lack the "requisite originality" for protection. The lawsuit arose when a telephone book publisher copied a telephone utility's northwest Kansas listings, after the utility had refused to license its white page listings to the publisher.

Writing for the Court, O'Connor said that, although the requisite level of creativity is extremely low for a copyright violation, "There is nothing remotely creative about arranging names alphabetically in a white-pages directory. It is an age-old practice, firmly rooted in tradition and so commonplace that it has come to be expected as a matter of course.... It is not only unoriginal, it is practically inevitable." Justice Blackmun concurred only in the judgment.

Punitive Damages

Pacific Mutual Life Insurance Co. v. Haslip, decided by a 7-1 vote, March 4, 1991; Blackmun wrote the opinion; O'Connor dissented; Souter took no part in the case.

Juries have broad discretion to decide punitive damages, even when the awards are greatly disproportionate to the actual damage suffered, as long as the awards are guided by reasonableness and are not "extreme." Punitive damages are awarded in civil cases to punish defendants or to deter future illegal conduct.

The case arose from a judgment for a woman who was defrauded out of her insurance coverage when an agent pocketed her premiums. The Court, allowing an award against an insurance company to stand, cited the jury's finding that the agent had been under the authority of the insurance company when he defrauded the woman and that Alabama's longstanding common law rule is that a company is liable for both compensatory and punitive damages for the fraud of its agents. *(See entry, p. 13; excerpts, p. 91)*

Securities

Gollust v. Mendell, decided by a 9-0 vote, June 10, 1991; Souter wrote the opinion.

For standing under an insider trading section of the Securities Exchange Act of 1934, a complaining party only must be the "owner of a security" of the corporation at the time the lawsuit is brought. Any security, including stock, notes, warrants, bonds, and debentures, will satisfy the standing requirement.

The unanimous Court said, however, that the person who brings the lawsuit must keep some financial interest in the litigation throughout its duration.

The relevant section of the 1934 law imposes strict liability on owners of more than 10 percent of a corporation's listed stock, and on the corporation's officers and directors, for any profits realized from a purchase and sale, or sale and purchase, of the stock within a six-month period. The question here was whether shareholders who filed a lawsuit against the "insiders" to recover illegal profits could continue the suit after a merger had caused an exchange of their original stock for cash and stock of a new corporate parent.

The Court held that a stockholder's properly instituted suit could continue after his interest in the issuer was exchanged in the merger.

Kamen v. Kemper Financial Services, Inc., decided by a 9-0 vote, May 20, 1991; Marshall wrote the opinion.

State law controls whether a shareholder in a derivative action under the Investment Company Act of 1940 first must make a request to directors to file a lawsuit. Most states require that a shareholder make a written demand on the board of directors before bringing a derivative suit. The demand asks the board to bring a suit or otherwise correct the wrongdoing. If the board refuses to act, the shareholder then may file the lawsuit. If the demand would be futile, under most state laws, the requirement is excused.

Marshall, writing for the unanimous Court, said when a gap occurs in the federal securities laws bearing on internal corporate powers, federal courts should combine the relevant state law with federal common law. Federal common law alone, Marshall noted, creates neither a futility exception nor a particular demand requirement.

The ruling reversed a lower court decision relying on federal common law to reject a shareholder's prior claim of demand futility when she tried to bring a derivative action on behalf of a mutual fund but had made no demand first on the fund's board of directors.

Lampf, Pleva, Lipkind, Prupis & Petigrow v. Gilberston, decided by a 5-4 vote, June 20, 1991; Blackmun wrote the opinion; Stevens, Souter, O'Connor, and Kennedy dissented.

Federal securities law, not state statutes, should govern the statute of limitations for cases brought under the federal antifraud provisions of the securities laws.

The Court said litigation based on 1933 and 1934 federal securities statutes must begin within one year after the discovery of the facts constituting the violation and within three years of the violation (or fraud-tainted investment) itself. The limits replace longer deadlines in state laws.

In this case, investors sued a law firm for its role in an allegedly fraudulent tax shelter plan. The defendants argued that allowing the case to be governed by a state statute of limitations would lead to forum shopping and compromise the policies of the federal securities laws.

Virginia Bankshares, Inc. v. Sandberg, decided by 9-0 and 5-4 votes, June 27, 1991; Souter wrote the opinion.

Proxy statements that contain directors' knowingly false statements of reasons for a recommended corporate transaction may be considered misstatements of material fact under § 14(a) of the 1934 Securities Exchange Act prohibiting fraudulent proxy materials. The law requires full and fair disclosure, and violations make the directors liable for damages.

The Court unanimously held that directors' recommendations, even though conclusory in form, may be challenged in a lawsuit. Justices said a shareholder would have considered the directors' reasons in deciding how to vote on a recommended corporate transaction, in this case a merger. But the Court added that liability exists only if the statement is factually incorrect or falsely states the directors' motivations for their recommendations.

In this case, the directors sent out proxy solicitations, although they were not required by state law for the merger at hand. In a separate part of the opinion, five justices said shareholders whose votes are not required by law to authorize the transaction cannot recover damages based on the proxy solicitation. The ruling significantly cut back on stockholders' ability to bring lawsuits under the 1934 law. Joining Souter in this part were Rehnquist, White, O'Connor, and Scalia, overturning a lower court ruling for shareholders who had asserted that they were underpaid when a bank bought up their stock.

Taxes

Cheek v. United States, decided by a 6-2 vote, January 8, 1991; White wrote the opinion; Blackmun and Marshall dissented; Souter took no part in the case.

A taxpayer who asserts a "good faith" belief that he does not have to pay taxes cannot be held criminally liable for willfully violating tax laws. Breaches of tax law require "willfulness," the Court said, to protect the average citizen from prosecution for innocent mistakes made because of the complexity of the tax laws.

The defendant here admitted he did not file returns but testified that he did not act willfully because he believed, based on his indoctrination by a tax-protester group, that the tax laws were unconstitutional.

In sending the case back to a trial court, the Court said that if the jury believes the defendant sincerely thought the Tax Code did not treat wages as income, as he asserted, the government would not have proven willfulness. Dissenting justices said that the ruling would encourage taxpayers "to cling to frivolous views of the law" to escape criminal prosecution.

Cottage Savings Association v. Commissioner of Internal Revenue, decided by a 7-2 vote, April 17, 1991; Marshall wrote the opinion; Blackmun and White dissented.

Financial institutions may deduct from their taxes paper losses from "reciprocal sales" of mortgage loans when the properties they exchange are materially different.

In 1791, the Supreme Court moved from New York to Philadelphia, joining the rest of the federal government. The Court remained in City Hall until 1800.

Cottage Savings Association simultaneously sold interests in 252 mortgages to four associations and purchased from them interests in 305 other mortgages. All of the loans were secured by single-family homes. The savings and loan was taking advantage of a rule adopted by the Federal Home Loan Bank Board that allowed thrifts to generate tax losses without book losses. It was intended for thrifts to obtain tax refunds without having to lower their net worth for accounting purposes.

On its 1980 federal income tax return, Cottage Savings claimed a deduction for the adjusted difference between the face value of the interests it traded and the fair market value of the interests it received. A court of appeals found that Cottage Savings was not entitled to the deduction because the losses were not actually sustained.

The Supreme Court, however, said as long as the property entitlements were not identical, their exchange allows the taxpayer the appreciated or depreciated value of the property.

Dennis v. Higgins, Director, Nebraska Department of Motor Vehicles, decided by a 7-2 vote, February 20, 1991; White wrote the opinion; Kennedy and Rehnquist dissented.

Lawsuits for violations of the Commerce Clause may be brought under Section 1983 of Title 42 of the U.S. Code, a civil rights law that allows individuals to sue for deprivation of "any rights, privileges, or immunities secured by the Constitution and [federal] laws." It permits winning parties to obtain attorneys' fees and court costs from the losing party.

The dispute arose after an Ohio-based trucker challenged a Nebraska motor carrier tax, specifically imposed on vehicles registered in other states, as discriminatory. The Court said the broad construction of Section 1983 and the idea of "rights" covers state law that might interfere with free interstate trade.

Freytag v. Commissioner of Internal Revenue, decided by 9-0 and 5-4 votes, June 27, 1991; Blackmun wrote the opinion; Scalia, O'Connor, Kennedy, and Souter dissented from part of the opinion.

Federal law authorizes the Tax Court's chief judge to assign any Tax Court proceeding, regardless of complexity or amount in controversy, to a temporary, special trial judge for a hearing and findings, the Court ruled unanimously.

Separately, five justices found that courts established under Article I of the Constitution, such as the Tax Court, are "Courts of Law" within the meaning of the Appointments Clause. Writing for the majority, Blackmun said those courts, like life-tenure judges appointed under Article III of the Constitution, exercise the judicial power of the United States. He said the Tax Court is independent of the executive and legislative branches, it exercises judicial power to the exclusion of any other function, and its role resembles that of the federal district courts.

James B. Beam Distilling Co. v. Georgia, decided by a 6-3 vote, June 20, 1991; Souter wrote the opinion; O'Connor, Rehnquist, and Kennedy dissented.

A 1984 Supreme Court decision striking down a Hawaii tax on out-of-state liquor as unconstitutional should be applied retroactively, the Court said in a case that could lead to the state of Georgia providing tax refunds to out-of-state liquor distillers who were subjected to higher taxes than in-state distillers. The 1984 Court decision ordered refunds from a similar tax found unconstitutional under the Commerce Clause. The majority in *Jim Beam* concluded that once the Court has applied a rule of law to parties in one civil case, the rule must be applied to all other litigants bringing similar claims. The Court reversed a decision of the Georgia Supreme Court and remanded the case.

The Court's ruling endorsed the idea that, when it applies retroactive relief—such as ordering a refund—in one case, subsequent lawsuits based on that ruling also can result in retroactive relief. The earlier decision was the Court's rejection of a Hawaii liquor tax scheme in *Bacchus Imports, Ltd. v. Dias.*

Leathers, Commissioner of Revenues of Arkansas v. Medlock; Medlock v. Leathers, Commissioner of Revenues of Arkansas, decided by a 7-2 vote, April 16, 1991; O'Connor wrote the opinion; Marshall and Blackmun dissented.

An Arkansas sales tax extended to cable television services, but with an exemption for print media, does not violate the First Amendment unless it is likely to inhibit the free exchange of ideas. At issue was a sales tax on personal property and services.

The Court acknowledged that cable services provide news and information and, as such, engage in speech and are part of the press. But the Court said taxing cable services differently from other media does not by itself raise First Amendment problems. The Court said cable companies could win the discrimination lawsuit only if the Arkansas tax scheme endangered the free expression of ideas.

Oklahoma Tax Commission v. Citizen Band Potawatomi Indian Tribe of Oklahoma, decided by a 9-0 vote, February 26, 1991; Rehnquist wrote the opinion.

In a case involving an Indian-run convenience store, the Court said a state may collect taxes on sales of goods to people who are not members of an Indian tribe on land held in trust for this tribe. But under the doctrine of tribal sovereign immunity, a state may not go to court to enforce collection of the taxes.

The Court, ruling on a store owned by the Citizen Band Potawatomi Indian Tribe that sold cigarettes and other items, said the tribe's sovereign immunity does not deprive Oklahoma of the authority to tax cigarette sales to nonmembers of the tribe at the tribe's store.

Rehnquist said states could sue store managers or seize goods that did not carry tax stamps.

Trinova Corp. v. Michigan Department of Treasury, decided by a 6-2 vote, February 19, 1991; Kennedy wrote the opinion; Stevens and Blackmun dissented; Souter took no part in the case.

Michigan's single-business tax levied against entities having "business activity" within the state and levied on the value added to merchandise does not violate either the Due Process Clause or the Commerce Clause. An Ohio corporation with a sales office in Michigan sued the state, alleging that the three-factor apportionment provision (using comparative payroll, capital, and profit figures) did not fairly represent the extent of its business activity within the state.

But the Supreme Court ruled that the tax meets the tests for validity by not discriminating against interstate commerce by having a "rational relationship" between the income attributed to the state and the in-state value of the enterprise. The Court said its job was not to attempt to devise the best method of tax apportionment but "to ensure that each state taxes only its fair share of an interstate transaction."

United States v. Centennial Savings Bank FSB (Resolution Trust Corporation, Receiver), decided by 7-2 and 9-0 votes, February 17, 1991; Marshall wrote the opinion; Blackmun and White dissented.

Centennial realized tax-deductible losses when it exchanged mortgage interests with another lender, the Court held in a ruling similar to its decision in *Cottage Savings Association v. Commissioner of Internal Revenue.*

The Court also ruled unanimously, however, that penalties collected from depositors who make early withdrawals cannot be excluded from a financial institution's taxable income. The Court said the income could be considered arising from a "discharge of indebtedness" and exempt from taxes only when the income comes from the forgiveness of an obligation to repay that is assumed when a transaction originally is made.

Civil Procedure

Business Guides, Inc. v. Chromatic Communications Enterprises, Inc., decided by a 5-4 vote, February 26, 1991; O'Connor wrote the opinion; Kennedy, Marshall, Stevens, and Scalia dissented.

A federal civil procedure rule intended to discourage frivolous court filings applies to clients as well as their attorneys. The Court said that Rule 11 of the Federal Rules of Civil Procedure clearly states that a party who signs a pleading or other paper without first making a "reasonable inquiry" into the merits of the allegations shall be sanctioned. Even if a represented party signs the pleading, when he need not have under the rule, he can be sanctioned, the Court said, rejecting arguments that the duty should be limited to attorneys and pro se parties. Clients should not have a more lenient standard, the majority said.

The four dissenting justices argued, in an opinion by Kennedy, that Rule 11 is intended to control attorneys' behavior. He said the Court's ruling could lead "citizens who seek the aid of the federal courts [to] risk money damages or other sanctions if they do not satisfy some objective standard of care in the preparation or litigation of a case."

Carnival Cruise Lines, Inc. v. Shute, decided by a 7-2 vote, April 17, 1991; Blackmun wrote the opinion; Stevens and Marshall dissented.

A provision of a cruise line's standard passenger ticket requiring any disputes arising from the terms of the ticket to be filed in a Florida court can be enforced. The Supreme Court said that although the forum-selection clause was not the subject of bargaining it was freely negotiated.

The dispute stemmed from a lawsuit brought by a Washington woman who had slipped and fallen on a deck mat while the ship sailed near Mexico and who tried to sue the cruise line in her home state. Blackmun said for the Court that the cruise line has a special interest in limiting where lawsuits might be filed, given that it could be subject to claims in several forums. He added that the forum requirement makes clear to all potential parties where a claim must be brought and that passengers likely gain the benefit of reduced fares because a cruise line effectively saves money by limiting where it can be sued.

Connecticut v. Doehr, decided by a 9-0 vote, June 6, 1991; White wrote the opinion.

A Connecticut statute that authorizes a person's property to be subject to a lien without prior notice or a hearing, without a showing of extraordinary circumstances, and without a requirement that the person seeking to have the property seized post a bond violated the Due Process Clause of the Fourteenth Amendment.

The Court said that states must provide a hearing before allowing one party to a civil lawsuit to obtain a property lien against the other party. "The risk of erroneous deprivation that the state permits here is substantial," White said for the unanimous Court. Connecticut was one of only a few states that did not require notice or a procedure for a party to challenge an attachment judgment.

Edmonson v. Leesville Concrete Co., Inc., decided by a 6-3 vote, June 3, 1991; Kennedy wrote the opinion; O'Connor, Rehnquist, and Scalia dissented. (Also listed with jury decisions under Criminal Law section.)

Potential jurors in civil cases cannot be excluded by lawyers because of the would-be jurors' race. The Court extended to a case involving a negligence claim a 1986 criminal law rule that barred prosecutors from using peremptory strikes to exclude jurors solely because they were of the same race as the criminal defendant.

A certain number of peremptory jury challenges are allowed for both parties to a dispute and permit potential jurors to be rejected without reason.

"Race discrimination within the courtroom raises serious questions as to the fairness of the proceedings conducted there," Kennedy wrote for the Court. While acknowledging that the conduct of private parties usually is outside the scope of the Constitution, he said, "Racial bias mars the integrity of the judicial system and prevents the idea of democratic government from becoming a reality."

O'Connor, dissenting, said race discrimination in peremptory challenges was "abhorrent," but she asserted that the guarantee of equal protection in jury selection did not extend to disputes between private parties. "The government is not responsible for everything that occurs in a courtroom," she said. "The government is not responsible for a peremptory challenge by a private litigant." *(See entry, p. 26; excerpts, p. 147)*

Firstier Mortgage Co., also known as Realbanc, Inc. v. Investors Mortgage Insurance Co., decided by a 9-0 vote, January 15, 1991; Marshall wrote the opinion.

A bench ruling may be considered a "final decision" under federal appellate procedures that dictate the timing for filing notice of appeals after final decisions. In this case, one of the parties filed a notice of appeal after the federal district court announced from the bench that it intended to grant summary judgment for the other party, but before entry of the judgment and before the parties, at the court's request, submitted proposed findings of fact and conclusions of law. The court entered its judgment about a month later.

Reversing an appeals court decision that the losing party violated federal appeals rules, the Court said federal rules of appellate procedure allow a notice of appeal filed from a court ruling that was not final to be considered an effective notice of appeal from a subsequently entered final judgment, as long as the bench ruling could have been appealed if immediately followed by the entry of judgment.

International Primate Protection League v. Administrators of Tulane Educational Fund, decided by an 8-0 vote, May 20, 1991; Marshall wrote the opinion; Scalia took no part in the case.

A lawsuit filed in state court challenging the treatment of monkeys used for medical experiments was improperly removed to federal court by the federal National Institutes of Health (NIH), one of the defendants.

A group of organizations and individuals seeking humane treatment of animals filed the suit in Louisiana civil district court. The monkeys were housed at a primate research center in Louisiana. NIH removed the suit to federal court, citing a statute that allows federal workers sued in their official capacity to remove to federal court. A federal appeals court eventually vacated an injunction protecting the monkeys and dismissed the case finding that the activists lacked standing.

The Supreme Court said the activists have standing to challenge the removal of the case. The unanimous Court said the animal rights groups have suffered an injury, by losing the right to sue in the forum of their choice, that can be traced to NIH's removal of the case. And if they prevail, the Court said, their injury will be redressed because the federal courts will lose subject matter jurisdiction and the case will be remanded. The Court also said that the NIH lacked authority to remove the case because the law it asserted applied to "officers," that is, individuals, acting in official capacity, not agencies.

Salve Regina College v. Russell, decided by a 6-3 vote, March 20, 1991; Blackmun wrote the opinion; Rehnquist, White, and Stevens dissented.

A federal court of appeals may not give a less stringent review to a district court's determination of state law than to a federal law determination. The court of appeals in this case did not adequately review the state law at the heart of the case, a majority of justices said.

The case stemmed from a nursing student who brought a lawsuit against the college after being asked to withdraw from the nursing program because of her obesity. She brought claims based on intentional infliction of emotional distress, invasion of privacy, and nonperformance by the college of an implied agreement to educate her. A district court judge directed a verdict for the college on the first two claims but put the third claim to a jury, which found for the student and awarded her $30,500. An appeals court upheld the verdict, deferring to the district court's determination of state law.

The Supreme Court said the court of appeals should have reviewed de novo (anew) the district court's determination of state law. Blackmun said for the majority, "Independent appellate review of legal issues best serves the dual goals of doctrinal coherence and economy of judicial administration. District judges preside alone over fast-paced trials: of necessity they devote much of their energy and resources to hearing witnesses and reviewing evidence."

Criminal Law

Capital Punishment

Lankford v. Idaho, decided by a 5-4 vote, May 20, 1991; Stevens wrote the opinion; Scalia, Rehnquist, White, and Souter dissented.

A murder defendant's right to due process was violated when a judge sentenced the defendant to death without the defendant earlier knowing the death penalty was being considered. A state prosecutor had told the defendant that he was seeking only life in prison, but the trial judge, who under Idaho law had full responsibility for determining the sentence, said the defendant's crimes were serious enough to warrant more severe punishment.

Reversing the sentence, the Supreme Court said that if the defendant's counsel had known that capital punishment was being considered, the counsel could have tried to rebut the grounds for it. As it stood, the defense counsel presented no evidence to counter the possible imposition of death, relying on the prosecutor's written notice.

Dissenting justices said that, in effect, the defendant had adequate notice because he knew he had been convicted of first-degree murder, which in Idaho means a possible punishment of death.

Parker v. Dugger, decided by a 5-4 vote, January 22, 1991; O'Connor wrote the opinion; White, Rehnquist, Scalia, and Kennedy dissented.

The Florida Supreme Court acted arbitrarily when, in considering an appeal of a death sentence, it failed to take into account evidence from the murder defendant that mitigated his crime.

This case began after a jury found that the mitigating circumstances of the defendant's crime outweighed the aggravating circumstances for capital punishment and recommended that the defendant be sentenced to life in prison. The mitigating factors at issue were not based on a statute. The trial judge, who had ultimate sentencing authority under Florida state law, overrode the jury's recommendation after finding no statutory mitigating circumstances related to the murder. He sentenced the defendant to death.

On appeal, the Florida Supreme Court concluded that there was not enough evidence to support two of the six aggravating factors that the trial judge relied upon in sentencing the defendant to death. Yet, the state's highest court then took the trial judge's findings of no mitigating circumstances. The U.S. Supreme Court said that the state court should have reweighed the evidence. Dissenting justices said that the state court properly deferred to the trial judge's findings.

Payne v. Tennessee, decided by a 6-3 vote, June 27, 1991; Rehnquist wrote the opinion; Marshall, Blackmun, and Stevens dissented.

Evidence of a victim's character and the impact of a crime on a victim's family may be used against a murder defendant in a sentencing hearing for capital punishment. The majority said the Eighth Amendment, which bans cruel and unusual punishment, does not bar a capital sentencing jury from considering these factors.

In allowing "victim impact statements," the Court overruled two earlier cases (*Booth v. Maryland* (1987) and *South Carolina v. Gathers* (1989)) that prohibited such evidence from being introduced. The Court's assumption had been that the information would call too much attention to the victim's character, instead of the defendant's blameworthiness, and would be difficult for the defendant to rebut.

Writing for the majority, Rehnquist said, "We are now of the view that a state may properly conclude that for the jury to assess meaningfully the defendant's moral culpability and blameworthiness, it should have before it at the sentencing phase evidence of the specific harm caused by the defendant." He said adherence to a precedent usually is the "best policy" but is "not an inexorable command."

The abandonment of recent rulings provoked a spirited dissent. Marshall wrote, "Power, not reason, is the new currency of this court's decisionmaking.... Neither the law nor the facts supporting *Booth* and *Gathers* underwent any change in the last four years. Only the personnel of this court did." *(See entry, p. 35; excerpts, p. 175)*

Schad v. Arizona, decided by a 5-4 vote, June 21, 1991; Souter wrote the opinion; White, Marshall, Blackmun, and Stevens dissented.

An Arizona law allowing a jury to forgo agreement on the type of first-degree murder that a defendant committed does not violate a defendant's right to due process of law. At issue was whether a first-degree murder conviction was valid under jury instructions that did not require unanimity on whether the defendant was guilty of premeditated murder or felony murder. Felony murder differs from premeditated murder in that it does not require that the defendant commit the killing or even intend to kill; the defendant only must be involved in the underlying felony.

Souter, writing for himself and three justices, said a jury may reach one verdict based on any combination of the alternative findings, as long as jurors agree the defendant was guilty of first-degree murder. He said the elements for jury findings on the two types of murder were similar. Scalia concurred in the judgment but on broader grounds.

White wrote for dissenting justices, "A verdict that simply pronounces a defendant 'guilty of first-degree murder' provides no clues as to whether the jury agrees that the ... elements of premeditated murder or the ... elements of felony murder have been proven beyond a reasonable doubt. Instead, it is entirely possible that half of the jury believed the defendant was guilty of premeditated murder and not guilty of felony murder/robbery, while half believed exactly the reverse."

Criminal Procedure

Demarest v. Manspeaker, decided by a 9-0 vote, January 8, 1991; Rehnquist wrote the opinion.

Federal law requires payment of witness fees to a convicted state prisoner who testifies at a federal trial under a writ of habeas corpus ad testificandum (used to order a prisoner to give testimony).

In 1810, the Court took occupancy of a courtroom in the Capitol designed especially for it. The Supreme Court chamber was home to the Court until 1860.

The Court said the statute makes clear that the fees provision referring to a "witness in attendance at any court of the United States" includes prisoners unless they otherwise are exempted in the statute. This case involved a Colorado inmate who appeared as a defense witness in a federal criminal trial and then was denied witness fees by the U.S. attorney. The Supreme Court rejected the federal officials' contention that the reimbursement of fees applied only to persons who testified under a subpoena.

Peretz v. United States, decided by a 5-4 vote, June 27, 1991; Stevens wrote the opinion; Marshall, White, Blackmun, and Scalia dissented.

Magistrates may supervise jury selection in a felony trial if the parties agreed to have magistrates fill in for federal judges, a five-justice majority said. The Court said the Federal Magistrates Act's "additional duties" clause allows a magistrate to supervise jury selection.

Magistrates, who have some but not all of the powers of judges, handle preliminary court proceedings and generally have jurisdiction to try minor offenses. They are not appointed to the bench for life as are federal judges. In this case, a magistrate presided over the jury selection after the defendant's lawyer consented to the procedure. However, the defendant then was convicted on drug charges and on appeal said it was an error to have the magistrate select the jury.

The Court said a defendant has no constitutional right to have a judge preside at jury selection if he has raised no objection to the judge's absence. Dissenting justices said the decision "contorted" a 1989 ruling (*Gomez v. United States*), which said that the magistrates act does not authorize magistrates to conduct jury selection at a felony trial, by asserting that the presence of consent is relevant.

Touby v. United States, decided by a 9-0 vote, May 20, 1991; O'Connor wrote the opinion.

The U.S. attorney general has broad power to classify drugs as illegal substances. The Court's ruling upheld a 1984 federal law aimed at so-called designer drugs. The defendant was found guilty of manufacturing the drug "Euphoria" and asserted that Congress improperly delegated legislative power to the attorney general.

Under the 1984 law, Congress gave the attorney general emergency power to temporarily designate drugs as illegal substances if the attorney general found it was "necessary to avoid an imminent hazard to the public safety." Usual procedures for clarifying illegal drugs often consist of lengthy delays. The Court said the law was not an unconstitutional delegation by Congress of its legislative powers.

United States v. R. Enterprises, Inc., decided by a 9-0 vote, January 22, 1991; O'Connor wrote the opinion.

A grand jury may issue a subpoena duces tecum (for specific documents or papers) without having to show that the materials would be relevant to a criminal investigation and admissible at trial. The Court said that the standard for relevancy in its 1974 decision in *United States v. Nixon* does not apply in a grand jury proceeding.

The case arose from a subpoena issued by a federal grand jury that was investigating allegations of interstate transportation of obscene materials. The targeted companies moved to quash the subpoenas, arguing that they called for production of materials irrelevant to the grand jury's investigation.

In upholding the subpoenas, the Supreme Court commented on the unique role of the grand jury to decide whether a crime has occurred. The Court said a grand jury traditionally has been able to compel the production of evidence without the procedural and evidentiary restraints governing the conduct of criminal trials. Still, it said, a grand jury investigation is subject to limits of federal procedure, and a district court may quash or modify a subpoena if compliance would be unreasonable or oppressive.

Habeas Corpus

Coleman v. Thompson, Warden, decided by a 6-3 vote, June 24, 1991; O'Connor wrote the opinion; Blackmun, Marshall, and Stevens dissented.

A death row inmate may not file a habeas corpus petition in federal court if he failed to abide by state court procedural rules. The convicted murderer in this case missed a deadline for filing an appeal at the state level by three days.

Petitions for habeas corpus are used by inmates to challenge the constitutionality of their convictions and sentences. Repetitive petitions for habeas corpus long have been a concern of a majority on the Court because inmates use successive petitions to delay their executions.

The Court said an inmate's petition for habeas corpus review should be barred unless he could show cause for the procedural default and actual prejudice as a result of the alleged violation of federal law or unless he could demonstrate that failure to consider the claims would result in a fundamental miscarriage of justice.

This decision reversed a 1963 ruling, in *Fay v. Noia*, that allowed most prisoners to file habeas corpus petitions in federal court unless they deliberately had bypassed state review. O'Connor, writing for the majority, explained that states must have first opportunity to correct their mistakes and that federal courts generally may not review a state court's denial of a state prisoner's constitutional claim if the state's rejection is independent of a federal question and supports the prisoner's continued custody.

Dissenting, Blackmun said the ruling continued the Court's "crusade to erect petty procedural barriers" to habeas corpus petitions.

McCleskey v. Zant, Superintendent, Georgia Diagnostic and Classification Center, decided by a 6-3 vote, April 16, 1991; Kennedy wrote the opinion; Marshall, Blackmun, and Stevens dissented.

Death row prisoners should be allowed one round of federal court review through petitions for habeas corpus, after state court appeals are exhausted, barring extraordinary circumstances. The six-justice majority said that a prisoner may file only one habeas corpus petition in federal court unless good reason exists for not having raised any new constitutional error on the first round. The prisoner also is required to show that he suffered "actual prejudice" from the error he asserts.

Under earlier court rulings, second and subsequent habeas corpus petitions were dismissed out of hand only if a prisoner deliberately withheld grounds for appeal (possibly to raise the arguments in later petitions). Dissenting justices asserted that the majority "exercises legislative power" by establishing tougher standards. *(See entry, p. 21; excerpts, p. 120)*

Ylst, Warden v. Nunnemaker, decided by a 6-3 vote, June 24, 1991; Scalia wrote the opinion; Blackmun, Marshall, and Stevens dissented.

A state court's failure to explain why it denied a prisoner's petition for habeas corpus is not a sufficient reason to give the prisoner a federal habeas corpus hearing. The inmate in this case had broken a state procedural rule for filing petitions for habeas corpus. In a petition to the U.S. Supreme Court, he said the "procedural bar" to further court review should be lifted because the state court did not explain why it would not hear his case. Petitions for habeas corpus are used by inmates to allege constitutional violations in their cases.

The Court said that the defendant did not overcome a presumption that the California Supreme Court's last unexplained order considered the merits of his argument. Dissenting justices referred to their dissent in *Coleman v. Thompson.*

Imprisonment

McCarthy v. Bronson, Warden, decided by a 9-0 vote, May 20, 1991; Stevens wrote the opinion.

Federal magistrates, not only federal judges, may hear cases involving prison conditions when the inmates have waived a right to a jury trial.

A 1976 federal law authorizes magistrates to hear and make findings on prisoner confinement. But the defendant in this case said that only a federal judge could hear a case arising from a specific complaint—that guards had used excessive force when they transferred him from one cell to another. The Supreme Court rejected the argument, saying that magistrates may hear, in addition to challenges to ongoing prison conditions, specific complaints from individual inmates.

Wilson v. Seiter, decided by a 5-4 vote, June 17, 1991; Scalia wrote the opinion; White, Marshall, Blackmun, and Stevens dissented.

A prisoner who claims that the conditions of his confinement violate the Eighth Amendment's prohibition on cruel and unusual punishment must show a culpable state of mind, "deliberate indifference," on the part of prison officials.

An inmate in Nelsonville, Ohio, made a number of allegations about the prison, among them overcrowding, inadequate heating, and unsanitary conditions. He sought declaratory and injunctive relief, as well as $900,000 in compensatory and punitive damages. He said that the conditions were ongoing and systemic and that, as a result, the mental state of mind of prison officials should not be relevant.

The majority rejected that argument and said the prisoner failed to show "intent" on the part of prison officials in creating the bad conditions: "Our cases say the offending conduct must be wanton," Scalia wrote. The majority upheld a lower court test for liability that the prison officials be shown to have acted "maliciously and sadistically for the very purpose of causing harm."

Dissenting justices said that proving inhumane conditions should be enough. White wrote, "The ultimate result of today's decision, I fear, is that 'serious deprivations of basic human needs' will go unredressed due to an unnecessary and meaningless search for 'deliberate indifference.' "

Interrogation

Arizona v. Fulminante, decided by separate 5-4 decisions, March 26, 1991; White first wrote an opinion for five justices saying that a defendant's confession, based on the proper standard of totality of the circumstances, was coerced (Rehnquist, O'Connor, Kennedy, and Souter dissented); Rehnquist then wrote for five justices that a coerced confession used at trial does not necessarily taint a conviction (White, Marshall, Blackmun, and Stevens dissented); finally, White wrote for a new coalition of five justices that in this case the confession was not "harmless error" (Rehnquist, O'Connor, and Scalia dissented; Souter did not sign on to either side for this part of the opinion).

The important ruling here was that a coerced confession does not automatically destroy a conviction. That decision reversed a 1967 ruling establishing that it was a denial of due process to use a forced confession against a defendant, regardless of other evidence. In the 1967 case, *Chapman v. California*, the Court held that a coerced confession would never be "harmless error" and must result in reversal of the conviction.

Rehnquist, writing for five justices on the critical part of the case, said if other evidence was enough to convict the defendant, a compelled confession may be "harmless error"—and thus not dictate a new trial. White, dissenting, said the Court had overruled a "vast body of precedent." He said, "Permitting a coerced confession to be part of the evidence . . . is inconsistent with the thesis that ours is not an inquisitorial system" of justice. *(See entry, p. 18; excerpts, p. 111)*

McNeil v. Wisconsin, decided by a 6-3 vote, June 13, 1991; Scalia wrote the opinion; Stevens, Marshall, and Blackmun dissented.

Police may interrogate a suspect without his lawyer being present even though the suspect just appeared with a lawyer at a hearing involving another crime. The Court said a suspect's invocation of the Sixth Amendment right to counsel during a judicial proceeding does not constitute an invocation of the right-to-counsel derived from the Fifth Amendment guarantee against self-incrimination in another crime.

Writing for the majority, Scalia said the Sixth Amendment right accompanies specific offenses. The defendant here appeared at a bail hearing for armed robbery with his counsel; later he was questioned, after waiving his Miranda rights, about a murder case.

Minnick v. Mississippi, decided by a 6-2 vote, December 3, 1990; Kennedy wrote the opinion; Scalia and Rehnquist dissented; Souter took no part in the decision.

Once a suspect has invoked his right to counsel, police may not resume questioning him in custody without the suspect having his lawyer present, even if he has consulted with counsel in the meantime. The Court extended a rule, established in *Edwards v. Arizona* (1981), requiring the police to stop interrogation after the accused asks for a lawyer.

The defendant had met with an attorney who told him not to talk. The police later told the defendant he could not refuse to answer questions about the case.

Jury Selection

Edmonson v. Leesville Concrete Co., Inc., decided by a 6-3 vote, June 3, 1991; Kennedy wrote the opinion; O'Connor, Rehnquist, and Scalia dissented. (This case also is listed under Civil Procedure. *(For description of case, see p. 52)*

Ford v. Georgia, decided by a 9-0 vote, February 19, 1991; Souter wrote the opinion.

The Georgia Supreme Court made a mistake when it concluded that a defendant had not properly argued that the jury selection in his case violated equal protection under law, the high Court held unanimously. The Supreme Court also ruled that the state court erred in barring the claim as untimely under a state procedural rule.

The Court said that although the defendant's pretrial motion did not mention the Equal Protection Clause, and his new trial motion cited the Sixth Amendment instead of the Fourteenth, the pretrial motion's reference to a pattern of excluding black potential members "over a long period of time" constituted an equal protection claim based on the evidentiary theory derived from *Swain v. Alabama* (1985). *Swain* preceded the Court's landmark ruling in *Baston v. Kentucky* that potential jurors could not be excluded on the basis of race.

In *Swain v. Alabama*, the Court said that purposefully excluding members of the defendant's race from his jury denied the defendant equal protection under the Fourteenth Amendment. But it held at the time that the defendant would have to prove a pattern of racial discrimination in prior cases as well as his own to prevail. The defendant in this case alleged that the county prosecutor "over a long period of time" excluded black persons from juries when the issues to be tried involved members of another race.

Hernadez v. New York, decided by a 6-3 vote, May 28, 1991; Kennedy wrote the opinion; Blackmun, Stevens, and Marshall dissented.

A prosecutor who struck from a jury pool bilingual Hispanics did not violate the constitutional guarantee of equal protection of the law, because the trial court found that the potential jurors were not eliminated because of race. The prosecutor excluded the Hispanics from a jury in a murder trial that involved Spanish-language testimony. He told the judge that after talking to the Hispanics he believed they would not accept an interpreter's English translation of the Spanish testimony. The defendant moved for a mistrial after the prosecutor dismissed the jurors.

The Supreme Court noted that the prosecutor had offered a reason other than race for his peremptory strike and said the trial judge acted within his broad discretion to accept the explanation. Stevens, dissenting, said, the explanation by the prosecutor "was insufficient to dispel the existing inference of racial animus."

Mu'min v. Virginia, decided by a 5-4 vote, May 30, 1991; Rehnquist wrote the opinion; Marshall, Blackmun, Stevens, and Kennedy dissented.

A criminal defendant does not have a right to ask potential jurors how much they know about a crime as long as they promise to be fair. The Court said a trial court's refusal of a defense request to question prospective jurors about their knowledge of a case and specific contents of news reports did not violate his constitutional right to be tried by an impartial jury.

A trial judge has wide discretion on jury selection, the majority said. Dissenting justices asserted that the trial judge has to do more to assess jurors' impartiality when they have been exposed to prejudicial pretrial publicity.

Powers v. Ohio, decided by a 7-2 vote, April 1, 1991; Kennedy wrote the opinion; Scalia and Rehnquist dissented.

A criminal defendant may object to race-based exclusions of jurors through peremptory challenges whether or not the defendant and the excluded jurors share the same race. The decision expanded the right of criminal defendants, stemming from the landmark *Batson v. Kentucky* (1986), to object to a prosecutor's use of peremptory challenges to exclude persons because of race.

A certain number of peremptory jury challenges are allowed for both parties to a dispute and permit potential jurors to be rejected without giving a reason. On trial was a white defendant who objected to the prosecution's elimination of several black potential jurors.

Kennedy, writing for the Court, said, "Racial discrimination in the selection of jurors casts doubt on the integrity of the judicial process and places the fairness of a criminal proceeding in doubt." He said that if only blacks were able to challenge prosecutors' exclusion of blacks from juries the process would condone arbitrary exclusion: "An individual juror does not have a right to sit on any particular petit jury, but he or she does possess the right not to be excluded from one on account of race."

Rape Shield Law

Michigan v. Lucas, decided by a 7-2 vote, May 20, 1991; O'Connor wrote the opinion; Stevens and Marshall dissented.

The Confrontation Clause of the Sixth Amendment does not guarantee that an alleged rapist may introduce evidence of a prior romantic relationship with the alleged victim. The defendant had been barred from introducing such evidence at trial because he failed to meet a rule that he notify prosecutors within ten days after arraignment that he would seek to introduce such testimony.

The majority rejected the defendant's argument that the ten-day rule violated his constitutional right to confront his accuser. It said the state's "notice-and-hearing requirement" served legitimate interests of protecting rape victims against surprise, harassment, and unnecessary invasions of privacy.

Search and Seizure

California v. Acevedo, decided by a 6-3 vote, May 30, 1991; Blackmun wrote the opinion; White, Stevens, and Marshall dissented.

Police do not need a warrant for a search of a car and all closed containers inside, if police have probable cause that a container in the car holds contraband but lack probable cause for the entire vehicle. Justice Blackmun said the decision would end confusion from conflicting Court decisions about what can be searched when police stop a driver and have probable cause to believe a vehicle contains evidence, justifying an exception to the constitutional bar to warrantless searches. He asserted that questions over whether probable cause in a specific case covers the whole car or only particular containers had burdened effective law enforcement.

In a dissent, Stevens said by broadening the "automobile exception" to the Fourth Amendment warrant requirement, the majority undermined constitutional protections against unreasonable law enforcement practices. He said in this particular case no exigent circumstances existed to waive the Court's prior rules against warrantless searches. Addressing Blackmun's concerns about effective police work, Stevens wrote ironically: "No impartial observer could criticize this Court for hindering the progress of the war on drugs. On the contrary, decisions like the one the Court makes today will support the conclusion that this Court has become a loyal foot soldier in the executive [branch]'s fight against crime."

California v. Hodari D., decided by a 7-2 vote, April 23, 1991; Scalia wrote the opinion; Stevens and Marshall dissented.

A youth who was running from police and dropped cocaine as he was being pursued was not "seized" within the meaning of the Fourth

Amendment. The Court ruled that to constitute a seizure of the person either physical force or submission to an officer's show of authority must have occurred.

A lower court ruled that the cocaine should be suppressed because it was the fruit of an illegal search—the police did not have the requisite "reasonable suspicion" required to justify stopping the defendant. But the Supreme Court ruled that, because no actual restraint occurred before the youth discarded the cocaine, there was no unconstitutional search or seizure. Discovery of the cocaine was not the result of improper police conduct, the Court said, and therefore could be admitted at trial.

County of Riverside, California v. McLaughlin, decided by a 5-4 vote, May 13, 1991; O'Connor wrote the opinion; Marshall, Blackmun, Stevens, and Scalia dissented.

An individual may be jailed for up to forty-eight hours without a hearing before a magistrate to determine whether his arrest was proper. Writing for the majority, O'Connor cited burdened criminal justice systems and said local courts need flexibility to combine the probable cause hearing with a bail hearing or arraignment.

The Supreme Court met in the old Senate chamber on the first floor of the Capitol from 1860 to 1935.

Scalia, who usually is with the majority limiting defendants' rights, said in a dissent that twenty-four hours should be the limit: "While in recent years we have invented novel applications of the Fourth Amendment to release the unquestionably guilty, we today repudiate one of its core applications so that the presumptively innocent may be left in jail."

Florida v. Bostick, decided by a 6-3 vote, June 20, 1991; O'Connor wrote the opinion; Marshall, Blackmun, and Stevens dissented.

Police may approach passengers on buses and ask to search their luggage for illegal drugs without suspicion that the passengers are engaged in wrongdoing. O'Connor said the ruling flowed from prior decisions allowing random searches in other public places. She stressed that the defendant had the right to refuse.

Marshall wrote for dissenting justices that the policy bears the mark of "coercion and unjustified intrusion." He said it violates the "core" of the Fourth Amendment prohibition on unreasonable searches.

Florida v. Jimeno, decided by a 7-2 vote, May 23, 1991; Rehnquist wrote the opinion; Marshall and Stevens dissented.

A criminal suspect's Fourth Amendment right to be free from unreasonable searches is not violated when, after he gives police permission to search his car, officers open a closed container found within the car that might reasonably hold the object of the search. The Court said that, once a stopped motorist authorizes the search of the car for narcotics, he allows a search of all containers inside the car.

Dissenting justices said consent to a search of car interior does not naturally mean consent to search closed containers such as bags and briefcases.

Sentencing

Braxton v. United States, decided by a 9-0 vote, May 28, 1991; Scalia wrote the opinion.

In a limited ruling, the Court said a federal district judge had misapplied a provision of the *U.S. Sentencing Commission Guidelines Manual*, which requires a court to use the guideline that most fits the conviction. The lower court sentenced the defendant, who pleaded guilty to assault and firearms charges, as if he had been convicted of an attempt-to-kill count.

Burns v. United States, decided by a 5-4 vote, June 13, 1991; Marshall wrote the opinion; Souter, White, O'Connor, and Rehnquist dissented.

A federal judge cannot give a defendant a harsher sentence than the range set by federal sentencing guidelines, without providing advance notice to the parties that he is considering a departure from the guidelines and giving the reason for the step. "Notice must specifically identify the ground on which the district court is contemplating an upward departure," the Court said.

Marshall wrote that the Federal Rule of Criminal Procedure "contemplates full adversarial testing of the issues relevant to a Guidelines sentence" and requires that a defendant be given a chance to argue against the sentence.

Souter said in a dissent: "For all this attentive concern with procedure, neither [the federal sentencing rule] nor any other provision of the Sentencing Reform Act expressly requires advance notice of a district court's intention to depart sua sponte from the Guidelines range."

Chapman v. United States, decided by a 7-2 vote, May 30, 1991; Rehnquist wrote the opinion; Stevens and Marshall dissented.

When the weight of the hallucinogenic drug LSD is being considered to determine sentencing, federal guidelines require that the blotter paper used to carry the drug be included in the weight. Defendants were convicted of selling ten sheets of blotter paper containing LSD. They argued that the weight of the drug should be only the weight of the LSD itself (.005 grams), not including the weight of the paper on which it had been sprayed (total 5.7 grams). Sentences generally are harsher the greater the amount of the drug involved, and defendants convicted of distributing more than 1 gram of LSD get a five-year minimum prison term under federal law.

The majority said that, because the statute at issue refers to a "mixture or substance containing a detectable amount," the entire mixture or substance is to be weighed when calculating the sentence.

Dissenting justices said the decision would punish more severely those who sell small quantities of LSD in weighty carriers, instead of those who sell large quantities of LSD in lighter carriers.

Gozlon-Peretz v. United States, decided by a 9-0 vote, February 19, 1991; Kennedy wrote the opinion.

All drug offenses specified by the 1986 Anti-Drug Abuse Act fall under the requirements of "supervised release," as defined by the 1987 Sentencing Reform Act's provisions. At issue were offenses committed during the period after the drug law was enacted but before the Sentencing Reform Act's provisions for supervised release became effective. The difference is the time between October 27, 1986, and November 1, 1987.

The unanimous Court spurned the defendant's argument that because the sentencing guidelines did not become effective until November 1, 1987, the term "supervised release" as used in the drug act had no significance before that date, and the courts had no power to impose it.

Harmelin v. Michigan, decided by a 5-4 vote, June 27, 1991; Scalia wrote the opinion; White, Blackmun, Marshall, and Stevens dissented.

A state may require life in prison without parole for a first-time drug offense without violating the constitutional ban on cruel and unusual punishment. Scalia, writing for a five-justice majority, said that consideration of whether an individual deserves the particular statutory penalty is only necessary when a court is considering capital punishment.

In another part of his opinion, which did not command a majority, Scalia said that severe, mandatory penalties may be cruel, but they are not unusual in the constitutional sense because they have been used in various forms throughout the country's history.

Dissenting justices argued that Scalia's distinction between capital and noncapital crimes was flawed and that the Court's past cases required proportionality in the idea of "cruel and unusual" punishment.

Miscellaneous Criminal Cases

Burns v. Reed, decided by a 6-3 vote, May 30, 1991; White wrote the opinion; Scalia, Blackmun, and Marshall dissented in part.

A state prosecuting attorney is absolutely immune from liability for damages under a civil rights law for participating in a warrant hearing at which he withheld information critical to a defendant's rights. But, the Court said, a prosecutor is not immune from lawsuit for the legal advice given to the police on the case. The key, according to the Court's analysis, is whether the prosecutor's conduct is "intimately associated with the judicial phase of the criminal process."

During a hearing on probable cause for a warrant, through a prosecutor's questioning of a police officer, it emerged that a defendant had confessed to shooting one of her sons while they slept. But neither the officer nor the prosecutor told the judge that the confession was made under hypnosis or that the defendant otherwise had denied guilt.

White said that participation in the hearing was similar to a prosecutor's conduct before a grand jury, protected by absolute immunity.

Moskal v. United States, decided by a 5-3 vote, December 3, 1990; Marshall wrote the opinion; Scalia, O'Connor, and Kennedy dissented; Souter took no part in the decision.

If a person receives genuine vehicle titles, knowing that they contain fraudulently tendered odometer readings, he does so knowing they have been "falsely made" in violation of federal law. The defendant had been involved in a "title washing" scheme in which automobile titles that were altered to reflect rolled-back odometer mileage figures were sent from Pennsylvania to Virginia. In Virginia, authorities were unaware of the alterations and issued titles using the false figures.

The Court rejected an argument by the defendant that the doctrine of lenity required the Court to interpret the statute as applying only to forged or counterfeited securities, as some courts had held. The Supreme

Court said the doctrine applies only to those situations in which reasonable doubt exists about a statute's intended scope—after consideration of the language and structure, legislative history, and motivating policies of the statute.

Scalia wrote for dissenting justices that "falsely made" refers to the tools of counterfeiting, and not to the tools of misrepresentation. "If the Rule of Lenity means anything, it means that the Court ought not to do what it does today: use an ill-defined general purpose to override an unquestionably clear term of art, and (to make matters worse) give the words a meaning that even one unfamiliar with the term of art would imagine."

Yates v. Evatt, Commissioner, South Carolina Department of Corrections, decided by a 9-0 vote, May 28, 1991; Souter wrote the opinion.

The South Carolina Supreme Court failed to apply the proper harmless error standard of a 1967 case (*Chapman v. California*) to jury instructions that were found unconstitutional. *Chapman* stands for the proposition that an error is harmless only if it appears "beyond a reasonable doubt that the error complained of did not contribute to the verdict obtained."

In throwing out the defendant's murder conviction, the Court ruled unanimously that the judge's error in jury instructions that allowed the jury to presume the defendant acted with malice was not a "harmless error" and that the state Supreme Court had "employed a deficient standard of review" in the case.

Federal Regulation

Arcadia, Ohio v. Ohio Power Co., decided by an 8-0 vote, November 27, 1990; Scalia wrote the opinion; Souter took no part in the case.

A section of the Federal Power Act that governs overlapping jurisdictions of the Securities and Exchange Commission (SEC) and Federal Energy Regulatory Commission (FERC) does not apply to a case in which the SEC authorized a power company to buy coal from an SEC-approved affiliate at a price equal to the affiliate's actual costs and then the FERC declared unreasonable the resulting charges the power company was to pass on to customers.

A federal court of appeals held that FERC's disallowance of the charges was precluded by the Federal Power Act. But the Supreme Court said, "Never before this case has [that act] been used as a general conflicts provision, policing the entire border between the two agencies." The Court sent the case back to the lower court and suggested the

FERC's decision might be flawed for other reasons, for example, because one of its own regulations states that when the price of fuel purchased from an affiliate "is subject to the jurisdiction of a regulatory body, such cost shall be deemed to be reasonable and includable" in wholesale rates.

FMC Corp. v. Holliday, decided by a 7-1 vote, November 27, 1990; O'Connor wrote the opinion; Stevens dissented; Souter took no part in the case.

State laws that bar insurance companies from going after court awards that an accident victim wins in a tort case are preempted by the federal Employee Retirement Income Security Act of 1974 (ERISA). At issue was a Pennsylvania "motor vehicle financial responsibility" law that said "there shall be no right of subrogation or reimbursement from a claimant's tort recovery" of benefits paid under an insurance policy. An accident victim argued that the Pennsylvania law blocked her insurance company from seeking money she won in a lawsuit to reimburse earlier insurance benefits paid.

O'Connor wrote that Congress had intended ERISA to protect from state insurance laws self-funding insurance plans, such as the one in this case: "It [ERISA] is plainly directed at any law of any state purporting to regulate insurance companies, insurance contracts, banks, trust companies, or investment companies."

Ingersoll-Rand Co. v. McClendon, decided by a 9-0 vote, December 3, 1990; O'Connor wrote the opinion.

The federal Employee Retirement Income Security Act of 1974 (ERISA) preempts a state common law claim by workers who assert that they were fired because an employer did not want to pay them benefits under an ERISA-covered pension plan.

The Court said that workers must file under the federal law, which does not allow punitive damages as some state laws permit fired workers to win. The case originated when a Texas worker who had been at his job for more than nine years alleged that he was fired so his company could avoid paying him pension benefits, which were due to vest within a few months. He sought damages for wrongful discharge in state court under tort and contract theories.

Martin, Secretary of Labor v. Occupational Safety and Health Review Commission, decided by a 9-0 vote, March 20, 1991; Marshall wrote the opinion.

Final authority for interpreting ambiguous standards under the 1970 Occupational Safety and Health Act (OSHA) rests with the secretary of labor, not with the Occupational Safety and Health Review Commission.

The act gives distinct regulatory tasks to both the labor secretary and the review commission—the former with setting and enforcing

The Supreme Court building, where the Court presides today, opened in 1935.

workplace health and safety standards and the latter with carrying out adjudicatory functions. In this case, after the secretary found that a steel manufacturer had provided some of its employees with loose-fitting respirators that exposed them to impermissible coke emission levels, the secretary cited the company and assessed a fine. The commission vacated the citation, ruling that the facts did not establish a violation of the regulation cited. (The regulation used required only that an employer train employees in the proper use of respirators. Another regulation, not mentioned in the violation, stated the employer's obligation to assure a proper fit.)

The Court said federal courts should defer to the secretary when the secretary and the commission give reasonable but conflicting interpretations of regulations under the act. Marshall, writing for the Court, said Congress did not intend to sever the power to interpret OSHA regulations from the secretary's power to promulgate and enforce them.

Melkonyan v. Sullivan, Secretary of Health and Human Services, decided by a 9-0 vote, June 10, 1991; O'Connor wrote the opinion.

A winning party in a civil rights action against the United States may be awarded attorneys' fees, court costs, and other expenses under the Equal Access to Justice Act. But the winning party must submit to the district court an application for fees and expenses within thirty days of a "final judgment" in the action. The Court ruled that the law requires a final judgment to be entered by a court, before the thirty-day deadline starts to run, and rejected an argument by the secretary of health and human services that final judgment includes decisions made by administrative agencies.

Metropolitan Washington Airports Authority v. Citizens for the Abatement of Aircraft Noise, Inc., decided by a 6-3 vote, June 17, 1991; Stevens wrote the opinion; White, Rehnquist, and Marshall dissented.

An interstate airport authority, initiated by Congress to be independent but whose directors were subject to veto power by a review board composed of members of Congress, violated the separation of powers doctrine. The Court said Congress exceeded its powers by dictating in such detail the structure of the airport authority, its membership, and powers.

The airport agency grew out of the 1986 Metropolitan Airports Act, in which Congress gave control of two airports to an agency created by a compact between the District of Columbia and Virginia. Washington-area residents had challenged the airport authority, attempting to head off a proposed renovation plan at National Airport that they said would cause noise from takeoffs and landings to become even worse.

Writing for the majority, Stevens said the airport authority set-up "provides a blueprint for extensive expansion of the legislative power beyond its constitutionally-confined role." Dissenting justices called it an "innovative and otherwise lawful governmental experiment" and said that the separation of powers doctrine should not apply to an agency created by state law.

Mobil Oil Exploration & Producing Southeast, Inc. v. United Distribution Cos.; Federal Energy Regulatory Commission v. United Distribution Cos., decided by an 8-0 vote, January 8, 1991; White wrote the opinion; Kennedy took no part in the case.

The Federal Energy Regulatory Commission had the authority, as part of commission rules adopted in 1986, to set a new single ceiling price for gas from older wells. The Court upheld the government's power to lift price controls on some natural gas and reinstated the federal regulations that allowed gas producers to raise some prices charged to pipeline companies. "Congress found the need to encourage new gas production sufficiently pressing to deal with the matter directly but was content to leave old gas pricing within the discretion of the commission to alter as conditions warranted," White wrote.

The 1986 rules let producers of old gas raise their prices and stop selling to pipeline companies unwilling to pay higher prices.

United States v. Gaubert, decided by a 9-0 vote, March 26, 1991; White wrote the opinion.

The federal government cannot be sued for damages arising from banking regulators' negligent handling of the day-to-day operations of troubled savings and loan institutions.

The Court said a regulator is shielded from liability under the Federal Tort Claims Act because his actions presumably flow from policies at the heart of federal banking statutes, which grant broad discretion to control savings and loans.

The lawsuit by a former owner of a Texas-based savings and loan alleged that government regulators ran the thrift into financial ruin through mismanagement of the institution.

Wisconsin Public Intervenor v. Mortier, decided by a 9-0 vote, June 21, 1991; White wrote the opinion.

The Federal Insecticide, Fungicide and Rodenticide Act (FIFRA) does not preempt local governments' regulation of residents' pesticide use. The 1972 FIFRA regulates the production, sale, and use of pesticides.

The Court said that, while the federal law was intended to be comprehensive to protect the environment from pesticides, it does not prohibit localities from providing more control. The law said explicitly that states have the power to control pesticide use, but courts differed in their interpretations of whether localities have similar authority. At issue was a small Wisconsin town's ban on aerial spraying and a challenge by tree growers and farmers. The town's ban was upheld.

State Regulation

State Elections

Renne, San Francisco City Attorney v. Geary, decided by a 6-3 vote, June 17, 1991; Kennedy wrote the opinion; White, Marshall, and Blackmun dissented.

Democratic political activists who sued the state of California over its law prohibiting political parties from endorsing, supporting, or opposing candidates for nonpartisan offices did not demonstrate a dispute ripe for resolution by the federal courts.

City and county officials, following the state law, banned any references to party endorsements on voter pamphlets, and the party leaders claimed the pamphlet rules violated the First Amendment. The Court said their allegations failed to show any actual threat to a particular individual's or group's free speech rights.

Campaign Finance

McCormick v. United States, decided by a 6-3 vote, May 23, 1991; White wrote the opinion; Stevens, Blackmun, and O'Connor dissented.

An extortion conviction under the Hobbs Act, arising from an elected official's receipt of a campaign contribution, requires a "quid pro quo," the realization of some benefit to the contributor, as a condition that the money be given.

The defendant in the case was a West Virginia state legislator who first sponsored legislation favoring foreign medical school graduates unable to pass state licensing exams and then later sought money from the doctors. The Court said payments are illegal only when they are taken in return for a promise to perform or not to perform a special act.

State Immunity

Blatchford, Commissioner, Department of Community and Regional Affairs of Alaska v. Native Village of Noatak, decided by a 6-3 vote, June 24, 1991; Scalia wrote the opinion; Blackmun, Marshall, and Stevens dissented.

The Eleventh Amendment, which shields states from being sued in federal courts by individuals seeking money damages, bars Indian tribes from suing state governments for money damages for violations of their constitutional rights.

Two Alaska native villages tried to bring a claim against a state agency official to win payment of money allegedly owed under a state revenue sharing statute.

Siegert v. Gilley, decided by a 6-3 vote, May 23, 1991; Rehnquist wrote the opinion; Marshall, Blackmun, and Stevens dissented.

A clinical psychologist who claimed that his former employer, a federal hospital, infringed his "liberty" interests by giving him a bad recommendation failed to state a claim for a violation of any constitutional right.

Writing for the Court, Rehnquist said an injury to reputation by itself is not a protected liberty interest. He said the psychologist failed to claim the violation of a clearly established constitutional right.

Dissenting justices said that a violation of the psychologist's liberty rights arose out of his inability to get a new job: "We have repeatedly recognized that an individual suffers the loss of a protected liberty interest where government action has operated to bestow a badge of loyalty or infamy, with an attendant foreclosure from other employment opportunity," Marshall wrote.

The chief justice of the United States sits at the center of the bench, with the senior associate justice at his immediate right and the second senior associate justice at his immediate left. The other justices take their places in alternating order of seniority.

Individual Rights

Abortion Rights

Rust v. Sullivan, decided by a 5-4 vote, May 23, 1991; Rehnquist wrote the opinion; Blackmun, Marshall, Stevens, and O'Connor dissented.

An administrative agency may forbid workers at publicly funded clinics from counseling pregnant women on abortion. The Court said Title X of the Public Health Service Act of 1970 may be read to bar not only abortions but also abortion counseling. Congress stipulated in that law that no federal funds could be used in "programs where abortion is a method of family planning."

In the 1980s, the Ronald Reagan administration, consistent with its effort to stem abortions, had used the language to try to stop abortion counseling at federally funded clinics. But those who unsuccessfully challenged the "gag rule"—doctors, health clinics, and the city and state of New York—said the statute meant only what it said explicitly: no money for abortions. *(See entry, p. 23; excerpts, p. 132)*

Civil Rights

Astoria Federal Savings & Loan Association v. Solimino, decided by a 9-0 vote, June 10, 1991; Souter wrote the opinion.

A worker whose age discrimination claim was reviewed and rejected by a state administrative agency is not precluded from filing a lawsuit in federal court. After the New York State Division of Human Rights rejected the discrimination complaint by a sixty-three-year-old man who was fired from a savings and loan, the worker, instead of appealing to state court, filed a lawsuit in federal court.

Souter wrote for the unanimous Court that the worker was entitled to federal court review of his complaint under the Age Discrimination in Employment Act, even though his claim previously had been reviewed by a state agency. He said the 1967 law makes clear that collateral estoppel (a bar to further litigation because of a prior judgment in the case) does not apply to state agency findings, as distinguished from court findings.

Board of Education of Oklahoma City Public Schools v. Dowell, decided by a 5-3 vote, January 15, 1991; Rehnquist wrote the opinion; Marshall, Blackmun, and Stevens dissented; Souter took no part in the case.

Formerly segregated school districts may be freed of school busing orders if they can prove that any elements of past discrimination have been removed to all "practicable" extent. Stressing that school desegregation decrees were meant to be temporary, the Supreme Court said a federal court may lift a desegregation order if the school district has complied with the decree in good faith and eliminated "the vestiges of past discrimination."

In a step toward returning the Oklahoma City schools to local control, the Court rejected a tougher standard imposed by an appeals court for determining whether school desegregation orders may be dissolved.

Regarding the standard that should be used, Chief Justice Rehnquist said, "In considering whether the vestiges of de jure segregation had been eliminated as far as practicable, the district court should look not only at student assignments, but to every facet of school operations." The decision did not define how a court would measure whether all practicable efforts had been made.

Marshall, who as a civil rights lawyer had argued the landmark *Brown v. Board of Education* case before the Court, said for the dissenting justices that a desegregation decree should not be lifted as long as the "stigmatic injury" of racial discrimination sought to be eliminated by the 1954 *Brown* ruling persisted.

Equal Employment Opportunity Commission v. Arabian American Oil Co., decided by a 6-3 vote, March 26, 1991; Rehnquist wrote the opinion; Marshall, Blackmun, and Stevens dissented.

Title VII of the 1964 Civil Rights Act does not cover U.S. workers employed in overseas offices of U.S.-based companies. The case was brought by a naturalized U.S. citizen who was born in Lebanon. He was working in Saudi Arabia for a U.S.-based company and alleged that his boss fired him after subjecting him to racial, religious, and ethnic slurs. Title VII bars job discrimination on the basis of an individual's race, color, religion, sex, or national origin.

Rehnquist wrote for the majority that while it was "plausible" that Congress wanted Title VII to apply to U.S. multinational firms, no persuasive evidence existed to demonstrate such. He dismissed arguments by the Equal Employment Opportunity Commission that Title VII has broad jurisdiction, saying much of the wording was "boilerplate language which can be found in any number of congressional acts, none of which have ever been held to apply overseas." He also noted that Congress did not provide guidelines for overseas enforcement.

Gilmer v. Interstate/Johnson Lane Corp., decided by a 7-2 vote, May 13, 1991; White wrote the opinion; Stevens and Marshall dissented.

A worker's claim under the Age Discrimination in Employment Act of 1967 can be subjected to compulsory arbitration if the worker previously signed an agreement to arbitrate all employment disputes. The worker was a securities representative with several stock exchanges, including the New York Stock Exchange, which required in its registration application that workers agree to arbitration.

At age sixty-two, the worker was fired from his firm. He contended that the compulsory arbitration process was biased and ran counter to the underlying goals of the age discrimination law.

Rejecting those arguments, White wrote for the majority that the age bias law, like other federal statutes, is subject to the government's policy favoring arbitration.

Gregory et al., Judges v. Ashcroft, Governor of Missouri, decided by a 7-2 vote, June 20, 1991; O'Connor wrote the opinion; Blackmun and Marshall dissented.

Missouri's mandatory retirement requirement for judges does not violate the Age Discrimination in Employment Act of 1967. The Court said the authority of a state to determine the qualifications of its governmental officials lies "at the heart of representative government" and is reserved under the Tenth Amendment.

The Missouri Constitution sets a mandatory retirement age of seventy for most state judges. The judges in this case filed a lawsuit saying that the provision violated the federal age discrimination law as well as the Equal Protection Clause of the Fourteenth Amendment.

O'Connor, writing for the majority, said Congress did not intend for the age discrimination law to cover judges because they are not "employees," as defined in the law. More importantly, she said, to interfere with Missouri's decision to establish a qualification for its judges would upset the usual constitutional balance of federal and state powers.

International Union, United Automobile, Aerospace & Agricultural Implement Workers of America, UAW v. Johnson Controls, Inc., decided by 9-0 and 5-4 votes; March 20, 1991; Blackmun wrote the opinion; White, Rehnquist, Kennedy, and Scalia dissented from a key portion of the opinion.

Companies may not exclude women from jobs that might harm a developing or potential fetus. The justices divided, however, over standards in federal antidiscrimination law. Five justices said that Congress intended to forbid all hiring practices based on a worker's ability to have children. Blackmun said for that majority that "Congress has left this choice to the woman as hers to make." He was joined by Marshall, Stevens, O'Connor, and Souter.

Four justices (White, Rehnquist, Kennedy, and Scalia) said situations could arise in which a company, because of personal injury liability and workplace costs, excludes women based on hazards to the unborn. White said that Title VII of the 1964 Civil Rights Act could be satisfied if an employer showed that excluding women from certain jobs was reasonably necessary to avoid major lawsuits. *(See entry, p. 16; excerpts, p. 102)*

Irwin v. Veterans Administration, decided by 7-1 and 6-2 votes, December 3, 1990; Rehnquist wrote the opinion; Stevens dissented in one

The wording of the saying carved on the front of the Supreme Court building—"Equal Justice Under Law"—was decided by architect Cass Gilbert and Chief Justice William Howard Taft.

part; White and Marshall dissented in another; Souter took no part in the case.

Deadlines for filings under Title VII of the 1964 Civil Rights Act that are tied to giving notice to one of the parties may be triggered when the party's attorney is notified. The Court said that notice to an attorney's office, which is acknowledged by a representative of that office, qualifies as notice to the client.

The seven-justice majority said if the rule were otherwise factual disputes could arise about when actual notice was received. Justices White and Marshall dissented from a portion of the Court's opinion holding that the thirty-day time period is subject to equitable tolling.

Stevens v. Department of the Treasury, decided by a 9-0 vote, April 24, 1991; Blackmun wrote the opinion.

A federal employee who intends to bring an age discrimination complaint directly to federal court must notify the Equal Employment Opportunity Commission (EEOC) of his intent to file the action within 180 days after the alleged incident occurred but need not file suit within 30 days of giving notice. The Court said a lower court misread a federal statute when it said an employee had to notify the EEOC within 30 days prior to bringing the lawsuit.

Here the employee had given notice 176 days after the alleged discrimination. He filed suit more than 30 days later.

First Amendment

Barnes, Prosecuting Attorney of St. Joseph County, Indiana v. Glen Theatre, Inc., decided by a 5-4 vote, June 21, 1991; Rehnquist wrote the opinion; White, Marshall, Blackmun, and Stevens dissented.

States may ban nude dancing as part of public indecency laws without breaching the First Amendment right of expression. The Court said a law intended to protect social order and morality may incidentally infringe on nude dancing as a form of expression. The lawsuit was brought by Indiana clubs that wanted to provide totally nude dancing. The state's public indecency law required dancers to wear pasties and a G-string.

Rehnquist wrote for the Court, "The requirement that the dancers don pasties and a G-string does not deprive the dance of whatever erotic message it conveys; it simply makes the message less graphic. The perceived evil that Indiana seeks to address is not erotic dancing, but public nudity."

Dissenting justices said no compelling state interest existed to override First Amendment concerns and said, "dancing is an ancient art form and inherently embodies the expression and communication of ideas and emotions." *(See entry, p. 31; excerpts, p. 163)*

Cohen v. Cowles Media, Inc., dba Minneapolis Star & Tribune Co., decided by a 5-4 vote, June 24, 1991; White wrote the opinion; Blackmun, Marshall, Souter, and O'Connor dissented.

The First Amendment does not shield the news media from lawsuits if they break promises of confidentiality to their sources. The Court said a state doctrine of promissory estoppel, which protects people who rely to their detriment on promises from others, applies to all citizens' daily transactions without targeting or singling out the press.

This dispute arose from the 1982 Minnesota gubernatorial race, in which a political consultant associated with the Republican campaign offered to turn over negative information about the Democratic lieutenant governor candidate to reporters on the promise of confidentiality. After two newspapers printed the name of the consultant, believing he was part of a smear campaign, he was fired from his job. He then sued the newspapers, alleging breach of contract and fraudulent misrepresentation.

In ruling that the First Amendment does not bar action for a broken contract, the Court said any resulting constraint on truthful reporting "is no more than the incidental, and constitutionally insignificant, consequence of applying to the press a generally applicable law that requires those who make certain kinds of promises to keep them."

Dissenting justices said First Amendment protection for the reporting of truthful information should supersede a state's interest in enforcing a newspaper's promise of confidentiality. *(See entry, p. 33; excerpts, p. 171)*

Gentile v. State Bar of Nevada, decided by separate 5-4 votes, June 27, 1991; Kennedy and Rehnquist wrote for the differing majorities.

The free speech rights of lawyers may be curtailed if their comments present "substantial likelihood of material prejudice," Rehnquist wrote in a part of the Court's ruling rejecting a higher "clear and present danger standard." The chief justice, joined by Justices White, Scalia, Souter, and, in part, O'Connor, said the "substantial likelihood of material prejudice" standard is a constitutionally permissible balance between the First Amendment rights of attorneys in pending cases and the state's interest in fair trials.

In another part of the ruling, Kennedy found that the Nevada rule at issue, as interpreted by the Nevada Supreme Court, was impermissibly vague. He, joined by Marshall, Blackmun, Stevens, and O'Connor, said a "safe harbor provision" in the law misled a lawyer into thinking that he could hold a press conference without fear of discipline. The safe harbor section said that an attorney could "state without elaboration" the general nature of the defense.

The case arose from a press conference that a defense lawyer held the day after his client was indicted on criminal charges. The Nevada State Bar filed a complaint against the lawyer saying that the statements he made violated a state Supreme Court rule prohibiting a lawyer from making extrajudicial statements to the press that he knows or reasonably should know will have a "substantial likelihood of materially prejudicing" a trial.

Masson v. The New Yorker, decided by a 7-2 vote, June 20, 1991; Kennedy wrote the opinion; White and Scalia dissented.

Fabricated quotes may be libelous if they are published with knowledge of falsity or give a different meaning to what the speaker actually said. This case arose from articles, and a subsequent book, written by Janet Malcolm about Jeffrey Masson, a psychoanalyst who was fired from his job as projects director of the Sigmund Freud Archives after disputing some of Freud's theories. Masson challenged some of the direct quotations attributed to him in the stories, saying they were fabricated. Many of the quotes made him sound boastful and, in one of the more damning quotes, Malcolm wrote that he said he was considered an "intellectual gigolo," a phrase he said he never used. Malcolm sued for libel.

Kennedy, writing for the Court majority, said that the question for a jury would be whether Malcolm acted with knowledge of falsity or reckless disregard for the truth of the passages in question. He said that, in general, quotation marks should signify a verbatim reproduction. Still, he said, the common law of libel does not concern itself with slight inaccuracies; it concentrates instead on what is the truth. He said a deliberate alteration of a plaintiff's words does not mean knowledge of falsity unless the alteration is a material change in the statement's meaning.

The majority, sending the case back to a jury, went on to say that, while the use of quotations to attribute words not spoken is important to that inquiry, the idea that any alteration beyond correction of grammar or syntax by itself proves falsity is rejected. As an example, he said the practical necessity of editing and making intelligible a speaker's perhaps rambling comments renders it misleading to suggest that a quotation must be reconstructed with complete accuracy.

The two dissenting justices said that evidence that a quotation is false should be enough to get the case to a jury.

Voting Rights

Chisom v. Roemer, Governor of Louisiana; United States v. Roemer, Governor of Louisiana, decided by a 6-3 vote, June 20, 1991; Stevens wrote the opinion; Scalia, Rehnquist, and Kennedy dissented.

The federal Voting Rights Act applies to elections for state Supreme Court justices. The Court rejected an argument that judges are not "representatives" covered by the act, which makes it illegal for states to engage in voting practices or draw district boundaries that cause discrimination on the basis of race.

A lower court dismissed a challenge by New Orleans voters to the way Louisiana sets up judicial districts. The court held that the Voting Rights Act did not apply to judges because its use of the term "representative" covered only legislators and executive officials, not judges. Stevens said the term is broad enough to cover any winners of popular elections. Dissenting justices cited a lack of explicit intent in the act to apply the terms to judges. *(See entry, p. 28; excerpts, p. 155)*

Houston Lawyers' Association v. Attorney General of Texas; League of United Latin American Citizens et al. v. Attorney General of Texas et al., decided by a 6-3 vote, June 20, 1991; Stevens wrote the opinion; Scalia, Rehnquist, and Kennedy dissented.

The Voting Rights Act applies to elections for state trial judges, the Court ruled in a companion decision to *Chisom v. Roemer*. This case involved the election of trial judges in Texas and a challenge to local law by black and Hispanic citizens. *(See entry, p. 28; excerpts, p. 155)*

Clark v. Roemer, decided by a 9-0 vote, June 3, 1991; Kennedy wrote the opinion.

A special election for state judgeships should not have been allowed by a federal judge without approval by the U.S. attorney general, as required by the Voting Rights Act. The act bars procedures that cause a "denial or abridgement of the right of any citizen of the United States to vote on account of race or color."

The case arose from a lawsuit filed by black registered voters and a voting rights organization in Louisiana challenging the validity of Louisiana's election plan for the selection of certain judges. The challengers said the plan diluted minority voting strength. A district court ruled that, despite the valid objections to some of the judgeships, including by the U.S. attorney general, elections for those seats could go forward and the winners could take their seats. The Supreme Court said the lower court should have enjoined the election.

Labor

Air Courier Conference of America v. American Postal Workers Union, AFL-CIO, decided by a 9-0 vote, February 26, 1991; Rehnquist wrote the opinion.

Postal employees may not challenge the U.S. Postal Service's use of private courier services known as "international remailing." The Court said the workers are not within the "zone of interests" of the Private Express Statutes, regulating mail delivery, so they do not have standing to challenge the postal service's use of private couriers to handle certain international delivery.

Under international remailing, private couriers are used to deposit with foreign postal services letters destined for foreign addresses. Rehnquist wrote for the unanimous Court that for standing the unions must show that the alleged adverse effect on postal workers' employment opportunities is within the zone of interests covered by the postal statutes. The Court said that this cannot be done, because the language and legislative history of the statutes demonstrates that Congress was concerned not with protecting postal employment or furthering postal job opportunities, but with the earning revenue for the postal service.

Air Line Pilots Association, International v. O'Neill, decided by a 9-0 vote, March 19, 1991; Stevens wrote the opinion.

In a decision clarifying standards for claims by workers against their union, the Court ruled that a pilot union's negotiation of a back-to-work agreement did not breach its duty of fair representation. The agreement permitted the airline to discriminate between striking pilots and nonstriking pilots in job openings. The Court said the rule that a union is liable if its actions are either "arbitrary, discriminatory, or in bad faith" applies to all union activity, including contract negotiation. The Court also made clear that union action is arbitrary only if it is outside a "wide range of reasonableness" to be "irrational."

The case arose out of a confrontation between Continental Airlines and a pilots union and a resulting back-to-work agreement. Striking pilots said the union had agreed to a bad bargain in a union settlement that put them behind all settling pilots for options for job positions, severance pay, and other benefits.

American Hospital Association v. National Labor Relations Board, decided by a 9-0 vote, April 23, 1991; Stevens wrote the opinion.

The Court upheld a National Labor Relations Board industrywide rule governing bargaining units for health care workers in acute care hospitals.

The rule says eight separate employee units may engage in collective bargaining in acute care hospitals, with exceptions for cases presenting "extraordinary circumstances." Hospitals opposed the rule, which opened the door for increased union organizing among their workers, arguing that the National Labor Relations Act required the board to make separate bargaining unit determinations "in each case." It was the first time the board promulgated a rule defining employee bargaining units in a particular industry.

Stevens wrote for the unanimous Court that, if a disagreement arises about the appropriateness of a bargaining unit, the board still would be able to step in and resolve the dispute.

Groves v. Ring Screw Works, Ferndale Fastener Division, decided by a 9-0 vote, December 10, 1990; Stevens wrote the opinion.

The federal Labor Management Relations Act gives judges authority to hear labor disputes unless a collective bargaining agreement between a union and management expressly forbids it. The Court reinstated a lawsuit by two union workers who had been fired and who had sued in federal district court.

Their Michigan employer argued that the union agreed that if the voluntary mediation process were unsuccessful (in this case over the employees' discharge), then the only alternative a union has was either a strike or lockout.

The unanimous Court said that when a collective bargaining agreement spells out voluntary grievance procedures and permits the parties to resort to strikes and lockouts and does not mention judicial remedies, no presumption may be made that the union cannot turn to the courts.

International Organization for Masters, Mates & Pilots v. Brown, decided by a 9-0 vote, February 20, 1991; Stevens wrote the opinion.

Labor unions must acquiesce to all "reasonable" requests from candidates to distribute campaign literature for union elections, even when a union rule might prohibit such distribution. The test of federal labor law is whether a candidate's distribution request is reasonable, the Court said.

From October to April or May, the Court hears oral arguments, which are open to the public.

The Court ruled unanimously that a maritime industry union violated the law when it denied a candidate for union presidency its membership mailing list. Justices said a broad interpretation of the candidate's right flows from the law's basic purpose of ensuring free and democratic union elections by offsetting the inherent advantage incumbent union leadership has over rank-and-file challengers.

Lehnert v. Ferris Faculty Association, decided by 8-1 and 5-4 votes, May 30, 1991; Blackmun wrote the opinion; Marshall dissented in part; and Scalia, O'Connor, Kennedy, and Souter dissented in part.

Public employee unions cannot use fees collected from nonmembers covered by an "agency shop" arrangement to pay for political activity or public relations that does not arise from the collective bargaining agreement, without violating the First Amendment. Marshall dissented from this part of the opinion, saying he would have allowed expenses aimed at getting funding from state legislatures to be assessed.

The Court further divided over how to determine for which activities unions lawfully may collect. Blackmun, who announced the Court's opinion, devised a three-part test for determining the constitutionality of using nonmembers' funds for various union expenses. Workers who object to the spending can be charged only for union activities that are "germane" to collective bargaining, are justified by the government's interest in labor peace and avoiding "free riders," and do not add significantly to the burden on free speech that is inherent in an agency shop. He was joined by Rehnquist, White, Marshall, and Stevens. Separately, Scalia, O'Connor, Kennedy, and Souter said "contributions can be compelled only for the costs of performing the union's statutory duties as exclusive bargaining agent."

Litton Financial Printing Division v. National Labor Relations Board, decided by a 5-4 vote, June 13, 1991; Kennedy wrote the opinion; Marshall, Blackmun, Scalia, and Stevens dissented.

A union member's grievance that arises after the expiration of a collective bargaining agreement can be arbitrated only if it involves incidents that happened before the agreement expired or the infringement of a right that survived the end of the agreement. The case began when an employer refused to arbitrate grievances filed by workers who were laid off about a year after expiration of a union contract requiring arbitration.

The Court's ruling limited a presumption that grievances that occur after a collective bargaining pact has expired can be arbitrated. Marshall, in a dissent, said the majority's rule means that the merits of a post-contract grievance would have to be determined before a court could decide whether arbitration should be ordered.

Pauley, Survivor of Pauley v. Bethenergy Mines, Inc.; Clinchfield Coal Co. v. Director, Office of Workers' Compensation Programs, United States Department of Labor; Consolidation Coal Co. v.

Director, Office of Workers' Compensation Programs, United States Department of Labor, decided by a 7-1 vote, June 24, 1991; Blackmun wrote the opinion; Scalia dissented; Kennedy took no part in the case.

In a ruling upholding federal regulations that make it easier for coal mining companies to deny benefits to miners who allege black lung disease, the Court said companies must have sufficient opportunity to rebut the evidence. It said they may try to show that the workers do not suffer from black lung disease or that work in the mines did not cause their disease.

The Court ruled that Labor Department interim regulations relating to the government's ability to rebut the presumption that a miner has black lung disease meet a test in federal law that they must not be more restrictive than regulations from the 1960s. The majority said it was deferring to the Labor Department's interpretation that its rulings conformed to federal law.

Miscellaneous

Article 17 of Warsaw Convention

Eastern Airlines, Inc. v. Floyd, decided by a 9-0 vote, April 17, 1991; Marshall wrote the opinion.

In a case arising from a near plane crash, the Court ruled that Article 17 of the Warsaw Convention does not allow recovery for purely mental injuries. Passengers had sued Eastern Airlines for mental distress stemming from an incident in which their flight between Miami and the Bahamas narrowly avoided crashing.

The Court said damages are allowed only for "bodily injuries," according to its translation of the French text of Article 17.

Border Dispute

Illinois v. Kentucky, decided by a 9-0 vote, May 28, 1991; Souter wrote the opinion.

Resolving a dispute between Illinois and Kentucky over their common boundary, the Court said the boundary is the line of the low-water mark of the Ohio River as it was in 1792. The Court adopted the recommendation of a special master that the Court find the boundary to be the "low-water mark on the northerly side of the Ohio River as it existed in the year 1792," instead of the river's northerly low-water mark "as it exists from time to time."

The ruling favored Illinois and could affect the regulation of fishing and boating rights on the river.

Immigration Law

McNary, Commissioner of Immigration and Naturalization v. Haitian Refugee Center, decided by a 7-2 vote, February 20, 1991; Stevens wrote the opinion; Rehnquist and Scalia dissented.

Federal courts have the power to rule on constitutional challenges to the Immigration and Naturalization Service's procedures granting amnesty for certain alien farm workers.

The case arose from a class action lawsuit brought by Haitian farm workers who had been denied amnesty. They said the agency's application procedures for a program intended to benefit agricultural workers violated due process protections of the Fifth Amendment. The federal government asserted that Congress intended in the Immigration Reform and Control Act of 1986 to bar judicial review of the immigration service's procedures and to allow lawsuits only by individual aliens who faced deportation.

Stevens said that, because the immigration law does not clearly preclude federal jurisdiction and because the workers are seeking constitutional relief, a federal court may hear the claims.

Interstate River Compact

Oklahoma v. New Mexico, decided by a 5-4 vote, June 17, 1991; White wrote the opinion; Rehnquist, O'Connor, Scalia, and Kennedy dissented.

Under a 1952 Canadian River water-use agreement among Oklahoma, New Mexico, and Texas, New Mexico must count toward its allocation water that spills over the Conchas Dam and is stored in New Mexico's reservoirs downstream. New Mexico had refused to count the flood waters toward its river-compact limit.

"New Mexico is entitled to 200,000 acre feet of conservation storage below Conchas Dam," the majority said. "As we construe the Compact, if New Mexico has at any time stored more than that amount, it was not entitled to do so." A special master in the case had found that New Mexico had exceeded the compact limit.

The Court was unanimous in other findings of the water dispute.

Maritime Law

Exxon Corp. v. Central Gulf Lines, Inc., decided by a 9-0 vote, June 3, 1991; Marshall wrote the opinion.

Admiralty jurisdiction extends to claims arising from contracts between a principal and an agent, the Court held, overruling an 1855 case that had been interpreted as setting an automatic bar to admiralty jurisdiction over agency contracts. The case involved an unpaid fuel bill for a ship owned by Central Gulf Lines but chartered by its agent. A lower court had rejected Exxon's attempt to get a lien on the ship under the Federal Maritime Lien Act.

McDermott International, Inc. v. Wilander, decided by a 9-0 vote, February 19, 1991; O'Connor wrote the opinion.

A worker on a ship need not aid in the navigation of the vessel to qualify as a "seaman" under the Jones Act. This case arose after a paint foreman was injured while working on a ship in the Persian Gulf chartered by a firm under the Jones Act. While he was inspecting a pipe, a bolt in the pipe blew out under pressure, striking him on the head.

The act provides a cause of action in negligence for "any seaman" injured "in the course of his employment" but does not define "seaman." The Court rejected the ship contractor's argument that a seaman aids in the navigation of a vessel. The Court said the worker only needs to have employment-related connection to the vessel to be covered by the act.

Miles, individually and as administratrix of the succession of Torregano v. Apex Marine Corp., decided by an 8-0 vote, November 6, 1990; O'Connor wrote the opinion; Souter took no part in the case.

Families of seamen killed on the job may not win money damages for lost future earnings or "loss of society" under general maritime law. The mother of a seaman who was killed by a fellow crew member sued the owner of the ship for negligence—for failure to prevent the assault and for breach of the warranty of seaworthiness under general maritime law by hiring a crew member unfit to serve.

The Court said that general maritime law allows wrongful-death lawsuits but that damages are limited.

Torts

United States v. Smith, decided by an 8-1 vote, March 20, 1991; Marshall wrote the opinion; Stevens dissented.

A combination of federal laws protects military doctors practicing at overseas installations from liability lawsuits. The case was brought by a family alleging that an Army doctor had negligently injured their child during his birth in a U.S. Army hospital in Italy.

Writing for the Court, Marshall said the Federal Employees Liability Reform and Tort Compensation Act protects government workers from lawsuits even when an exception in the Federal Tort Claims Act precludes recovery against the government itself.

Case Excerpts

Following are excerpts from some of the most important rulings of the Supreme Court's 1990-1991 term. They appear in the order in which they were announced.

No. 89-1279

Pacific Mutual Life Insurance Company, Petitioner v. Cleopatra Haslip et al.

On writ of certiorari to the Supreme Court of Alabama

[March 4, 1991]

JUSTICE BLACKMUN delivered the opinion of the Court.

This case is yet another that presents a challenge to a punitive damages award.

I

In 1981, Lemmie L. Ruffin, Jr., was an Alabama-licensed agent for petitioner Pacific Mutual Life Insurance Company. He also was a licensed agent for Union Fidelity Life Insurance Company. Pacific Mutual and Union are distinct and nonaffiliated entities. Union wrote group health insurance for municipalities. Pacific Mutual did not.

Respondents Cleopatra Haslip, Cynthia Craig, Alma M. Calhoun, and Eddie Hargrove were employees of Roosevelt City, an Alabama municipality. Ruffin, presenting himself as an agent of Pacific Mutual, solicited the city for both health and life insurance for its employees. The city was interested. Ruffin gave the city a single proposal for both coverages. The city approved and, in August 1981, Ruffin prepared separate applications for the city and its employees for group health with Union and for individual life policies with Pacific Mutual. This packaging of health insurance with life insurance, although from different and unrelated insurers, was not unusual. Indeed, it tended to boost life insurance sales by minimizing the loss of customers who wished to have both health and life protection. The initial premium payments were taken by Ruffin and submitted to the insurers with the applications. Thus far, nothing is claimed to have been out of line. Respondents were among those with the health coverage.

An arrangement was made for Union to send its billings for health premiums to Ruffin at Pacific Mutual's Birmingham office. Premium payments were to be effected through payroll deductions. The city clerk each month issued a check for those premiums. The check was sent to Ruffin or picked up by him. He, however, did not remit to Union the premium payments received from the city; instead, he misappropriated most of them. In late 1981, when Union did not receive payment, it sent notices of lapsed health coverage to respondents in care of Ruffin and Patrick Lupia, Pacific Mutual's agent-in-charge of its Birmingham office. Those notices were not forwarded to respondents. Although there is some evidence to the contrary, the trial court found that respondents did not know that their health policies had been canceled.

II

Respondent Haslip was hospitalized on January 23, 1982. She incurred hospital and physician's charges. Because the hospital could not confirm health coverage, it required Haslip, upon her discharge, to make a payment upon her bill. Her physician, when he was not paid, placed her account with a collection agency. The agency obtained a judgment against Haslip and her credit was adversely affected.

In May 1982, respondents filed this suit, naming as defendants Pacific Mutual (but not Union) and Ruffin, individually and as a proprietorship, in the Circuit Court for Jefferson County, Ala. It was alleged that Ruffin collected premiums but failed to remit them to the insurers so that respondents' respective health insurance policies lapsed without their knowledge. Damages for fraud were claimed. The case against Pacific Mutual was submitted to the jury under a theory of *respondeat superior.*

Following the trial court's charge on liability, the jury was instructed that if it determined there was liability for fraud, it could award punitive damages. That part of the instructions is set forth in the margin. Pacific Mutual made no objection on the ground of lack of specificity in the instructions and it did not propose a more particularized charge. No evidence was introduced as to Pacific Mutual's financial worth. The jury returned general verdicts for respondents against Pacific Mutual and Ruffin in the following amounts:

Haslip:	$1,040,000	Calhoun:	15,290
Craig:	12,400	Hargrove:	10,288

Judgments were entered accordingly.

On Pacific Mutual's appeal, the Supreme Court of Alabama, by a divided vote, affirmed. In addition to issues not now before us, the court ruled that, while punitive damages are not recoverable in Alabama for misrepresentation made innocently or by mistake, they are recoverable for deceit or willful fraud, and that on the evidence in this case a jury could not have concluded that Ruffin's misrepresentations were made either innocently or mistakenly. The majority then specifically upheld the punitive damages award.

One Justice concurred in the result without opinion. Two Justices dissented in part on the ground that the award of punitive damages violated Pacific Mutual's due process rights under the Fourteenth Amendment.

Pacific Mutual, but not Ruffin, then brought the case here. It challenged punitive damages in Alabama as the product of unbridled jury discretion and as violative of its due process rights. We stayed enforcement of the Haslip judgment, and then granted certiorari, ____ U.S. ____ (1990), to review the punitive damages procedures and award in the light of the long-enduring debate about their propriety.

[III omitted]

IV

Two preliminary and overlapping due process arguments raised by Pacific Mutual deserve attention before we reach the principal issue in controversy. Did Ruffin act within the scope of his apparent authority as an agent of Pacific Mutual? If so, may Pacific Mutual be held responsible for Ruffin's fraud on a theory of *respondeat superior?*

Pacific Mutual was held responsible for the acts of Ruffin. The insurer mounts a challenge to this result on substantive due process grounds, arguing that it was not shown that either it or its Birmingham manager was aware that Ruffin was collecting premiums contrary to his contract; that Pacific Mutual had no notice of the actions complained of prior to the filing of the complaint in this litigation; that it did not authorize or ratify Ruffin's conduct; that his contract with the company forbade his collecting any premium other than the initial one submitted with an application; and that Pacific Mutual was held liable and punished for unauthorized actions of its agent for acts performed on behalf of another company. Thus, it is said, when punitive damages were imposed on Pacific Mutual, the focus for determining the amount of those damages shifted from Ruffin, where it belonged, to Pacific Mutual, and obviously and unfairly contributed to the amount of the punitive damages and their disproportionality. Ruffin was acting not to benefit Pacific Mutual but for his own benefit, and to hold Pacific Mutual liable is "beyond the point of fundamental fairness," embodied in due process. It is said that the burden of the liability comes to rest on Pacific Mutual's other policy holders.

The jury found that Ruffin was acting as an employee of Pacific Mutual when he defrauded respondents. The Supreme Court of Alabama did not disturb that finding. There is no occasion for us to question it, for it is amply supported by the record. Ruffin had actual authority to sell Pacific Mutual life insurance to respondents. The insurer derived economic benefit from those life insurance sales. Ruffin's defalcations related to the life premiums as well as to the health premiums. Thus, Pacific Mutual cannot plausibly claim that Ruffin was acting wholly as an agent of Union when he defrauded respondents....

Before the frauds in this case were effectuated, Pacific Mutual had received notice that its agent Ruffin was engaged in a pattern of fraud identical to those perpetrated against respondents. There were complaints to the Birmingham office about the absence of coverage purchased through Ruffin. The Birmingham manager was also advised of Ruffin's receipt of non-initial premiums made payable to him, a practice in violation of company policy.

Alabama's common-law rule is that a corporation is liable for both compensatory and punitive damages for fraud of its employee effected within the scope of his employment. We cannot say that this does not rationally advance the State's interest in minimizing fraud. Alabama long has applied this rule in the insurance context, for it has determined that an insurer is more likely to prevent an agent's fraud if given sufficient financial incentive to do so.... If an insurer were liable for such damages only upon proof that it was at fault independently, it would have an incentive to minimize oversight of its agents. Imposing liability without independent fault deters fraud more than a less stringent rule. It therefore rationally advances the State's goal. We cannot say this is a violation of Fourteenth Amendment due process....

V

Under the traditional common-law approach, the amount of the punitive award is initially determined by a jury instructed to consider the gravity of the wrong and the need to deter similar wrongful conduct. The jury's determination is then reviewed by trial and appellate courts to ensure that it is reasonable.

This Court more than once has approved the common-law method for assessing punitive awards.... So far as we have been able to determine, every state and federal court that has considered the question has ruled that the common-law method for assessing punitive damages does not in itself violate due process. . . . This, however, is not the end of the matter. It would be just as inappropriate to say that, because punitive damages have been recognized for so long, their imposition is never unconstitutional. . . . [O]ur task today is to determine whether the Due Process Clause renders the punitive damages award in this case constitutionally unacceptable.

VI

One must concede that unlimited jury discretion . . . in the fixing of punitive damages may invite extreme results that jar one's constitutional sensibilities. We need not, and indeed we cannot, draw a mathematical bright line between the constitutionally acceptable and the constitutionally unacceptable that would fit every case. We can say, however, that general concerns of reasonableness and adequate guidance from the court when the case is tried to a jury properly enter into the constitutional calculus. . . .

1. We have carefully reviewed the [judge's] instructions to the jury. . . . [They] gave the jury significant discretion in its determination of punitive damages. But that discretion was not unlimited. It was confined to deterrence and retribution, the state policy concerns sought to be advanced. And if punitive damages were to be awarded, the jury "must take into consideration the character and the degree of the wrong as shown by the evidence and necessity of preventing similar wrong." The instructions thus enlightened the jury as to the punitive damages' nature and purpose, identified the damages as punishment for civil wrongdoing of the kind involved, and explained that their imposition was not compulsory.

These instructions, we believe, reasonably accommodated Pacific Mutual's interest in rational decisionmaking and Alabama's interest in meaningful individualized assessment of appropriate deterrence and retribution. . . . As long as the discretion is exercised within reasonable constraints, due process is satisfied. . . .

2. Before the trial in this case took place, the Supreme Court of Alabama had established post-trial procedures for scrutinizing punitive awards. In *Hammond* v. *City of Gadsden* (1986), it stated that trial courts are "to reflect in the record the reasons for interfering with a jury verdict, or refusing to do so, on grounds of excessiveness of the damages." Among the factors deemed "appropriate for the trial court's consideration" are the "culpability of the defendant's conduct," the "desirability of discouraging others from similar conduct," the "impact upon the parties," and "other factors, such as the impact on innocent third parties." The *Hammond* test ensures meaningful and adequate review by the trial court whenever a jury has fixed the punitive damages.

3. By its review of punitive awards, the Alabama Supreme Court provides an additional check on the jury's or trial court's discretion. It first undertakes a comparative analysis. It then applies the detailed substantive standards it has developed for evaluating punitive awards. In particular, it makes its review to ensure that the award does "not exceed an amount that will accomplish society's goals of punishment and deterrence." This appellate review makes certain that the punitive damages are reasonable in their amount and rational in light of their purpose to punish what has occurred and to deter its repetition. . . .

The application of these standards, we conclude, imposes a sufficiently definite and meaningful constraint on the discretion of Alabama fact finders in awarding punitive damages. The Alabama Supreme Court's post-verdict review ensures that punitive damages awards are not grossly out of proportion to the severity of the offense and have some understandable relationship to compensatory damages. . . . Alabama plaintiffs do not enjoy a windfall because they have the good fortune to have a defendant with a deep pocket. . . .

Pacific Mutual thus had the benefit of the full panoply of Alabama's procedural protections. The jury was adequately instructed. The trial court conducted a post-verdict hearing that conformed with *Hammond*. . . .

We are aware that the punitive damages ward in this case is more than 4 times the amount of compensatory damages, is more than 200 times the out-of-pocket expenses of respondent Haslip, and, of course, is much in excess of the fine that could be imposed for insurance fraud. . . . While the monetary comparisons are wide and, indeed, may be close to the line, the award here did not lack objective criteria. We conclude, after careful consideration, that in this case it does not cross the line into the area of constitutional impropriety. Accordingly, Pacific Mutual's due process challenge must be, and is, rejected.

The judgment of the Supreme Court of Alabama is affirmed.

It is so ordered.

JUSTICE SOUTER took no part in the consideration or decision of this case.

JUSTICE SCALIA, concurring in the judgment.

. . . Since it has been the traditional practice of American courts to leave punitive damages (where the evidence satisfies the legal requirements for imposing them) to the discretion of the jury; and since in my view a process that accords with such a tradition and does not violate the Bill of Rights necessarily constitutes "due" process; I would approve the procedure challenged here without further inquiry into its "fairness" or "reasonableness." I therefore concur only in the judgment of the Court. . . . We have expended much ink upon the due-process implications of punitive damages, and the fact-specific nature of the Court's opinion guarantees that we and other courts will expend much more in the years to come. Since jury-assessed punitive damages are a part of our living tradition that dates back prior to 1868, I would end the suspense and categorically affirm their validity.

JUSTICE KENNEDY, concurring in the judgment.

Historical acceptance of legal institutions serves to validate them not because history provides the most convenient rule of decision but because we have confidence that a long-accepted legal institution would not have survived if it rested upon procedures found to be either irrational or unfair. For this reason, JUSTICE SCALIA's historical approach to questions of procedural due process has much to commend it. I cannot say with the confidence maintained by JUSTICE SCALIA, however, that widespread adherence to a historical practice always forecloses further inquiry when a party challenges an ancient institution or procedure as violative of due process. But I agree that the judgment of history should govern the outcome in the case before us. Jury determination of punitive damages has such long and principled recognition as a central part of our system that no further evidence of its essential fairness or rationality ought to be deemed necessary. . . .

That is not to say that every award of punitive damages by a jury will satisfy constitutional norms. A verdict returned by a biased or prejudiced jury no doubt violates due process, and the extreme amount of an award compared to the actual damage inflicted can be some evidence of bias or prejudice in an appropriate case. One must recognize the difficulty of making the showing required to prevail on this theory. In my view, however, it provides firmer guidance and rests on sounder jurisprudential foundations than does the approach espoused by the majority. While seeming to approve the common law method for assessing punitive damages, the majority nevertheless undertakes a detailed examination of that method as applied in the case before us. It is difficult to comprehend on what basis the majority believes the common-law method might violate due process in a particular case after it has approved that method as a general matter, and this tension in its analysis now must be resolved in some later case.

In my view, the principles mentioned above and the usual protections given by the laws of the particular State must suffice until judges or legislators authorized to do so initiate systemwide change. We do not have the authority, as do judges in some of the States, to alter the rules of the common law respecting the proper standard for awarding punitive damages and the respective roles of the jury and the court in making that determination. Were we sitting as state court judges, the size and recurring unpredictability of punitive damages awards might be a convincing argument to reconsider those rules or to urge a reexamination by the legislative authority. We are confined in this case, however, to interpreting the Constitution, and from this perspective I agree that we must reject the arguments advanced by the petitioner.

For these reasons I concur in the judgment of the Court.

JUSTICE O'CONNOR, dissenting.

Punitive damages are a powerful weapon. Imposed wisely and with restraint, they have the potential to advance legitimate state interests. Imposed indiscriminately, however, they have a devastating potential for harm. Regrettably, common-law procedures for awarding punitive damages fall into the latter category. States routinely authorize civil juries to impose punitive damages without providing them any meaningful instructions on how to do so. . . .

In my view, such instructions are so fraught with uncertainty that they defy rational implementation. Instead, they encourage inconsistent and unpredictable results by inviting juries to rely on private beliefs and personal predilections. Juries are permitted to target unpopular defendants, penalize unorthodox or controversial views, and redistribute wealth. Multimillion dollar losses are inflicted on a whim. While I do not question the general legitimacy of punitive damages, I see a strong need to provide juries with standards to constrain their discretion so that they may exercise their power wisely, not capriciously or maliciously. The Constitution requires as much.

The Court today acknowledges that dangers may lurk, but holds that they did not materialize in this case. They did materialize, however. They always do, because such dangers are part-and-parcel of common-law punitive damages procedures. As is typical, the trial court's instructions in this case provided no meaningful standards to guide the jury's decision to impose punitive damages or to fix the amount. Accordingly, these instructions were void for vagueness. Even if the Court disagrees with me on this point, it should still find that Pacific Mutual was denied procedural due process. Whether or not the jury instructions were so vague as to be unconstitutional, they plainly offered less guidance than is required under the due process test set out in *Mathews* v. *Eldridge,* 424 U.S. 319, 335 (1976). The most modest of procedural safeguards would have made the process substantially more rational without impairing any legitimate governmental interest. The Court relies heavily on the State's mechanism for postverdict judicial review, but this is incapable of curing a grant of standardless discretion to the jury. *Post hoc* review tests only the amount of the award, not the procedures by which that amount was determined. Alabama's common-law scheme is so lacking in fundamental fairness that the propriety of any specific award is irrelevant. *Any* award of punitive damages rendered under these procedures, no matter how small the amount, is constitutionally infirm.

. . . Unfortunately, Alabama's punitive damages scheme is indistinguishable from the common-law schemes employed by many States. The Court's holding will therefore substantially impede punitive damages reforms. Because I am concerned that the Court today sends the wrong signal, I respectfully dissent.

I

A

. . . Alabama's punitive damages scheme required a jury to make two decisions: (1) whether or not to impose punitive damages against the defendant, and (2) if so, in what amount. On the threshold question of whether or not to impose punitive damages, the trial court instructed the jury as follows: "Imposition of punitive damages is *entirely discretionary* with the jury, that means you don't have to award it unless this jury *feels* that you should do so."

This instruction is a vague as any I can imagine. It speaks of discretion, but suggests *no* criteria on which to base the exercise of that discretion. Instead of reminding the jury that its decision must rest on a factual or legal predicate, the instruction suggests that the jury may do whatever it "feels" like. It thus invites individual jurors to rely upon emotion, bias, and personal predilections of every sort. . . .

The vagueness question is not even close. This is not a case where a State has ostensibly provided a standard to guide the jury's discretion. Alabama, making no pretensions whatsoever, gives civil juries complete, unfettered, and unchanneled discretion to determine whether or not to impose punitive damages. Not only that, the State *tells* the jury that it has complete discretion. This is a textbook example of the void-for-vagueness doctrine. Alabama's common-law scheme is unconstitutionally vague. . . .

B

If an Alabama jury determines that punitive damages are appropriate in a particular case, it must then fix the amount. Here, the trial court instructed the jury: "Should you award punitive damages, in fixing the amount, you must take into consideration the character and the degree of the wrong as shown by the evidence and [the] necessity of preventing similar wrong."

The Court concludes that this instruction sufficiently limited the jury's discretion, but I cannot share this conclusion. Although the instruction ostensibly provided some guidance, this appearance is deceiving. As [former] Justice William J. Brennan said of a similar instruction: "Guidance like this is scarcely better than no guidance at all. I do not suggest that the instruction itself was in error; indeed, it appears to have been a correct statement of [state] law. The point is, rather, that the instruction reveals a deeper flaw: the fact that punitive damages are imposed by juries guided by little more than an admonition to do what they think is best." . . . [T]he trial court did not suggest what relation, if any, should exist between the harm caused and the size of the award, nor how to measure the deterrent effect of a particular award. It provided no information to the jury about criminal fines for comparable conduct or the range of punitive damages awards in similar cases. Nor did it identify the limitations dictated by retributive and deterrent principles, or advise the jury to refrain from awarding more than necessary to meet these objectives. In short, the trial court's instruction identified the ultimate destination, but did not tell the jury how to get there. Due process may not require a detailed roadmap, but it certainly requires directions of some sort. . . .

II

. . . Compounding the problem, punitive damages are quasi-criminal punishment. Unlike compensatory damages, which serve to allocate an existing loss between two parties, punitive damages are specifically designed to exact punishment in excess of actual harm to make clear that the defendant's misconduct was especially reprehensible. Hence, there is a stigma attached to an award of punitive damages that does not accompany a purely compensatory award. The punitive character of punitive damages means that there is more than just money at stake. This factor militates in favor of strong procedural safeguards.

. . . Over the last 20 years, the Court has repeatedly criticized common-law punitive damages procedures on the ground that they invite discriminatory and otherwise illegitimate awards. . . . For this reason, the Court has forbidden the award of punitive damages in certain defamation suits brought by private plaintiffs, and in unfair representation suits brought against labor unions under the Railway Labor Act. . . .

Even if judicial review of award amounts could potentially minimize the evils of standardless discretion, Alabama's review procedure is not up to the task. For one thing, Alabama courts cannot review whether a jury properly applied permissible factors, because juries are not told which factors are permissible and which are not. Making effective review even more unlikely, the primary component of Alabama's review mechanism is deference. The State Supreme Court insists that a jury's award of punitive damages carries a "presumption of correctness" that a defendant must overcome before remittitur is appropriate. . . . When Pacific Mutual challenged the State's procedures governing awards of punitive damages, the trial court simply deferred to the jury. The judge noted that he "would in all likelihood have rendered a lesser amount," but that the verdict was not excessive or unfair because "[t]he jury was composed of male and female, white and black and . . . acted conscientiously throughout the trial." Relying on the trial judge's refusal to disturb the verdict, the State Supreme Court afforded it a double dose of deference, stating that "jury verdicts are presumed correct, and that presumption is strengthened when the presiding judge refuses to grant a new trial.". . .

III

. . . I would require Alabama to adopt some method, either through its legislature or its courts, to constrain the discretion of juries in deciding whether or not to impose punitive damages and in fixing the amount of such awards. As a number of effective procedural safeguards are available, we need not dictate to the States the precise manner in which they must address the problem. We should permit the States to experiment with different methods and to adjust these methods over time.

This conclusion is neither ground-breaking nor remarkable. It reflects merely a straightforward application of our Due Process Clause jurisprudence. . . . Why, then, is it consigned to a dissent rather than a majority opinion? It may be that the Court is reluctant to afford procedural due process to Pacific Mutual because it perceives that such a ruling would force us to evaluate the constitutionality of every State's punitive damages scheme. I am confident, though, that if we announce what the Constitution requires and allow the States sufficient flexibility to respond, the constitutional problems will be resolved in time without any undue burden on the federal courts. Indeed, it may have been our hesitation that has inspired a flood of petitions for certiorari. For more than 20 years, this Court has criticized common-law punitive damages procedures, but has shied away from its duty to step in, hoping that the problems would go away. It is now clear that the problems are getting worse, and that the time has come to address them squarely. The Court does address them today. In my view, however, it offers an incorrect answer.

□□□

No. 89-1215

International Union, United Automobile, Aerospace and Agricultural Implement Workers of America, UAW, et. al., Petitioners v. Johnson Controls, Inc.

On writ of certiorari to the United States Court of Appeals for the Seventh Circuit

[March 20, 1991]

JUSTICE BLACKMUN delivered the opinion of the Court.

In this case we are concerned with an employer's gender-based fetal-protection policy. May an employer exclude a fertile female employee from certain jobs because of its concern for the health of the fetus the woman might conceive?

I

Respondent Johnson Controls, Inc., manufactures batteries. In the manufacturing process, the element lead is a primary ingredient. Occupational exposure to lead entails health risks, including the risk of harm to any fetus carried by a female employee.

Before the Civil Rights Act of 1964 became law, Johnson Controls did not employ any woman in a battery-manufacturing job. In June 1977, however, it announced its first official policy concerning its employment of women in lead-exposure work:

> "[P]rotection of the health of the unborn child is the immediate and direct responsibility of the prospective parents. While the medical profession and the company can support them in the exercise of this responsibility, it cannot assume it for them without simultaneously infringing their rights as persons.
>
> ". . . . Since not all women who can become mothers wish to become mothers (or will become mothers), it would appear to be illegal discrimination to treat all who are capable of pregnancy as though they will become pregnant."

Consistent with that view, Johnson Controls "stopped short of excluding women capable of bearing children from lead exposure" but emphasized that a woman who expected to have a child should not choose a job in which she would have such exposure. The company also required a woman who wished to be considered for employment to sign a statement that she had been advised of the risk of having a child while she was exposed to lead. The statement informed the woman that although there was evidence "that women exposed to lead have a higher rate of abortion," this evidence was "not as clear . . . as the relationship between cigarette smoking and cancer," but that it was, "medically speaking, just good sense not to run that risk if you want children and do not want to expose the unborn child to risk, however small. . . ."

Five years later, in 1982, Johnson Controls shifted from a policy of warning to a policy of exclusion. Between 1979 and 1983, eight employees became pregnant while maintaining blood lead levels in excess of 30 micrograms per deciliter. This appeared to be the critical level noted by the Occupational Health and Safety Administration (OSHA) for a worker who was planning to have a family. The company responded by announcing a broad exclusion of women from jobs that exposed them to lead:

> ". . . [I]t is [Johnson Controls'] policy that women who are pregnant or who are capable of bearing children will not be placed into jobs involving lead exposure or which could expose them to lead through the exercise of job bidding, bumping, transfer or promotion rights."

The policy defined "women . . . capable of bearing children" as "[a]ll women except those whose inability to bear children is medically documented." It further stated that an unacceptable work station was one where, "over the past year," an employee had recorded a blood lead level of more than 30 micrograms per deciliter or the work site had yielded an air sample containing a lead level in excess of 30 micrograms per cubic meter.

II

In April 1984, petitioners filed in the United States District Court for the Eastern District of Wisconsin a class action challenging Johnson Controls' fetal-protection policy as sex discrimination that violated Title VII of the Civil Rights Act of 1964, as amended. Among the individual plaintiffs were petitioners Mary Craig, who had chosen to be sterilized in order to avoid losing her job, Elsie Nason, a 50-year-old divorcee, who had suffered a loss in compensation when she was transferred out of a job where she was exposed to lead, and Donald Penney, who had been denied a request for a leave of absence for the purpose of lowering his lead level because he intended to become a father. Upon stipulation of the parties, the District Court certified a class consisting of "all past, present and future production and maintenance employees" in United Auto Workers bargaining units at nine of Johnson Controls' plants "who have been and continue to be affected by [the employer's] Fetal Protection Policy implemented in 1982."

The District Court granted summary judgment for defendant-respondent Johnson Controls. Applying a three-part business necessity defense derived from fetal-protection cases in the Courts of Appeals for the Fourth and Eleventh Circuits, the District Court concluded that while "there is a disagreement among the experts regarding the effect of lead on the fetus," the hazard to the fetus through exposure to lead was established by "a considerable body of opinion"; that although "[e]xpert opinion has been provided which holds that lead also affects the reproductive abilities of men and women . . . [and] that these effects are as great as the effects of exposure of the fetus . . . a great body of experts are of the opinion that the fetus is more vulnerable to levels of lead that would not affect adults"; and that petitioners had "failed to establish that there is an acceptable alternative policy which would protect the fetus." The court stated that, in view of this disposition of the business necessity defense, it did not "have to undertake a bona fide occupational qualification's (BFOQ) analysis."

The Court of Appeals for the Seventh Circuit, sitting en banc, affirmed the summary judgment by a 7-to-4 vote. The majority held that the proper standard for evaluating the fetal-protection policy was the defense of business necessity; that Johnson Controls was entitled to summary judgment under that defense; and that even if the proper standard was a BFOQ, Johnson Controls still was entitled to a summary judgment.

The Court of Appeals first reviewed fetal-protection opinions from the Eleventh and Fourth Circuits. Those opinions established the three-step business necessity inquiry: whether there is a substantial health risk to the fetus; whether transmission of the hazard to the fetus occurs only through women; and whether there is a less discriminatory alternative equally capable of preventing the health hazard to the fetus. . . .

Applying this business necessity defense, the Court of Appeals ruled that Johnson Controls should prevail. Specifically, the court concluded that there was no genuine issue of material fact about the substantial health-risk factor because the parties agreed that there was a substantial risk to a fetus from lead exposure. The Court of Appeals also concluded that, unlike the evidence of risk to the fetus from the mother's exposure, the evidence of risk from the father's exposure, which petitioners presented, "is, at best, speculative and unconvincing." Finally, the court found that petitioners had waived the issue of less discriminatory alternatives by not adequately presenting it. . . .

Having concluded that the business necessity defense was the appropriate framework and that Johnson Controls satisfied that standard, the court proceeded to discuss the BFOQ defense and concluded that Johnson Controls met that test, too. The en banc majority ruled that industrial safety is part of the essence of respondent's business, and that the fetal-protection policy is reasonably necessary to further that concern. . . .

With its ruling, the Seventh Circuit became the first Court of Appeals to hold that a fetal-protection policy directed exclusively at women could qualify as a BFOQ. We granted certiorari to resolve the obvious conflict between the Fourth, Seventh, and Eleventh Circuits on this issue, and to address the important and difficult question whether an employer, seeking to protect potential fetuses, may discriminate against women just because of their ability to become pregnant.

III

The bias in Johnson Controls' policy is obvious. Fertile men, but not fertile women, are given a choice as to whether they wish to risk their reproductive health for a particular job. Section 703(a) of the Civil Rights Act of 1964 prohibits sex-based classifications in terms and conditions of employment, in hiring and discharging decisions, and in other employment decisions that adversely affect an employee's status. Respondent's fetal-protection policy explicitly discriminates against women on the basis of their sex. The policy excludes women with childbearing capacity from lead-exposed jobs and so creates a facial classification based on gender. . . .

Nevertheless, the Court of Appeals assumed, as did the two appellate courts who already had confronted the issue, that sex-specific fetal-protection policies do not involve facial discrimination. These courts analyzed the policies as though they were facially neutral, and had only a discriminatory effect upon the employment opportunities of women. Consequently, the courts looked to see if each employer in question had established that its policy was justified as a business necessity. The business necessity standard is more lenient for the employer than the statutory BFOQ defense. The Court of Appeals here went one step further and invoked the burden-shifting framework set forth in *Wards Cove Packing Co.* v. *Atonio* (1989), thus requiring petitioners to bear the burden of persuasion on all questions. The court assumed that because the asserted reason for the sex-based exclusion (protecting women's unconceived offspring) was ostensibly benign, the policy was not sex-based discrimination. That assumption, however, was incorrect.

First, Johnson Controls' policy classifies on the basis of gender and childbearing capacity, rather than fertility alone. Respondent does not seek to protect the unconceived children of all its employees. Despite evidence in the record about the debilitating effect of lead exposure on the male reproductive system, Johnson Controls is concerned only with the harms that may befall the unborn offspring of its female employees. . . . Johnson Controls' policy is facially discriminatory because it requires only a female employee to produce proof that she is not capable of reproducing.

Our conclusion is bolstered by the Pregnancy Discrimination Act of 1978 (PDA), in which Congress explicitly provided that, for purposes of Title VII, discrimination "on the basis of sex" includes discrimination "because of or on the basis of pregnancy, childbirth, or related medical conditions." "The Pregnancy Discrimination Act has now made clear that, for all Title VII purposes, discrimination based on a woman's pregnancy is, on its face, discrimination because of her sex." *Newport News Shipbuilding & Dry Dock Co.* v. *EEOC* (1983). . . .

. . . [T]he absence of a malevolent motive does not convert a facially discriminatory policy into a neutral policy with a discriminatory effect. Whether an employment practice involves disparate treatment through explicit facial discrimination does not depend on why the employer discriminates but rather on the explicit terms of the discrimination. . . .

IV

Under § 703(e)(1) of Title VII, an employer may discriminate on the basis of "religion, sex, or national origin in those certain instances where religion, sex, or national origin is a bona fide occupational qualification reasonably necessary to the normal operation of that particular business or enterprise." We therefore turn to the question whether Johnson Controls' fetal-protection policy is one of those "certain instances" that come within the BFOQ exception.

The BFOQ defense is written narrowly, and this Court has read it narrowly. . . .

In *Dothard* v. *Rawlinson* [1977], this Court indicated that danger to a woman herself does not justify discrimination. We there allowed the employer to hire only male guards in contact areas of maximum-security male penitentiaries only because . . . the employment of a female guard would create real risks of safety to others if violence broke out because the guard was a woman. Sex discrimination was tolerated because sex was related to the guard's ability to do the job—maintaining prison security. . . .

Similarly, some courts have approved airlines' layoffs of pregnant flight attendants at different points during the first five months of pregnancy on the ground that the employer's policy was necessary to ensure the safety of passengers. . . . We stressed that in order to qualify as a BFOQ, a job qualification must relate to the "essence," or to the "central mission of the employer's business." . . .

Our case law, therefore, makes clear that the safety exception is limited to instances in which sex or pregnancy actually interferes with the employee's ability to perform the job. . . . Johnson Controls suggests, however, that we expand the exception to allow fetal-protection policies that mandate particular standards for pregnant or fertile women. We decline to do so. . . .

[V Omitted]

VI

A word about tort liability and the increased cost of fertile women in the workplace is perhaps necessary. One of the dissenting judges in this case expressed concern about an employer's tort liability and concluded that liability for a potential injury to a fetus is a social cost that Title VII does not require a company to ignore. It is correct to say that Title VII does not prevent the employer from having a conscience. The statute, however, does prevent sex-specific fetal-protection policies. These two aspects of Title VII do not conflict.

More than 40 States currently recognize a right to recover for a prenatal injury based either on negligence or on wrongful death. According to Johnson Controls, however, the company complies with the lead standard developed by OSHA and warns its female employees about the damaging effects of lead. . . . If, under general tort principles, Title VII bans sex-specific fetal-protection policies, the employer fully informs the woman of the risk, and the employer has not acted negligently, the basis for holding an employer liable seems remote at best. . . .

VII

Our holding today that Title VII, as so amended, forbids sex-specific fetal-protection policies is neither remarkable nor unprecedented. Concern for a woman's existing or potential offspring historically has been the excuse for denying women equal employment opportunities. Congress in the PDA prohibited discrimination on the basis of a woman's ability to become pregnant. We do no more than hold that the Pregnancy Discrimination Act means what it says.

It is no more appropriate for the courts than it is for individual employers to decide whether a woman's reproductive role is more important to herself and her family than her economic role. Congress has left this choice to the woman as hers to make.

The judgment of the Court of Appeals is reversed and the case is remanded for further proceedings consistent with this opinion.

It is so ordered.

JUSTICE WHITE, with whom THE CHIEF JUSTICE and JUSTICE KENNEDY join, concurring in part and concurring in the judgment.

The Court properly holds that Johnson Controls' fetal protection policy overtly discriminates against women, and thus is prohibited by Title VII unless it falls within the bona fide occupational qualification (BFOQ) exception.... The Court erroneously holds, however, that the BFOQ defense is so narrow that it could never justify a sex-specific fetal protection policy. I nevertheless concur in the judgment of reversal because on the record before us summary judgment in favor of Johnson Controls was improperly entered by the District Court and affirmed by the Court of Appeals.

I

In evaluating the scope of the BFOQ defense, the proper starting point is the language of the statute. Title VII forbids discrimination on the basis of sex, except "in those certain instances where ... sex ... is a bona fide occupational qualification reasonably necessary to the normal operation of that particular business or enterprise." For the fetal protection policy involved in this case to be a BFOQ, therefore, the policy must be "reasonably necessary" to the "normal operation" of making batteries, which is Johnson Controls' "particular business." Although that is a difficult standard to satisfy, nothing in the statute's language indicates that it could *never* support a sex-specific fetal protection policy.

On the contrary, a fetal protection policy would be justified under the terms of the statute if, for example, an employer could show that exclusion of women from certain jobs was reasonably necessary to avoid substantial tort liability. Common sense tells us that it is part of the normal operation of business concerns to avoid causing injury to third parties, as well as to employees, if for no other reason than to avoid tort liability and its substantial costs. This possibility of tort liability is not hypothetical; every State currently allows children born alive to recover in tort for prenatal injuries caused by third parties, and an increasing number of courts have recognized a right to recover even for prenatal injuries caused by torts committed prior to conception.

The Court dismisses the possibility of tort liability by no more than speculating that if "Title VII bans sex-specific fetal-protection policies, the employer fully informs the woman of the risk, and the employer has not acted negligently, the basis for holding an employer liable seems remote at best." Such speculation will be small comfort to employers. First, it is far from clear that compliance with Title VII will pre-empt state tort liability, and the Court offers no support for that proposition.

Second, although warnings may preclude claims by injured *employees*, they will not preclude claims by injured children because the general rule is that parents cannot waive causes of action on behalf of their children, and the parents' negligence will not be imputed to the children.... Compliance with OSHA standards, for example, has been held not to be a defense to state tort or criminal liability. Moreover, it is possible that employers will be held strictly liable, if, for example, their manufacturing process is considered "abnormally dangerous."...

Prior decisions construing the BFOQ defense confirm that the defense is broad enough to include considerations of cost and safety of the sort that could form the basis for an employer's adoption of a fetal protection policy....

The Pregnancy Discrimination Act (PDA), contrary to the Court's assertion, did not restrict the scope of the BFOQ defense. The PDA was only an amendment to the "Definitions" section of Title VII, and did not purport to eliminate or alter the BFOQ defense. Rather, it merely clarified Title VII to make it clear that pregnancy and related conditions are included within Title VII's antidiscrimination provisions. As we have already recognized, "the purpose of the PDA was simply to make the treatment of pregnancy consistent with general Title VII principles."...

In enacting the BFOQ standard, "Congress did not ignore the public interest in safety." The court's narrow interpretation of the BFOQ defense in this case, however, means that an employer cannot exclude even *pregnant* women from an environment highly toxic to their fetuses. It is foolish to think that Congress intended such a result, and neither the language of the BFOQ exception nor our cases requires it.

II

Despite my disagreement with the Court concerning the scope of the BFOQ defense, I concur in reversing the Court of Appeals because that court erred in affirming the District Court's grant of summary judgment in favor of Johnson Controls. First, the Court of Appeals erred in failing to consider the level of risk-avoidance that was part of Johnson Controls' "normal operation." Although the court did conclude that there was a "substantial risk" to fetuses from lead exposure in fertile women, it merely meant that there was a high risk that *some* fetal injury would occur absent a fetal protection policy. That analysis, of course, fails to address the *extent* of fetal injury that is likely to occur. If the fetal protection policy insists on a risk-avoidance level substantially higher than other risk levels tolerated by Johnson Controls such as risks to employees and consumers, the policy should not constitute a BFOQ.

Second, even without more information about the normal level of risk at Johnson Controls, the fetal protection policy at issue here reaches too far. This is evident both in its presumption that, absent medical documentation to the contrary, all women are fertile regardless of their age, and in its exclusion of presumptively fertile women from positions that might result in a promotion to a position involving high lead exposure. There has been no showing that either of those aspects of the policy is reasonably necessary to ensure safe and efficient operation of Johnson Controls' battery-manufacturing business. Of course, these infirmities in the company's policy do not warrant invalidating the entire fetal protection program.

Third, it should be recalled that until 1982 Johnson Controls operated without an exclusionary policy, and it has not identified any grounds for believing that its current policy is reasonably necessary to its normal operations. Although it is now more aware of some of the dangers of lead exposure, it has not shown that the risks of fetal harm or the costs associated with it have substantially increased. . . .

Finally, the Court of Appeals failed to consider properly petitioners' evidence of harm to offspring caused by lead exposure in males. The court considered that evidence only in its discussion of the business necessity standard, in which it focused on whether *petitioners* had met their burden of proof. The burden of proving that a discriminatory qualification is a BFOQ, however, rests with the employer. . . .

JUSTICE SCALIA, concurring in the judgment.

I generally agree with the Court's analysis, but have some reservations, several of which bear mention.

First, I think it irrelevant that there was "evidence in the record about the debilitating effect of lead exposure on the male reproductive system." Even without such evidence, treating women differently "on the basis of pregnancy" constitutes discrimination "on the basis of sex," because Congress has unequivocally said so.

Second, the Court points out that "Johnson Controls has shown no factual basis for believing that all or substantially all women would be unable to perform safely . . . the duties of the job involved." In my view, this is . . . entirely irrelevant. By reason of the Pregnancy Discrimination Act, it would not matter if all pregnant women placed their children at risk in taking these jobs, just as it does not matter if no men do so. . . .

Last, the Court goes far afield, it seems to me, in suggesting that increased cost alone—short of "costs . . . so prohibitive as to threaten survival of the employer's business"—cannot support a BFOQ defense. I agree with JUSTICE WHITE's concurrence that nothing in our prior cases suggests this, and in my view it is wrong. I think, for example, that a shipping company may refuse to hire pregnant women as crew members on long voyages because the on-board facilities for foreseeable emergencies, though quite feasible, would be inordinately expensive. In the present case, however, Johnson has not asserted a cost-based BFOQ.

I concur in the judgment of the Court.

□□□

No. 89-839

Arizona, Petitioner v. Oreste C. Fulminante

On writ of certiorari to the Supreme Court of Arizona

[March 26, 1991]

JUSTICE WHITE delivered the opinion of the Court.

The Arizona Supreme Court ruled in this case that respondent Oreste Fulminante's confession, received in evidence at his trial for murder, had been coerced and that its use against him was barred by the Fifth and Fourteenth Amendments to the United States Constitution. The court also held that the harmless-error rule could not be used to save the conviction. We affirm the judgment of the Arizona court, although for different reasons than those upon which that court relied.

I

Early in the morning of September 14, 1982, Fulminante called the Mesa, Arizona, Police Department to report that his 11-year-old stepdaughter, Jeneane Michelle Hunt, was missing. He had been caring for Jeneane while his wife, Jeneane's mother, was in the hospital. Two days later, Jeneane's body was found in the desert east of Mesa. She had been shot twice in the head at close range with a large caliber weapon, and a ligature was around her neck. Because of the decomposed condition of the body, it was impossible to tell whether she had been sexually assaulted.

Fulminante's statements to police concerning Jeneane's disappearance and his relationship with her contained a number of inconsistencies, and he became a suspect in her killing. When no charges were filed against him, Fulminante left Arizona for New Jersey. Fulminante was later convicted in New Jersey on federal charges of possession of a firearm by a felon.

Fulminante was incarcerated in the Ray Brook Federal Correctional Institution in New York. There he became friends with another inmate, Anthony Sarivola, then serving a 60-day sentence for extortion. The two men came to spend several hours a day together. Sarivola, a former police officer, had been involved in loansharking for organized crime but then became a paid informant for the Federal Bureau of Investigation. While at Ray Brook, he masqueraded as an organized crime figure. After becoming friends with Fulminante, Sarivola heard a rumor that Fulminante was suspected of killing a child in Arizona. Sarivola then raised the subject with Fulminante in several conversations, but Fulminante repeatedly denied any involvement in Jeneane's death. During one conversation, he told Sarivola that Jeneane had been killed by bikers looking for drugs; on another occasion, he said he did not know what had happened. Sarivola passed this information on to an agent of the Federal Bureau of Investigation, who instructed Sarivola to find out more.

Sarivola learned more one evening in October 1983, as he and Fulminante walked together around the prison track. Sarivola said that he knew Fulminante was "starting to get some tough treatment and whatnot" from other inmates because of the rumor. Sarivola offered to protect Fulminante from his fellow inmates, but told him, " 'You have to tell me about it,' you know. I mean, in other words, 'For me to give you any help.' " Fulminante then admitted to Sarivola that he had driven Jeneane to the desert on his motorcycle, where he choked her, sexually assaulted her, and made her beg for her life, before shooting her twice in the head.

Sarivola was released from prison in November 1983. Fulminante was released the following May, only to be arrested the next month for another weapons violation. On September 4, 1984, Fulminante was indicted in Arizona for the first-degree murder of Jeneane.

Prior to trial, Fulminante moved to suppress the statement he had given Sarivola in prison, as well as a second confession he had given to Donna Sarivola, then Anthony Sarivola's fiancee and later his wife, following his May 1984 release from prison. He asserted that the confession to Sarivola was coerced, and that the second confession was the "fruit" of the first. Following the hearing, the trial court denied the motion to suppress, specifically finding that, based on the stipulated facts, the confessions were voluntary. The State introduced both confessions as evidence at trial, and on December 19, 1985, Fulminante was convicted of Jeneane's murder. He was subsequently sentenced to death.

Fulminante appealed.... After considering the evidence at trial as well as the stipulated facts before the trial court on the motion to suppress, the Arizona Supreme Court held that the confession was coerced, but initially determined that the admission of the confession at trial was harmless error, because of the overwhelming nature of the evidence against Fulminante. Upon Fulminante's motion for reconsideration, however, the court ruled that this Court's precedent precluded the use of the harmless-error analysis in the case of a coerced confession. The Court therefore reversed the conviction and ordered that Fulminante be retried without the use of the confession to Sarivola. Because of differing views in the state and federal courts over whether the admission at trial of a coerced confession is subject to a harmless-error analysis, we granted the State's petition for certiorari [to call up the case for review]. Although a majority of this Court finds that such a confession is subject to a harmless-error analysis, for the reasons set forth below, we affirm the judgment of the Arizona court.

II

We deal first with the State's contention that the court below [Arizona Supreme Court] erred in holding Fulminante's confession to have been coerced. The State argues that it is the totality of the circumstances that determines whether Fulminante's confession was coerced, but contends that rather than apply this standard, the Arizona court applied a "but for" test, under which the court found that but for the promise given by Sarivola, Fulminante would not have confessed. In support of this argument, the State points to the Arizona court's reference to *Bram* v. *United States* (1897).... [I]t is clear this passage from *Bram,* which under current precedent does not state the standard for determining the voluntariness of a confession, was not relied on by the Arizona court in reaching its conclusion. Rather, the court cited this language as part of a longer quotation from an Arizona case which accurately described the State's burden of proof for establishing voluntariness. Indeed, the Arizona Supreme Court stated that a "determination regarding the voluntariness of a confession . . . must be viewed in a totality of the circumstances," and under that standard plainly found that Fulminante's statement to Sarivola had been coerced....

Although the question is a close one, we agree with the Arizona Supreme Court's conclusion that Fulminante's confession was coerced. The Arizona Supreme Court found a credible threat of physical violence unless Fulminante confessed. Our cases have made clear that a finding of coercion need not depend upon actual violence by a government agent; a credible threat is sufficient. As we have said, "coercion can be mental as well as physical, and . . . the blood of the accused is not the only hallmark of an unconstitutional inquisition." *Blackburn* v. *Alabama* (1960)....

III

Four of us, JUSTICES MARSHALL, BLACKMUN, STEVENS, and myself, would affirm the judgment of the Arizona Supreme Court on the ground that the harmless-error rule is inapplicable to erroneously admitted coerced confessions. We thus disagree with the Justices who have a contrary view.

The majority today abandons what until now the Court has regarded as the "axiomatic [proposition] that a defendant in a criminal case is deprived of due process of law if his conviction is founded, in whole or in part, upon an involuntary confession, without regard for the truth or falsity of the confession."... The Court has repeatedly stressed that the view that the admission of a coerced confession can be harmless error because of the other evidence to support the verdict is "an impermissible doctrine."... Today, a majority of the Court, without any justification overrules this vast body of precedent without a word and in so doing dislodges one of the fundamental tenets of our criminal justice system.

In extending to coerced confessions the harmless error rule of *Chapman* v. *California* (1967), the majority declares that because the Court has applied that analysis to numerous other "trial errors," there is no reason that it should not apply to an error of this nature as well. The four of us remain convinced, however, that we should abide by our cases that have refused to apply the harmless error rule to coerced confessions, for a coerced confession is fundamentally different from other types of erroneously admitted evidence to which the rule has been applied....

Chapman specifically noted three constitutional errors that could not be categorized as harmless error: using a coerced confession against a defendant in a criminal trial, depriving a defendant of counsel, and trying a defendant before a biased judge. The majority attempts to distinguish the use of a coerced confession from the other two errors listed in *Chapman* by drawing a meaningless dichotomy between "trial errors" and "structural defects" in the trial process....

This effort fails, for our jurisprudence on harmless error has not classified so neatly the errors at issue....

... [P]ermitting a coerced confession to be part of the evidence on which a jury is free to base its verdict of guilty is inconsistent with the thesis that ours is not an inquisitorial system of criminal justice....

The search for truth is indeed central to our system of justice, but "certain constitutional rights are not, and should not be, subject to harmless-error analysis because those rights protect important values that are unrelated to the truth-seeking function of the trial." *Rose* v. *Clark*. The right of a defendant not to have his coerced confession used against him is among those rights....

IV

Since five Justices have determined that harmless error analysis applies to coerced confessions, it becomes necessary to evaluate under that ruling the admissibility of Fulminante's confession to Sarivola. *Chapman* . . . made clear that "before a federal constitutional error can be held harmless, the court must be able to declare a belief that it was harmless beyond a reasonable doubt." . . . In so doing, it must be determined whether the State has met its burden of demonstrating that the admission of the confession to Sarivola did not contribute to Fulminante's conviction. Five of us are of the view that the State has not carried its burden and accordingly affirm the judgment of the court below reversing petitioner's conviction. . . .

First, the transcript discloses that both the trial court and the State recognized that a successful prosecution depended on the jury believing the two confessions. Absent the confessions, it is unlikely that Fulminante would have been prosecuted at all, because the physical evidence from the scene and other circumstantial evidence would have been insufficient to convict. Indeed, no indictment was filed until nearly two years after the murder. Although the police had suspected Fulminante from the beginning, as the prosecutor acknowledged in his opening statement to the jury "[W]hat brings us to Court, what makes this case fileable, and prosecutable and triable is that later, Mr. Fulminante confesses this crime to Anthony Sarivola and later, to Donna Sarivola, his wife." . . .

Second, the jury's assessment of the confession to Donna Sarivola could easily have depended in large part on the presence of the confession to Anthony Sarivola. Absent the admission at trial of the first confession, the jurors might have found Donna Sarivola's story unbelievable. Fulminante's confession to Donna Sarivola allegedly occurred in May 1984, on the day he was released from Ray Brook, as she and Anthony Sarivola drove Fulminante from New York to Pennsylvania. Donna Sarivola testified that Fulminante, whom she had never before met, confessed in detail about Jeneane's brutal murder in response to her casual question concerning why he was going to visit friends in Pennsylvania instead of returning to his family in Arizona. Although she testified that she was "disgusted" by Fulminante's disclosures, she stated that she took no steps to notify authorities of what she had learned. In fact, she claimed that she barely discussed the matter with Anthony Sarivola, who was in the car and overheard Fulminante's entire conversation with Donna. Despite her disgust for Fulminante, Donna Sarivola later went on a second trip with him. Although Sarivola informed authorities that he had driven Fulminante to Pennsylvania, he did not mention Donna's presence in the car or her conversation with Fulminante. Only when questioned by authorities in June 1985 did Anthony Sarivola belatedly recall the confession to Donna more than a year before, and only then did he ask if she would be willing to discuss the matter with authorities.

Although some of the details in the confession to Donna Sarivola were corroborated by circumstantial evidence, many, including details that Jeneane was choked and sexually assaulted, were not. . . .

Third, the admission of the first confession led to the admission of other evidence prejudicial to Fulminante. For example, the State introduced evidence that Fulminante knew of Sarivola's connections with organized crime in an attempt to explain why Fulminante would have been motivated to confess to Sarivola in seeking protection. Absent the confession, this evidence would have had no relevance and would have been inadmissible at trial. The Arizona Supreme Court found that the evidence of Sarivola's connections with organized crime reflected on Sarivola's character, not Fulminante's, and noted that the evidence could have been used to impeach Sarivola. This analysis overlooks the fact that had the confession not been admitted, there would have been no reason for Sarivola to testify and thus no need to impeach his testimony. Moreover, we cannot agree that the evidence did not reflect on Fulminante's character as well, for it depicted him as someone who willingly sought out the company of criminals. It is quite possible that this evidence led the jury to view Fulminante as capable of murder.

Finally, although our concern here is with the effect of the erroneous admission of the confession on Fulminante's conviction, it is clear that the presence of the confession also influenced the sentencing phase of the trial. Under Arizona law, the trial judge is the sentencer. At the sentencing hearing, the admissibility of information regarding aggravating circumstances is governed by the rules of evidence applicable to criminal trials. § 13-703(C). In this case, "based upon admissible evidence produced at the trial," the judge found that only one aggravating circumstance existed beyond a reasonable doubt, *i.e.,* that the murder was committed in "an *especially* heinous, cruel, and depraved manner." In reaching this conclusion, the judge relied heavily on evidence concerning the manner of the killing and Fulminante's motives and state of mind which could only be found in the two confessions. . . .

Because a majority of the Court has determined that Fulminante's confession to Anthony Sarivola was coerced and because a majority has determined that admitting this confession was not harmless beyond a reasonable doubt, we agree with the Arizona Supreme Court's conclusion that Fulminante is entitled to a new trail at which the confession is not admitted. Accordingly the judgment of the Arizona Supreme Court is

Affirmed.

CHIEF JUSTICE REHNQUIST, with whom JUSTICE O'CONNOR joins, JUSTICE KENNEDY and JUSTICE SOUTER join as to Parts I and II, and JUSTICE SCALIA joins as to Parts II and

III, delivering the opinion of the Court as to Part II, and dissenting as to Parts I and III.

The Court today properly concludes that the admission of an "involuntary" confession at trial is subject to harmless error analysis. Nonetheless, the independent review of the record which we are required to make shows that respondent Fulminante's confession was not in fact involuntary. And even if the confession were deemed to be involuntary, the evidence offered at trial, including a second, untainted confession by Fulminante, supports the conclusion that any error here was certainly harmless.

I

. . . The admissibility of a confession such as that made by respondent Fulminante depends upon whether it was voluntarily made. . . .

The Supreme Court of Arizona stated that the trial court committed no error in finding the confession voluntary based on the record before it. But it overturned the trial court's finding of voluntariness based on the more comprehensive trial record before it, which included, in addition to the facts stipulated at the suppression hearing, a statement made by Sarivola at the trial that "the defendant had been receiving 'rough treatment from the guys, and if the defendant would tell the truth, he could be protected.' " . . .

. . . I am at a loss to see how the Supreme Court of Arizona reached the conclusion that it did. Fulminante offered no evidence that he believed that his life was in danger or that he in fact confessed to Sarivola in order to obtain the proffered protection. Indeed, he had stipulated that "[a]t no time did the defendant indicate he was in fear of other inmates nor did he ever seek Mr. Sarivola's 'protection' " Sarivola's testimony that he told Fulminante that "if [he] would tell the truth, he could be protected," adds little if anything to the substance of the parties' stipulation. . . . The fact that Sarivola was a government informant does not by itself render Fulminante's confession involuntary, since we have consistently accepted the use of informants in the discovery of evidence of a crime as a legitimate investigatory procedure consistent with the Constitution. The conversations between Sarivola and Fulminante were not lengthy, and the defendant was free at all times to leave Sarivola's company. Sarivola at no time threatened him or demanded that he confess; he simply requested that he speak the truth about the matter. Fulminante was an experienced habitue of prisons, and presumably able to fend for himself. In concluding on these facts that Fulminante's confession was involuntary, the Court today embraced a more expansive definition of that term than is warranted by any of our decided cases.

II

Since this Court's landmark decision in *Chapman* . . . in which we adopted the general rule that a constitutional error does not automatically require reversal of a conviction, the Court has applied harmless error analysis to a wide range of errors and has recognized that most constitutional errors can be harmless. . . .

The common thread connecting these cases is that each involved "trial error"—error which occurred during the presentation of the case to the jury, and which may therefore be quantitatively assessed in the context of other evidence presented in order to determine whether its admission was harmless beyond a reasonable doubt. In applying harmless-error analysis to these many different constitutional violations, the Court has been faithful to the belief that the harmless-error doctrine is essential to preserve the "principle that the central purpose of a criminal trial is to decide the factual question of the defendant's guilt or innocence, and promotes public respect for the criminal process by focusing on the underlying fairness of the trial rather than on the virtually inevitable presence of immaterial error." . . .

It is evident from a comparison of the constitutional violations which we have held subject to harmless error, and those which we have held not, that involuntary statements or confessions belong in the former category. The admission of an involuntary confession is a "trial error," similar in both degree and kind to the erroneous admission of other types of evidence. The evidentiary impact of an involuntary confession, and its effect upon the composition of the record, is indistinguishable from that of a confession obtained in violation of the Sixth Amendment . . . or of a prosecutor's improper comment on a defendant's silence at trial. . . . When reviewing the erroneous admission of an involuntary confession, the appellate court, as it does with the admission of other forms of improperly admitted evidence, simply reviews the remainder of the evidence against the defendant to determine whether the admission of the confession was harmless beyond a reasonable doubt.

Nor can it be said that the admission of an involuntary confession is the type of error which "transcends the criminal process." This Court has applied harmless-error analysis to the violation of other constitutional rights similar in magnitude and importance and involving the same level of police misconduct. For instance, we have previously held that the admission of a defendant's statements obtained in violation of the Sixth Amendment is subject to harmless-error analysis. . . .

Of course an involuntary confession may have a more dramatic effect on the course of a trial than do other trial errors—in particular cases it may be devastating to a defendant—but this simply means that a reviewing court will conclude in such a case that its admission was not harmless error; it is not a reason for eschewing the harmless error test entirely. . . .

III

I would agree with the finding of the Supreme Court of Arizona in its initial opinion—in which it believed harmless-error analysis was applicable to the admission of involuntary confessions—that the admission of Fulminante's confession was harmless. Indeed, this seems to me to be a classic case of harmless error: a second confession giving more details of the crime than the first was admitted in evidence and found to be free of any constitutional objection. Accordingly, I would affirm the holding of the Supreme Court of Arizona in its initial opinion, and reverse the judgment which it ultimately rendered in this case.

JUSTICE KENNEDY, concurring in the judgment.

For the reasons stated by THE CHIEF JUSTICE, I agree that Fulminante's confession to Anthony Sarivola was not coerced. In my view, the trial court did not err in admitting this testimony. A majority of the Court, however, finds the confession coerced and proceeds to consider whether harmless-error analysis may be used when a coerced confession has been admitted at trial. . . . For the reasons given by JUSTICE WHITE in Part IV of his opinion, I cannot with confidence find admission of Fulminante's confession to Anthony Sarivola to be harmless error. . . .

In the interests of providing a clear mandate to the Arizona Supreme Court in this capital case, I deem it proper to accept in the case now before us the holding of five Justices that the confession was coerced and inadmissible. I agree with a majority of the Court that admission of the confession could not be harmless error when viewed in light of all the other evidence; and so I concur in the judgment to affirm the ruling of the Arizona Supreme Court.

□□□

No. 89-7024

Warren McCleskey, Petitioner v. Walter D. Zant, Superintendent, Georgia Diagnostic & Classification Center

On writ of certiorari to the United States Court of Appeals for the Eleventh Circuit

[April 16, 1991]

JUSTICE KENNEDY delivered the opinion of the Court.

The doctrine of abuse of the writ defines the circumstances in which federal courts decline to entertain a claim presented for the first time in a second or subsequent petition for a writ of habeas corpus. Petitioner Warren McCleskey in a second federal habeas petition presented a claim under *Massiah* v. *United States* 377 U.S. 201 (1964), that he failed to include in his first federal petition. The Court of Appeals for the Eleventh Circuit held that assertion of the *Massiah* claim in this manner abused the writ. Though our analysis differs from that of the Court of Appeals, we agree that the petitioner here abused the writ, and we affirm the judgment.

I

McCleskey and three other men, all armed, robbed a Georgia furniture store in 1978. One of the robbers shot and killed an off duty policeman who entered the store in the midst of the crime. McCleskey confessed to the police that he participated in the robbery. When on trial for both the robbery and the murder, however, McCleskey renounced his confession after taking the stand with an alibi denying all involvement. To rebut McCleskey's testimony, the prosecution called Offie Evans, who had occupied a jail cell next to McCleskey's. Evans testified that McCleskey admitted shooting the officer during the robbery and boasted that he would have shot his way out of the store even in the face of a dozen policemen.

Although no one witnessed the shooting, further direct and circumstantial evidence supported McCleskey's guilt of the murder. An eyewitness testified that someone ran from the store carrying a pearl-handled pistol soon after the robbery. Other witnesses testified that McCleskey earlier had stolen a pearl-handled pistol of the same caliber as the bullet that killed the officer. Ben Wright, one of McCleskey's accomplices, confirmed that during the crime McCleskey carried a white-handled handgun matching the caliber of the fatal bullet. Wright also testified that McCleskey admitted shooting the officer. Finally, the prosecutor introduced McCleskey's confession of participation in the robbery.

In December 1978, the jury convicted McCleskey of murder and sentenced him to death. Since his conviction, McCleskey has pursued direct and collateral remedies for more than a decade. We describe this procedural history in detail, both for a proper understanding of the case and as an illustration of the context in which allegations of abuse of the writ arise.

On direct appeal to the Supreme Court of Georgia, McCleskey raised six grounds of error. A summary of McCleskey's claims on direct appeal, as well as those he asserted in each of his four collateral proceedings, is set forth in the Appendix to this opinion. The portion of the appeal relevant for our purposes involves McCleskey's attack on Evans' rebuttal testimony. McCleskey contended that the trial court "erred in allowing evidence of [McCleskey's] oral statement admitting the murder made to [Evans] in the next cell, because the prosecutor had deliberately withheld such statement" in violation of *Brady* v. *Maryland.* A unanimous Georgia Supreme Court acknowledged that the prosecutor did not furnish Evans' statement to the defense, but ruled that because the undisclosed evidence was not exculpatory, McCleskey suffered no material prejudice and was not denied a fair trial under *Brady*. The court noted, moreover, that the evidence McCleskey wanted to inspect was "introduced to the jury in its entirety" through Evans' testimony, and that McCleskey's argument that "the evidence was needed in order to prepare a proper defense or impeach other witnesses ha[d] no merit because the evidence requested was statements made by [McCleskey] himself." The court rejected McCleskey's other contentions, and affirmed his conviction and sentence. We denied certiorari [for Supreme Court review].

McCleskey then initiated postconviction proceedings. In January 1981, he filed a petition for state habeas corpus relief. The amended petition raised 23 challenges to his murder conviction and death sentence. Three of the claims concerned Evans' testimony. First, McCleskey contended that the State violated his due process rights under *Giglio* v. *United States* (1972), by its failure to disclose an agreement to drop pending escape charges against Evans in return for his cooperation and testimony. Second, McCleskey reasserted his *Brady* claim that the State violated his due process rights by the deliberate withholding of the statement he made to Evans while in jail. Third, McCleskey alleged that admission of Evans' testimony violated the Sixth Amendment right to counsel as construed in *Massiah*. . . . On this theory, "[t]he introduction into evidence of [his] statements to [Evans], elicited in a situation created to include [McCleskey] to make incriminating statements without the assistance of counsel, violated [McCleskey's] right to counsel under the

Sixth Amendment to the Constitution of the United States."

At the state habeas corpus hearing, Evans testified that one of the detectives investigating the murder agreed to speak a word on his behalf to the federal authorities about certain federal charges pending against him. The state habeas court ruled that the *ex parte* recommendation did not implicate *Giglio,* and it denied relief on all other claims. The Supreme Court of Georgia denied McCleskey's application for a certificate of probable cause, and we denied his second petition for a writ of certiorari.

In December 1981, McCleskey filed his first federal habeas corpus petition in the United States District Court for the Northern District of Georgia, asserting 18 grounds for relief. The petition failed to allege the *Massiah* claim, but it did reassert the *Giglio* and *Brady* claims. Following extensive hearings in August and October 1983, the District Court held that the detective's statement to Evans was a promise of favorable treatment, and that failure to disclose the promise violated *Giglio.* The District Court further held that Evans' trial testimony may have affected the jury's verdict on the charge of malice murder. On these premises it granted relief.

The Court of Appeals reversed the District Court's grant of the writ. The court held that the State had not made a promise to Evans of the kind contemplated by *Giglio,* and that in any event the *Giglio* error would be harmless. The court affirmed the District Court on all other grounds. We granted certiorari limited to the question whether Georgia's capital sentencing procedures were constitutional, and denied relief.

McCleskey continued his postconviction attacks by filing a second state habeas corpus action in 1987 which, as amended, contained five claims for relief. One of the claims again centered on Evans' testimony, alleging the State had an agreement with Evans that it had failed to disclose. The state trial court held a hearing and dismissed the petition. The Supreme Court of Georgia denied McCleskey's application for a certificate of probable cause.

In July 1987, McCleskey filed a second federal habeas action, the one we now review. In the District Court, McCleskey asserted seven claims, including a *Massiah* challenge to the introduction of Evans' testimony. McCleskey had presented a *Massiah* claim, it will be recalled, in his first state habeas action when he alleged that the conversation recounted by Evans at trial had been "elicited in a situation created to induce" him to make an incriminating statement without the assistance of counsel. The first federal petition did not present a *Massiah* claim. The proffered basis for the *Massiah* claim in the second federal petition was a 21-page signed statement that Evans made to the Atlanta Police Department on August 1, 1978, two weeks before the trial began. The department furnished the document to McCleskey one month before he filed his second federal petition.

The statement related pretrial jailhouse conversations that Evans had with McCleskey and that Evans overheard between McCleskey and Bernard Dupree. By the statement's own terms, McCleskey participated in all the reported jail-cell conversations. Consistent with Evans' testimony at trial, the statement reports McCleskey admitting and boasting about the murder. It also recounts that Evans posed as Ben Wright's uncle and told McCleskey he had talked with Wright about the robbery and the murder.

In his second federal habeas petition, McCleskey asserted that the statement proved Evans "was acting in direct concert with State officials" during the incriminating conversations with McCleskey, and that the authorities "deliberately elicited" inculpatory admissions in violation of McCleskey's Sixth Amendment right to counsel. Among other responses, the State of Georgia contended that McCleskey's presentation of a *Massiah* claim for the first time in the second federal petition was an abuse of the writ.

The District Court held extensive hearings in July and August 1987 focusing on the arrangement the jailers had made for Evans' cell assignment in 1978. Several witnesses denied that Evans had been placed next to McCleskey by design or instructed to overhear conversations or obtain statements from McCleskey. McCleskey's key witness was Ulysses Worthy, a jailer at the Fulton County Jail during the summer of 1978. McCleskey's lawyers contacted Worthy after a detective testified that the 1978 Evans statement was taken in Worthy's office. The District Court characterized Worthy's testimony as "often confused and self-contradictory." Worthy testified that someone at some time requested permission to move Evans near McCleskey's cell. He contradicted himself, however, concerning when, why, and by whom Evans was moved, and about whether he overheard investigators urging Evans to engage McCleskey in conversation.

On December 23, 1987, the District Court granted McCleskey relief based upon a violation of *Massiah*. The court stated that the Evans statement "contains strong indication of an *ab initio* relationship between Evans and the authorities." In addition, the court credited Worthy's testimony suggesting that the police had used Evans to obtain incriminating information from McCleskey. Based on the Evans statement and portions of Worthy's testimony, the District Court found that the jail authorities had placed Evans in the cell adjoining McCleskey's "for the purpose of gathering incriminating information"; that "Evans was probably coached in how to approach McCleskey and given critical facts unknown to the general public"; that Evans talked with McCleskey and eavesdropped on McCleskey's conversations with others; and that Evans reported what he had heard to the authorities. These findings, in the District Court's view, established a *Massiah* violation.

In granting habeas relief, the District Court rejected the State's argument that McCleskey's assertion of the *Massiah* claim for the first time in the second federal petition constituted an abuse of the writ. The court ruled that McCleskey did not deliberately abandon the claim after raising it in his first state habeas petition. "This is not a case," the District Court reasoned, "where petitioner has reserved his proof or deliberately withheld his claim for a second petition." The District court also determined that when McCleskey filed his first federal petition, he did not know about either the 21-page Evans document or the identity of Worthy, and that the failure to discover the evidence for the first federal petition "was not due to [McCleskey's] inexcusable neglect."

The Eleventh Circuit reversed, holding that the District Court abused its discretion by failing to dismiss McCleskey's *Massiah* claim as an abuse of the writ. The Court of Appeals agreed with the District Court that the petitioner must "show that he did not deliberately abandon the claim and that his failure to raise it [in the first federal habeas proceeding] was not due to inexcusable neglect." Accepting the District Court's findings that at the first petition stage McCleskey knew neither the existence of the Evans statement nor the identity of Worthy, the court held that the District Court "misconstru[ed] the meaning of deliberate abandonment." Because McCleskey included a *Massiah* claim in his first state petition, dropped it in his first federal petition, and then reasserted it in his second federal petition, he "made a knowing choice not to pursue the claim after having raised it previously" that constituted a prima facie showing of "deliberate abandonment." The court further found the State's alleged concealment of the Evans statement irrelevant because it "was simply the catalyst that caused counsel to pursue the *Massiah* claim more vigorously" and did not itself "demonstrate the existence of a *Massiah* violation." The court concluded that McCleskey had presented no reason why counsel could not have discovered Worthy earlier. Finally, the court ruled that McCleskey's claim did not fall within the ends of justice exception to the abuse of the writ doctrine because any *Massiah* violation that may have been committed would have been harmless error.

McCleskey petitioned this Court for a writ of certiorari, alleging numerous errors in the Eleventh Circuit's abuse of the writ analysis. In our order granting the petition, we requested the parties to address the following additional question: "Must the State demonstrate that a claim was deliberately abandoned in an earlier petition for a writ of habeas corpus in order to establish that inclusion of that claim in a subsequent habeas petition constitutes abuse of the writ?"

II

The parties agree that the government has the burden of pleading abuse of the writ, and that once the government makes a proper submission, the petitioner must show that he has not abused the writ in seeking habeas relief. Much confusion exists though, on the standard for determining when a petitioner abuses the writ. Although the standard is central to the proper determination of many federal habeas corpus actions, we have had little occasion to define it. Indeed, there is truth to the observation that we have defined abuse of the writ in an oblique way, through dicta and denials of certiorari petitions or stay applications. . . . Today we give the subject our careful consideration. We begin by tracing the historical development of some of the substantive and procedural aspects of the writ, and then consider the standard for abuse that district courts should apply in actions seeking federal habeas corpus relief.

A

The Judiciary Act of 1789 empowered federal courts to issue writs of habeas corpus to prisoners "in custody, under or by colour of the authority of the United States." In the early decades of our new federal system, English common law defined the substantive scope of the writ. Federal prisoners could use the writ to challenge confinement imposed by a court that lacked jurisdiction, or detention by the executive without proper legal process.

. . . The major statutory expansion of the writ occurred in 1867, when Congress extended federal habeas corpus to prisoners held in state custody. For the most part, however, expansion of the writ has come through judicial decisionmaking. . . . [T]he Court began by interpreting the concept of jurisdictional defect with generosity to include sentences imposed without statutory authorization, and convictions obtained under an unconstitutional statute. Later, we allowed habeas relief for confinement under a state conviction obtained without adequate procedural protections for the defendant.

. . . With the exception of Fourth Amendment violations that a petitioner has been given a full and fair opportunity to litigate in state court, *Stone* v. *Powell* (1976), the writ today appears to extend to all dispositive constitutional claims presented in a proper procedural manner.

One procedural requisite is that a petition not lead to an abuse of the writ. . . .

[B omitted]

III

. . . [T]he doctrine of abuse of the writ refers to a complex and evolving body of equitable principles informed and controlled by historical usage, statutory developments, and judicial decisions. . . .

Although our decisions on the subject do not all admit of ready synthesis, one point emerges with clarity: Abuse of the writ is not confined to instances of deliberate abandonment. . . .

. . . Our recent decisions confirm that a petitioner can abuse the writ by raising a claim in a subsequent petition that he could have raised in his first, regardless of whether the failure to raise it earlier stemmed from a deliberate choice.

The inexcusable neglect standard demands more from a petitioner than the standard of deliberate abandonment. But we have not given the former term the content necessary to guide district courts in the ordered consideration of allegedly abusive habeas corpus petitions. . . . [A] review of our habeas corpus precedents leads us to decide that the same standard used to determine whether to excuse state procedural defaults should govern the determination of inexcusable neglect in the abuse of the writ context. . . .

. . . If re-examination of a conviction in the first round of federal habeas stretches resources, examination of new claims raised in a second or subsequent petition spreads them thinner still. These later petitions deplete the resources needed for federal litigants in the first instance, including litigants commencing their first federal habeas action. . . . And if re-examination of convictions in the first round of habeas offends federalism and comity, the offense increases when a State must defend its conviction in a second or subsequent habeas proceeding on grounds not even raised in the first petition.

The federal writ of habeas corpus overrides all these considerations, essential as they are to the rule of law, when a petitioner raises a meritorious constitutional claim in a proper manner in a habeas petition. Our procedural default jurisprudence and abuse of the writ jurisprudence help define this dimension of procedural regularity. Both doctrines impose on petitioners a burden of reasonable compliance with procedures designed to discourage baseless claims and to keep the system open for valid ones; both recognize the law's interest in finality; and both invoke equitable principles to define the court's discretion to excuse pleading and procedural requirements for petitioners who could not comply with them in the exercise of reasonable care and diligence. . . .

In procedural default cases, the cause standard requires the petitioner to show that "some objective factor external to the defense impeded counsel's efforts" to raise the claim in state court. Objective factors that constitute cause include " 'interference by officials' " that makes compliance with the state's procedural rule impracticable, and "a showing that the factual or legal basis for a claim was not reasonably available to counsel." In addition, constitutionally "ineffective assistance of counsel . . .

is cause." Attorney error short of ineffective assistance will not excuse a procedural default. Once the petitioner has established cause, he must show " 'actual prejudice' resulting from the errors of which he complains."

. . . When a prisoner files a second or subsequent application, the government bears the burden of pleading abuse of the writ. The government satisfies this burden if, with clarity and particularity, it notes petitioner's prior writ history, identifies the claims that appear for the first time, and alleges that petitioner has abused the writ. The burden to disprove abuse then becomes petitioner's. To excuse his failure to raise the claim earlier, he must show cause for failing to raise it and prejudice therefrom as those concepts have been defined in our procedural default decisions. . . . If petitioner cannot show cause, the failure to raise the claim in an earlier petition may nonetheless be excused if he or she can show that a fundamental miscarriage of justice would result from a failure to entertain the claim. . . .

The cause and prejudice standard should curtail the abusive petitions that in recent years have threatened to undermine the integrity of the habeas corpus process. . . .

We now apply these principles to the case before us.

IV

McCleskey based the *Massiah* claim in his second federal petition on the 21-page Evans document alone. Worthy's identity did not come to light until the hearing. The District Court found, based on the document's revelation of the tactics used by Evans in engaging McCleskey in conversation (such as his pretending to be Ben Wright's uncle and his claim that he was supposed to participate in the robbery), that the document established an *ab initio* relationship between Evans and the authorities. It relied on the finding and on Worthy's later testimony to conclude that the State committed a *Massiah* violation.

This ruling on the merits cannot come before us or any federal court if it is premised on a claim that constitutes an abuse of the writ. We must consider, therefore, the preliminary question whether McCleskey had cause for failing to raise the *Massiah* claim in his first federal petition. The District Court found that neither the 21-page document nor Worthy were known or discoverable before filing the first federal petition. Relying on these findings, McCleskey argues that his failure to raise the *Massiah* claim in the first petition should be excused. For reasons set forth below, we disagree.

That McCleskey did not possess or could not reasonably have obtained certain evidence fails to establish cause if other known or discoverable evidence could have supported the claim in any event. For cause to exist, the external impediment, whether it be government interference or the reasonable unavailability of the factual basis for the claim, must have prevented petitioner from raising the claim. Abuse of the writ doctrine examines *petitioner's* conduct: the question is whether petitioner possessed, or by reasonable means could have obtained, a sufficient basis to allege a claim in the first petition and pursue the matter through the habeas process. . . .

. . . It is essential at the outset to distinguish between two issues: (1) Whether petitioner knew about or could have discovered the 21-page document; and (2) whether he knew about or could have discovered the evidence the document recounted, namely the jail-cell conversations. The District Court's error lies in its conflation of the two inquiries, an error petitioner would have us perpetuate here.

The 21-page document unavailable to McCleskey at the time of the first petition does not establish that McCleskey had cause for failing to raise the *Massiah* claim at the outset. Based on testimony and questioning at trial, McCleskey knew that he had confessed the murder during jail-cell conversations with Evans, knew that Evans claimed to be a relative of Ben Wright during the conversations, and knew that Evans told the police about the conversations. Knowledge of these facts alone would put McCleskey on notice to pursue the *Massiah* claim in his first federal habeas petition as he had done in the first state habeas petition. . . .

By failing to raise the *Massiah* claim in 1981, McCleskey foreclosed the procedures best suited for disclosure of the facts needed for a reliable determination. . . .

As McCleskey lacks cause for failing to raise the *Massiah* claim in the first federal petition, we need not consider whether he would be prejudiced by his inability to raise the alleged *Massiah* violation at this late date.

We do address whether the Court should nonetheless exercise its equitable discretion to correct a miscarriage of justice. That narrow exception is of no avail to McCleskey. The *Massiah* violation, if it be one, resulted in the admission at trial of truthful inculpatory evidence which did not affect the reliability of the guilt determination. The very statement McCleskey now seeks to embrace confirms his guilt. . . .

The history of the proceedings in this case, and the burden upon the State in defending against allegations made for the first time in federal court some 9 years after the trial, reveal the necessity for the abuse of the writ doctrine. The cause and prejudice standard we adopt today leaves ample room for consideration of constitutional errors in a first federal habeas petition and in a later petition under appropriate circumstances. Petitioner has not satisfied this standard for excusing the omission of the *Massiah* claim from his first petition. The judgment of the Court of

Appeals is

Affirmed.

JUSTICE MARSHALL, with whom JUSTICE BLACKMUN and JUSTICE STEVENS join, dissenting.

Today's decision departs drastically from the norms that inform the proper judicial function. Without even the most casual admission that it is discarding longstanding legal principles, the Court radically redefines the content of the "abuse of the writ" doctrine, substituting the strict-liability "cause and prejudice" standard of *Wainwright* v. *Sykes,* 433 U.S. 72 (1977), for the good-faith "deliberate abandonment" standard of *Sanders* v. *United States,* 373 U.S. 1 (1963). This doctrinal innovation, which repudiates a line of judicial decisions codified by Congress in the governing statute and procedural rules, was by no means foreseeable when the petitioner in this case filed his first federal habeas application. Indeed, the new rule announced and applied today was not even *requested* by respondent at any point in this litigation. Finally, rather than remand this case for reconsideration in light of its new standard, the majority performs an independent reconstruction of the record, disregarding the factual findings of the District Court and applying its new rule in a manner that encourages state officials to *conceal* evidence that would likely prompt a petitioner to raise a particular claim on habeas. Because I cannot acquiesce in this unjustifiable assault on the Great Writ, I dissent.

I

. . . The Court in *Sanders* distinguished successive petitions raising previously asserted grounds from those raising previously unasserted grounds. With regard to the former class of petitions, the Court explained, the district court may give "[c]ontrolling weight . . . to [the] denial of a prior application" unless "the ends of justice would . . . be served by reaching the merits of the subsequent application." With regard to the latter, however, the district court *must* reach the merits of the petition *unless* "there has been an abuse of the writ. In determining whether the omission of the claim from the previous petition constitutes an abuse of the writ, the judgment of the district court is to be guided chiefly by the " '[equitable] principle that a suitor's conduct in relation to the matter at hand may disentitle him to the relief he seeks.' ". . .

What emerges from *Sanders* and its predecessors is essentially a good-faith standard. . . . [S]o long as the petitioner's previous application was based on a good-faith assessment of the claims available to him, the denial of the application does not bar the petitioner from availing himself of "new or additional information" in support of a claim not previously raised.

"Cause and prejudice"—the standard currently applicable to procedural defaults in state proceedings—imposes a much stricter test. As this Court's precedents make clear, a petitioner has *cause* for failing effectively to present his federal claim in state proceedings only when "some objective factor external to the defense impeded counsel's efforts to comply with the State's procedural rule. . . ." Under this test, the state of mind of counsel is largely irrelevant. Indeed, this Court has held that even counsel's *reasonable* perception that a particular claim is without factual or legal foundation does not excuse the failure to raise that claim in the absence of an objective, external impediment to counsel's efforts. In this sense, the cause component of the *Wainwright* v. *Sykes* test establishes a *strict-liability* standard.

Equally foreign to our abuse-of-the-writ jurisprudence is the requirement that a petitioner show "prejudice." Under *Sanders,* a petitioner who articulates a justifiable reason for failing to present a claim in a previous habeas application is not required in addition to demonstrate any particular degree of prejudice before the habeas court must consider his claim. If the petitioner demonstrates that his claim has merit, it is the State that must show that the resulting constitutional error was harmless beyond a reasonable doubt.

II

The real question posed by the majority's analysis is not *whether* the cause-and-prejudice test departs from the principles of *Sanders*—for it clearly does—but whether the majority has succeeded in *justifying* this departure as an exercise of this Court's common-lawmaking discretion. In my view, the majority does not come close to justifying its new standard.

A

Incorporation of the cause-and-prejudice test into the abuse-of-the-writ doctrine cannot be justified as an exercise of this Court's common-lawmaking discretion, because this Court has no discretion to exercise in this area. Congress has affirmatively ratified the *Sanders* good-faith standard in the governing statute and procedural rules, thereby insulating that standard from judicial repeal.

The abuse-of-writ doctrine is embodied in 28 U.S.C. § 2244(b) and in Habeas Corpus Rule 9(b). . . .

The majority concedes that § 2244(b) and Rule 9(b) codify *Sanders,* but concludes nonetheless that Congress did "not answer" all of the "questions" concerning the abuse-of-the-writ doctrine. The majority emphasizes that § 2244(b) refers to second or successive petitions from petitioners who have "deliberately withheld the newly asserted ground *or otherwise abused the writ*" without exhaustively cataloging the ways in which the writ may "otherwise" be "abused." From this "silenc[e]," the majority infers a congressional delegation of lawmaking power broad enough to encompass the engrafting of the cause-and-prejudice test onto the abuse-of-the-writ doctrine.

It is difficult to take this reasoning seriously. . . . Insofar as *Sanders* was primarily concerned with limiting dismissal of a second or subsequent petition to instances in which the petitioner had deliberately abandoned the new claim, the suggestion that Congress invested courts with the discretion to read this language out of the statute is completely irreconcilable with the proposition that § 2244(b) and Rule 9(b) codify *Sanders*. . . .

The majority tacitly acknowledges this constraint on the Court's interpretive discretion by suggesting that "cause" is tantamount to "inexcusable neglect." This claim, too, is untenable. The majority exaggerates when it claims that the "inexcusable neglect" formulation—which this Court has never applied in an abuse-of-the-writ decision—functions as an independent standard for evaluating a petitioner's failure to raise a claim in a previous habeas application. . . .

Confirmation that the majority today exercises legislative power not properly belonging to this Court is supplied by Congress' own recent consideration and rejection of an amendment to § 2244(b). It is axiomatic that this Court does not function as a backup legislature for the reconsideration of failed attempts to amend existing statutes. Yet that is exactly the effect of today's decision. . . .

[B omitted]

III

The manner in which the majority applies its new rule is as objectionable as the manner in which the majority creates that rule. As even the majority acknowledges, the standard that it announces today is not the one employed by the Court of Appeals, which purported to rely on *Sanders*. Where, as here, application of a different standard from the one applied by the lower court requires an in-depth review of the record, the ordinary course is to remand so that the parties have a fair opportunity to address, and the lower court to consider, all of the relevant issues. . . .

The majority's analysis of this case is dangerous precisely because it treats as irrelevant the effect that the State's disinformation strategy had on counsel's assessment of pursing the reasonableness of the *Massiah* claim. For the majority, all that matters is that no external obstacle barred

McCleskey from finding Worthy. But obviously, counsel's decision even to look for evidence in support of a particular claim has to be informed by what counsel reasonably perceives to be the prospect that the claim may have merit; in this case, by withholding the 21-page statement and by affirmatively misleading counsel as to the State's involvement with Evans, state officials created a climate in which McCleskey's first habeas counsel was perfectly justified in focusing his attentions elsewhere. The sum and substance of the majority's analysis is that McCleskey had no "cause" for failing to assert the *Massiah* claim because he did not try hard enough to pierce the State's veil of deception. Because the majority excludes from its conception of cause any recognition of how state officials can distort a petitioner's reasonable perception of whether pursuit of a particular claim is worthwhile, the majority's conception of "cause" creates an incentive for state officials to engage in this very type of misconduct. . . .

IV

Ironically, the majority seeks to defend its doctrinal innovation on the ground that it will promote respect for the "rule of law." Obviously, respect for the rule of law must start with those who are responsible for *pronouncing* the law. The majority's invocation of " 'the orderly administration of justice' " rings hollow when the majority itself tosses aside established precedents without explanation, disregards the will of Congress, fashions rules that defy the reasonable expectations of the persons who must conform their conduct to the law's dictates, and applies those rules in a way that rewards state misconduct and deceit. Whatever "abuse of the writ" today's decision is designed to avert pales in comparison with the majority's own abuse of the norms that inform the proper judicial function.

I dissent.

□□□

Nos. 89-1391 and 89-1392

Irving Rust, etc., et al., Petitioners v. Louis W. Sullivan, Secretary of Health and Human Services

New York, et al., Petitioners v. Louis W. Sullivan, Secretary of Health and Human Services

On writs of certiorari to the United States Court of Appeals for the Second Circuit

[May 23, 1991]

CHIEF JUSTICE REHNQUIST delivered the opinion of the Court.

[I omitted]
II

We begin by pointing out the posture of the cases before us. Petitioners are challenging the *facial* validity of the regulations. Thus, we are concerned only with the question whether, on their face, the regulations are both authorized by the Act, and can be construed in such a manner that they can be applied to a set of individuals without infringing upon constitutionally protected rights. Petitioners face a heavy burden in seeking to have the regulations invalidated as facially unconstitutional. "A facial challenge to a legislative Act is, of course, the most difficult challenge to mount successfully, since the challenger must establish that no set of circumstances exists under which the Act would be valid. The fact that [the regulations] might operate unconstitutionally under some conceivable set of circumstances is insufficient to render [them] wholly invalid." *United States* v. *Salerno* (1987). . . .

A

We need not dwell on the plain language of the statute because we agree with every court to have addressed the issue that the language is ambiguous. The language of § 1008—that "[n]one of the funds appropriated under this subchapter shall be used in programs where abortion is a method of family planning"—does not speak directly to the issues of counseling, referral, advocacy, or program integrity. . . .

The broad language of Title X plainly allows the Secretary's construction of the statute. By its own terms, § 1008 prohibits the use of Title X funds "in programs where abortion is a method of family planning." Title X does not define the term "method of family planning," nor does it enumerate what types of medical and counseling services are entitled to Title X funding. Based on the broad directives provided by Congress in Title X in general and § 1008 in particular, we are unable to say that the Secretary's construction of the prohibition in § 1008 to require a ban on counseling, referral, and advocacy within the Title X project, is impermissible. . . .

When we find, as we do here, that the legislative history is ambiguous and unenlightening on the matters with respect to which the regulations deal, we customarily defer to the expertise of the agency. Petitioners argue, however, that the regulations are entitled to little or no deference because they "reverse a longstanding agency policy that permitted nondirective counseling and referral for abortion," and thus represent a sharp break from the Secretary's prior construction of the statute. Petitioners argue that the agency's prior consistent interpretation of Section 1008 to permit nondirective counseling and to encourage coordination with local and state family planning services is entitled to substantial weight.

This Court has rejected the argument that an agency's interpretation "is not entitled to deference because it represents a sharp break with prior interpretations" of the statute in question. In *Chevron* [1984], we held that a revised interpretation deserves deference because "[a]n initial agency interpretation is not instantly carved in stone" and "the agency, to engage in informed rulemaking, must consider varying interpretations and the wisdom of its policy on a continuing basis." . . .

We find that the Secretary amply justified his change of interpretation with a "reasoned analysis." The Secretary explained that the regulations are a result of his determination, in the wake of the critical reports of the General Accounting Office (GAO) and the Office of the Inspector General (OIG), that prior policy failed to implement properly the statute and that it was necessary to provide "clear and operational guidance to grantees to preserve the distinction between Title X programs and abortion as a method of family planning." He also determined that the new regulations are more in keeping with the original intent of the statute, are justified by client experience under the prior policy, and are supported by a shift in attitude against the "elimination of unborn children by abortion." We believe that these justifications are sufficient to support the Secretary's revised approach. Having concluded that the plain language and legislative history are ambiguous as to Congress' intent in enacting Title X, we must defer to the Secretary's permissible construction of the statute.

B

We turn next to the "program integrity" requirements embodied at § 59.9 of the regulations, mandating separate facilities, personnel, and records. These requirements are not inconsistent with the plain language of Title X. Petitioners contend, however, that they are based on an impermissible construction of the statute because they frustrate the clearly expressed intent of Congress that Title X programs be an integral part of a broader, comprehensive, health-care system. They argue that this integration is impermissibly burdened because the efficient use of non-Title X funds by Title X grantees will be adversely affected by the regulations.

The Secretary defends the separation requirements of § 59.9 on the grounds that they are necessary to assure that Title X grantees apply federal funds only to federally authorized purposes and that grantees avoid creating the appearance that the government is supporting abortion-related activities. The program integrity regulations were promulgated in direct response to the observations in the GAO and OIG reports that "[b]ecause the distinction between the recipient's title X and other activities may not be easily recognized, the public can get the impression that Federal funds are being improperly used for abortion activities." . . .

III

Petitioners contend that the regulations violate the First Amendment . . . "free speech rights of private health care organizations that receive Title X funds, of their staff, and of their patients" by impermissibly imposing "viewpoint-discriminatory conditions on government subsidies" and thus penaliz[e] speech funded with non-Title X monies." Because "Title X continues to fund speech ancillary to pregnancy testing in a manner that is not evenhanded with respect to views and information about abortion, it invidiously discriminates on the basis of viewpoint." Relying on *Regan* v. *Taxation With Representation of Wash.* [1983], and *Arkansas Writers Project, Inc.* v. *Ragland* (1987), petitioners also assert that while the Government may place certain conditions on the receipt of federal subsidies, it may not "discriminate invidiously in its subsidies in such a way as to 'ai[m] at the suppression of dangerous ideas.' "

There is no question but that the statutory prohibition contained in § 1008 is constitutional. In *Maher* v. *Roe* [1977] we upheld a state welfare regulation under which Medicaid recipients received payments for services related to childbirth, but not for nontherapeutic abortions. The Court rejected the claim that this unequal subsidization worked a violation of the Constitution. We held that the government may "make a value judgment favoring childbirth over abortion, and . . . implement that judgment by the allocation of public funds." Here the Government is exercising the authority it possesses under *Maher* and [*Harris* v.] *McRae* to subsidize family planning services which will lead to conception and child birth, and declining to "promote or encourage abortion." The Government can, without violating the Constitution, selectively fund a program to encourage certain activities it believes to be in the public interest, without at the same time funding an alternate program which seeks to deal with the problem in another way. . . .

. . . This is not a case of the Government "suppressing a dangerous idea," but of a prohibition on a project grantee or its employees from engaging in activities outside of its scope. . . . When Congress established a National Endowment for Democracy to encourage other countries to adopt democratic principles, it was not constitutionally required to fund a program to encourage competing lines of political philosophy such as Communism and Fascism. . . .

We believe that petitioners' reliance upon our decision in *Arkansas Writers Project, supra*, is misplaced. That case involved a state sales tax which discriminated between magazines on the basis of their content. Relying on this fact, and on the fact that the tax "targets a small group within the press," . . . the Court held the tax invalid. But we have here not the case of a general law singling out a disfavored group on the basis of speech content, but a case of the Government refusing to fund activities, including speech, which are specifically excluded from the scope of the project funded.

Petitioners rely heavily on their claim that the regulations would not, in the circumstance of a medical emergency, permit a Title X project to refer a woman whose pregnancy places her life in imminent peril to a provider of abortions or abortion-related services. This case, of course, involves only a facial challenge to the regulations, and we do not have before us any application by the Secretary to a specific fact situation. On their face, we do not read the regulations to bar abortion referral or counseling in such circumstances. Abortion counseling as a "method of family planning" is prohibited, and it does not seem that a medically necessitated abortion in such circumstances would be the equivalent of its use as a "method of family planning." Neither § 1008 nor the specific restrictions of the regulations would apply. Moreover, the regulations themselves contemplate that a Title X project would be permitted to engage in otherwise prohibited abortion-related activity in such circumstances. Section 59.8(a)(2) provides a specific exemption for emergency care and requires Title X recipients "to refer the client immediately to an appropriate provider of emergency medical services." Section 59.5(b)(1) also requires Title X projects to provide "necessary referral to other medical facilities when medically indicated." . . .

Petitioners also contend that the restrictions on the subsidization of abortion-related speech contained in the regulations are impermissible because they condition the receipt of a benefit, in this case Title X funding, on the relinquishment of a constitutional right, the right to engage in abortion advocacy and counseling. Relying on *Perry* v. *Sindermann* (1972), and *FCC* v. *League of Women Voters of Cal.* (1984), petitioners argue that "even though the government may deny [a] . . . benefit for any number of reasons, there are some reasons upon which the government may not rely. It may not deny a benefit to a person on a basis that infringes his constitutionally protected interests—especially, his interest in freedom of speech."

Petitioners' reliance on these cases is unavailing, however, because here the government is not denying a benefit to anyone, but is instead simply insisting that public funds be spent for the purposes for which they were authorized. . . . The Title X *grantee* can continue to perform abortions, provide abortion-related services, and engage in abortion advocacy; it simply is required to conduct those activities through programs that are separate and independent from the project that receives Title X funds.

In contrast, our "unconstitutional conditions" cases involve situations in which the government has placed a condition on the *recipient* of the subsidy rather than on a particular program or service, thus effectively prohibiting the recipient from engaging in the protected conduct outside the scope of the federally funded program. In *FCC* v. *League of Women Voters of Cal.*, we invalidated a federal law providing that noncommercial television and radio stations that receive federal grants may not "engage in editorializing." Under that law, a recipient of federal funds was "barred absolutely from all editorializing" because it "is not able to segregate its activities according to the source of its funding" and thus "has no way of limiting the use of its federal funds to all noneditorializing activities." The effect of the law was that "a noncommercial educational station that receives only 1% of its overall income from [federal] grants is barred absolutely from all editorializing" and "barred from using even wholly private funds to finance its editorial activity." We expressly recognized, however, that were Congress to permit the recipient stations to "establish 'affiliate' organizations which could then use the station's facilities to editorialize with nonfederal funds, such a statutory mechanism would plainly be valid." Such a scheme would permit the station "to make known its views on matters of public importance through its nonfederally funded, editorializing affiliate without losing federal grants for its noneditorializing broadcast activities."

Similarly, in *Regan* we held that Congress could, in the exercise of its spending power, reasonably refuse to subsidize the lobbying activities of tax-exempt charitable organizations by prohibiting such organizations from using tax-deductible contributions to support their lobbying efforts. In so holding, we explained that such organizations remained free "to receive deductible contributions to support . . . nonlobbying activi-t[ies]." . . .

By requiring that the Title X grantee engage in abortion-related activity separately from activity receiving federal funding, Congress has, consistent with our teachings in *League of Women Voters* and *Regan*, not denied it the right to engage in abortion-related activities. Congress has merely refused to fund such activities out of the public fisc, and the Secretary has simply required a certain degree of separation from the Title X project in order to ensure the integrity of the federally funded program.

The same principles apply to petitioners' claim that the regulations abridge the free speech rights of the grantee's staff. Individuals who are voluntarily employed for a Title X project must perform their duties in accordance with the regulation's restrictions on abortion counseling and referral. The employees remain free, however, to pursue abortion-related activities when they are not acting under the auspices of the Title X project. The regulations, which govern solely the scope of the Title X project's activities, do not in any way restrict the activities of those persons acting as private individuals. The employees' freedom of expression is limited during the time that they actually work for the project; but this limitation is a consequence of their decision to accept employment in a project, the scope of which is permissibly restricted by the funding authority.

This is not to suggest that funding by the Government, even when coupled with the freedom of the fund recipients to speak outside the scope of the Government-funded project, is invariably sufficient to justify government control over the content of expression. For example, this Court has recognized that the existence of a Government "subsidy," in the form of Government-owned property, does not justify the restriction of speech in areas that have "been traditionally open to the public for expressive activity," *United States* v. *Kokinda* (1990).... Similarly, we have recognized that the university is a traditional sphere of free expression so fundamental to the functioning of our society that the Government's ability to control speech within that sphere by means of conditions attached to the expenditure of Government funds is restricted by the vagueness and overbreadth doctrines of the First Amendment, *Keyishian* v. *Board of Regents* (1967). It could be argued by analogy that traditional relationships such as that between doctor and patient should enjoy protection under the First Amendment from government regulation, even when subsidized by the Government. We need not resolve that question here, however, because the Title X program regulations do not significantly impinge upon the doctor-patient relationship. Nothing in them requires a doctor to represent as his own any opinion that he does not in fact hold. Nor is the doctor-patient relationship established by the Title X program sufficiently all-encompassing so as to justify an expectation on the part of the patient of comprehensive medical advice. The program does not provide postconception medical care, and therefore a doctor's silence with regard to abortion cannot reasonably be thought to mislead a client into thinking that the doctor does not consider abortion an appropriate option for her....

IV

We turn now to petitioners' argument that the regulations violate a woman's Fifth Amendment right to choose whether to terminate her pregnancy. We recently reaffirmed the long-recognized principle that

" 'the Due Process Clauses generally confer no affirmative right to governmental aid, even where such aid may be necessary to secure life, liberty, or property interests of which the government itself may not deprive the individual.' " *Webster*, 492 U.S. at ___, quoting *DeShaney* v. *Winnebago County Dept. of Social Services* (1989). The Government has no constitutional duty to subsidize an activity merely because the activity is constitutionally protected. . . .

Petitioners also argue that by impermissibly infringing on the doctor/patient relationship and depriving a Title X client of information concerning abortion as a method of family planning, the regulations violate a woman's Fifth Amendment right to medical self-determination and to make informed medical decisions free of government-imposed harm. They argue that under our decisions in *Akron* v. *Akron Center for Reproductive Health, Inc.* (1983), and *Thornburg* v. *American College of Obstetricians and Gynecologists* (1986), the government cannot interfere with a woman's right to make an informed and voluntary choice by placing restrictions on the patient/doctor dialogue.

In *Akron*, we invalidated a city ordinance requiring *all* physicians to make specified statements to the patient prior to performing an abortion in order to ensure that the woman's consent was "truly informed." Similarly, in *Thornburg*, we struck down a state statute mandating that a list of agencies offering alternatives to abortion and a description of fetal development be provided to *every* woman considering terminating her pregnancy through an abortion. . . . [B]oth cases required *all* doctors within their respective jurisdictions to provide *all* pregnant patients contemplating an abortion a litany of information, regardless of whether the patient sought the information or whether the doctor thought the information necessary to the patient's decision. Under the Secretary's regulations, however, a doctor's ability to provide, and a woman's right to receive, information concerning abortion and abortion-related services outside the context of the Title X project remains unfettered. It would undoubtedly be easier for a woman seeking an abortion if she could receive information about abortion from a Title X project, but the Constitution does not require that the Government distort the scope of its mandated program in order to provide that information.

Petitioners contend, however, that most Title X clients are effectively precluded by indigency and poverty from seeing a health care provider who will provide abortion-related services. But once again, even these Title X clients are in no worse position than if Congress had never enacted Title X. . . .

The Secretary's regulations are a permissible construction of Title X and do not violate either the First or Fifth Amendments to the Constitution. Accordingly, the judgment of the Court of Appeals is

Affirmed.

JUSTICE BLACKMUN, with whom JUSTICE MARSHALL joins, with whom JUSTICE STEVENS joins as to Parts II and III, and with whom JUSTICE O'CONNOR joins as to Part I, dissenting.

Casting aside established principles of statutory construction and administrative jurisprudence, the majority in these cases today unnecessarily passes upon important questions of constitutional law. In so doing, the Court, for the first time, upholds viewpoint-based suppression of speech solely because it is imposed on those dependent upon the Government for economic support. Under essentially the same rationale, the majority upholds direct regulation of dialogue between a pregnant woman and her physician when that regulation has both the purpose and the effect of manipulating her decision as to the continuance of her pregnancy. I conclude that the Secretary's regulation of referral, advocacy, and counseling activities exceeds his statutory authority, and, also, that the Regulations violate the First and Fifth Amendments of our Constitution. Accordingly, I dissent and would reverse the divided-vote judgment of the Court of Appeals.

I

. . . Whether or not one believes that these Regulations are valid, it avoids reality to contend that they do not give rise to serious constitutional questions. . . . [T]he question squarely presented by the Regulations—the extent to which the Government may attach an otherwise unconstitutional condition to the receipt of a public benefit—implicates a troubled area of our jurisprudence in which a court ought not entangle itself unnecessarily. . . .

[T]he Regulations impose viewpoint-based restrictions upon protected speech and are aimed at a woman's decision whether to continue or terminate her pregnancy. In both respects, they implicate core constitutional values. This verity is evidenced by the fact that two of the three Courts of Appeals that have entertained challenges to the Regulations have invalidated them on constitutional grounds. See *Massachusetts* v. *Secretary of Health and Human Services* (CA1 1990); *Planned Parenthood Federation of America* v. *Sullivan* (CA10 1990). . . . That a bare majority of this Court today reaches a different result does not change the fact that the constitutional questions raised by the Regulations are both grave and doubtful.

Nor is this a case in which the statutory language itself requires us to address a constitutional question. Section 1008 of the Public Health Service Act, 84 Stat. 1508, 42 U.S.C. § 300a-6, provides simply: "None of the funds appropriated under this title shall be used in programs where abortion is a method of family planning." The majority concedes that this language "does not speak directly to the issues of counseling, referral, advocacy, or program integrity," and that "the legislative history is ambiguous" in this respect. . . . Indeed, it would appear that our duty to avoid passing unnecessarily upon important constitutional questions is strongest where, as here, the language of the statute is decidedly ambiguous. It is both logical and eminently prudent to assume that when Congress intends to press the limits of constitutionality in its enactments, it will express that intent in explicit and unambiguous terms. . . .

Because I conclude that a plainly constitutional construction of § 1008 "is not only 'fairly possible' but entirely reasonable," I would reverse the judgment of the Court of Appeals on this ground without deciding the constitutionality of the Secretary's Regulations.

II

A

. . . Until today, the Court never has upheld viewpoint-based suppression of speech simply because that suppression was a condition upon the acceptance of public funds. Whatever may be the Government's power to condition the receipt of its largess upon the relinquishment of constitutional rights, it surely does not extend to a condition that suppresses the recipient's cherished freedom of speech based solely upon the content or viewpoint of that speech. This rule is a sound one, for, as the Court often has noted: " 'A regulation of speech that is motivated by nothing more than a desire to curtail expression of a particular point of view on controversial issues of general interest is the purest example of a "law . . . abridging the freedom of speech, or of the press." ' " . . .

It cannot seriously be disputed that the counseling and referral provisions at issue in the present cases constitute content-based regulation of speech. Title X grantees may provide counseling and referral regarding any of a wide range of family planning and other topics, save abortion. . . .

The Regulations are also clearly viewpoint-based. While suppressing speech favorable to abortion with one hand, the Secretary compels anti-abortion speech with the other. For example, the Department of Health and Human Services' own description of the Regulations makes plain that "Title X projects are *required* to facilitate access to prenatal care and social services, including adoption services, that might be needed by the pregnant client to promote her well-being and that of her child, while making it abundantly clear that the project is not permitted to promote abortion by facilitating access to abortion through the referral process."

Moreover, the Regulations command that a project refer for prenatal care each woman diagnosed as pregnant, irrespective of the woman's expressed desire to continue or terminate her pregnancy. If a client asks directly about abortion, a Title X physician or counselor is required to say, in essence, that the project does not consider abortion to be an appropriate method of family planning. Both requirements are antithetical to the First Amendment.

The Regulations pertaining to "advocacy" are even more explicitly viewpoint-based. These provide: "A Title X project may not *encourage, promote or advocate* abortion as a method of family planning." They explain: "This requirement prohibits actions to *assist* women to obtain abortions or *increase* the availability or accessibility of abortion for family planning purposes." The Regulations do not, however, proscribe or even regulate anti-abortion advocacy. These are clearly restrictions aimed at the suppression of "dangerous ideas."

Remarkably, the majority concludes that "the Government has not discriminated on the basis of viewpoint; it has merely chosen to fund one activity to the exclusion of another." But the majority's claim that the Regulations merely limit a Title X project's speech to preventive or preconceptional services rings hollow in light of the broad range of non-preventive services that the Regulations authorize Title X projects to provide. By refusing to fund those family-planning projects that advocate abortion *because* they advocate abortion, the Government plainly has targeted a particular viewpoint. The majority's reliance on the fact that the Regulations pertain solely to funding decisions simply begs the question. Clearly, there are some bases upon which government may not rest its decision to fund or not to fund. For example, the Members of the majority surely would agree that government may not base its decision to support an activity upon considerations of race. As demonstrated above, our cases make clear that ideological viewpoint is a similarly repugnant ground upon which to base funding decisions.

The majority's reliance upon *Regan* in this connection is also misplaced. That case stands for the proposition that government has no obligation to subsidize a private party's efforts to petition the legislature regarding its views. Thus, if the challenged Regulations were confined to non-ideological limitations upon the use of Title X funds for lobbying activities, there would exist no violation of the First Amendment. The advocacy Regulations at issue here, however, are not limited to lobbying but extend to all speech having the effect of encouraging, promoting, or advocating abortion as a method of family planning. Thus, in addition to their impermissible focus upon the viewpoint of regulated speech, the provisions intrude upon a wide range of communicative conduct, including the very words spoken to a woman by her physician. By manipulating the content of the doctor/patient dialogue, the Regulations upheld today force each of the petitioners "to be an instrument for fostering public adherence to an ideological point of view [he or she] finds unacceptable." This type of intrusive, ideologically based regulation of speech goes far beyond the narrow lobbying limitations approved in *Regan*, and cannot be justified simply because it is a condition upon the receipt of a governmental benefit.

B

The Court concludes that the challenged Regulations do not violate the First Amendment rights of Title X staff members because any limitation of the employees' freedom of expression is simply a consequence of their decision to accept employment at a federally funded project. But it has never been sufficient to justify an otherwise unconstitutional condition upon public employment that the employee may escape the condition by relinquishing his or her job. . . .

The majority attempts to circumvent this principle by emphasizing that Title X physicians and counselors "remain free . . . to pursue abortion-related activities when they are not acting under the auspices of the Title X project." "The regulations," the majority explains, "do not in any way restrict the activities of those persons acting as private individuals." Under the majority's reasoning, the First Amendment could be read to tolerate *any* governmental restriction upon an employee's speech so long as that restriction is limited to the funded workplace. This is a dangerous proposition, and one the Court has rightly rejected in the past. . . .

In the cases at bar, the speaker's interest in the communication is both clear and vital. In addressing the family-planning needs of their clients, the physicians and counselors who staff Title X projects seek to provide them with the full range of information and options regarding their health and reproductive freedom. Indeed, the legitimate expectations of the patient and the ethical responsibilities of the medical profession demand no less. "The patient's right of self-decision can be effectively exercised only if the patient possesses enough information to enable an intelligent choice. . . . The physician has an ethical obligation to help the patient make choices from among the therapeutic alternatives consistent with good medical practice." Current Opinions, the Council on Ethical and Judicial Affairs of the American Medical Association pgh. 8.08 (1989). . . . When a client becomes pregnant, the full range of therapeutic alternatives includes the abortion option, and Title X counselors' interest in providing this information is compelling.

The Government's articulated interest in distorting the doctor/patient dialogue—ensuring that federal funds are not spent for a purpose outside the scope of the program—falls far short of that necessary to justify the suppression of truthful information and professional medical opinion regarding constitutionally protected conduct. . . .

C

Finally, it is of no small significance that the speech the Secretary would suppress is truthful information regarding constitutionally protected conduct of vital importance to the listener. One can imagine no legitimate governmental interest that might be served by suppressing such information. Concededly, the abortion debate is among the most divisive and contentious issues that our Nation has faced in recent years. "But freedom to differ is not limited to things that do not matter much. That would be a mere shadow of freedom. The test of its substance is the right to differ as to things that touch the heart of the existing order." *West Virginia Board of Education* v. *Barnette* (1943).

III

By far the most disturbing aspect of today's ruling is the effect it will have on the Fifth Amendment rights of the women who, supposedly, are beneficiaries of Title X programs....

Until today, the Court has allowed to stand only those restrictions upon reproductive freedom that, while limiting the availability of abortion, have left intact a woman's ability to decide without coercion whether she will continue her pregnancy to term. *Maher,* ... *McRae,* and *Webster* [1989] are all to this effect. Today's decision abandons that principle, and with disastrous results.

Contrary to the majority's characterization, this is not a case in which individuals seek government aid in exercising their fundamental rights. The Fifth Amendment right asserted by petitioners is the right of a pregnant woman to be free from affirmative governmental *interference* in her decision. *Roe* v. *Wade* (1973), and its progeny are not so much about a medical procedure as they are about a woman's fundamental right to self-determination. Those cases serve to vindicate the idea that "liberty," if it means anything, must entail freedom from governmental domination in making the most intimate and personal of decisions....

It is crystal-clear that the aim of the challenged provisions—an aim the majority cannot escape noticing—is not simply to ensure that federal funds are not used to perform abortions, but to "reduce the incidence of abortion." As recounted above, the Regulations require Title X physicians and counselors to provide information pertaining only to childbirth, to refer a pregnant woman for prenatal care irrespective of her medical situation, and, upon direct inquiry, to respond that abortion is not an "appropriate method" of family planning.

The undeniable message conveyed by this forced speech, and the one that the Title X client will draw from it, is that abortion nearly always is an improper medical option. Although her physician's words, in fact, are strictly controlled by the Government and wholly unrelated to her particular medical situation, the Title X client will reasonably construe them as professional advice to forgo her right to obtain an abortion. As would most rational patients, many of these women will follow that perceived advice and carry their pregnancy to term, despite their needs to the contrary and despite the safety of the abortion procedure for the vast majority of them. Others, delayed by the Regulations' mandatory prenatal referral, will be prevented from acquiring abortions during the period in which the process is medically sound and constitutionally protected.

In view of the inevitable effect of the Regulations, the majority's conclusion that "[t]he difficulty that a woman encounters when a Title X project does not provide abortion counseling or referral leaves her in no different position than she would have been if the government had not enacted Title X" is insensitive and contrary to common human experience. Both the purpose and result of the challenged Regulations is to deny women the ability voluntarily to decide their procreative destiny. For these women, the Government will have obliterated the freedom to choose as surely as if it had banned abortions outright. The denial of this freedom is not a consequence of poverty but of the Government's ill-intentioned distortion of information it has chosen to provide.

The substantial obstacles to bodily self-determination that the Regulations impose are doubly offensive because they are effected by manipulating the very words spoken by physicians and counselors to their patients. In our society, the doctor/patient dialogue embodies a unique relationship of trust. The specialized nature of medical science and the emotional distress often attendant to health-related decisions requires that patients place their complete confidence, and often their very lives, in the hands of medical professionals. One seeks a physician's aid not only for medication or diagnosis, but also for guidance, professional judgment, and vital emotional support. Accordingly, each of us attaches profound importance and authority to the words of advice spoken by the physician. . . .

The manipulation of the doctor/patient dialogue achieved through the Secretary's Regulations is clearly an effort "to deter a woman from making a decision that, with her physician, is hers to make." As such, it violates the Fifth Amendment.

IV

In its haste further to restrict the right of every woman to control her reproductive freedom and bodily integrity, the majority disregards established principles of law and contorts this Court's decided cases to arrive at its preordained result. The majority professes to leave undisturbed the free speech protections upon which our society has come to rely, but one must wonder what force the First Amendment retains if it is read to countenance the deliberate manipulation by the Government of the dialogue between a woman and her physician. While technically leaving intact the fundamental right protected by *Roe* v. *Wade*, the Court, "through a relentlessly formalistic catechism," once again has rendered the right's substance nugatory. This is a course nearly as noxious as overruling *Roe* directly, for if a right is found to be unenforceable, even against flagrant attempts by government to circumvent it, then it ceases to be a right at all. This, I fear, may be the effect of today's decision.

JUSTICE STEVENS, dissenting.

In my opinion, the Court has not paid sufficient attention to the language of the controlling statute or to the consistent interpretation accorded the statute by the responsible cabinet officers during four different Presidencies and 18 years. . . .

The entirely new approach adopted by the Secretary in 1988 was not, in my view, authorized by the statute. The new regulations did not merely reflect a change in a policy determination that the Secretary had been authorized by Congress to make. Rather, they represented an assumption of policymaking responsibility that Congress had not delegated to the Secretary. . . .

Because I am convinced that the 1970 Act did not authorize the Secretary to censor the speech of grant recipients or their employees, I would hold the challenged regulations invalid and reverse the judgment of the Court of Appeals.

Even if I thought the statute were ambiguous, however, I would reach the same result for the reasons stated in JUSTICE O'CONNOR's dissenting opinion. As she also explains, if a majority of the Court had reached this result, it would be improper to comment on the constitutional issues that the parties have debated. . . .

JUSTICE O'CONNOR, dissenting.

"[W]here an otherwise acceptable construction of a statute would raise serious constitutional problems, the Court will construe the statute to avoid such problems unless such construction is plainly contrary to the intent of Congress." *Edward J. DeBartolo Corp.* v. *Florida Gulf Coast Building & Construction Trades Council* (1988). JUSTICE BLACKMUN has explained well why this long-standing canon of statutory construction applies in this case, and I join Part I of his dissent. Part II demonstrates why the challenged regulations, which constitute the Secretary's interpretation of § 1008 of the Public Health Service Act, 84 Stat. 1508, 42 U.S.C. § 300a-6, "raise serious constitutional problems": the restrictions on the speech of Title X fund recipients, restrictions directed precisely at speech concerning one of "the most divisive and contentious issues that our Nation has faced in recent years."

One may well conclude, as JUSTICE BLACKMUN does in Part II, that the regulations are unconstitutional for this reason. I do not join Part II of the dissent, however, for the same reason that I do not join Part III, in which JUSTICE BLACKMUN concludes that the regulations are unconstitutional under the Fifth Amendment. The canon of construction that JUSTICE BLACKMUN correctly applies here is grounded in large part upon our time-honored practice of not reaching constitutional questions unnecessarily. . . .

This Court acts at the limits of its power when it invalidates a law on constitutional grounds. In recognition of our place in the constitutional scheme, we must act with "great gravity and delicacy" when telling a coordinate branch that its actions are absolutely prohibited absent constitutional amendment. In this case, we need only tell the Secretary that his regulations are not a reasonable interpretation of the statute; we need not tell Congress that it cannot pass such legislation. If we rule solely on statutory grounds, Congress retains the power to force the constitutional question by legislating more explicitly. It may instead choose to do nothing. That decision should be left to Congress; we should not tell Congress what it cannot do before it has chosen to do it. It is enough in this case to conclude that neither the language nor the history of § 1008 compels the Secretary's interpretation, and that the interpretation raises serious First Amendment concerns. On this basis alone, I would reverse the judgment of the Court of Appeals and invalidate the challenged regulations.

□□□

No. 89-7743

Thaddeus Donald Edmonson, Petitioner v. Leesville Concrete Company, Inc.

On writ of certiorari to the United States Court of Appeals for the Fifth Circuit

[June 3, 1991]

JUSTICE KENNEDY delivered the opinion of the Court.

We must decide in the case before us whether a private litigant in a civil case may use peremptory challenges to exclude jurors on account of their race. Recognizing the impropriety of racial bias in the courtroom, we hold the race-based exclusion violates the equal protection rights of the challenged jurors. This civil case originated in a United States District

Court, and we apply the equal protection component of the Fifth Amendment's Due Process Clause.

I

Thaddeus Donald Edmonson, a construction worker, was injured in a job-site accident at Fort Polk, Louisiana, a federal enclave. Edmonson sued Leesville Concrete Company for negligence in the United States District Court for the Western District of Louisiana, claiming that a Leesville employee permitted one of the company's trucks to roll backward and pin him against some construction equipment. Edmonson invoked his Seventh Amendment right to a trial by jury.

During *voir dire* [jury selection], Leesville used two of its three peremptory challenges authorized by statute to remove black persons from the prospective jury. Citing our decision in *Batson* v. *Kentucky*, 476 U.S. 79 (1986), Edmonson, who is himself black, requested that the District Court require Leesville to articulate a race-neutral explanation for striking the two jurors. The District Court denied the request on the ground that *Batson* does not apply in civil proceedings. As impaneled, the jury included 11 white persons and 1 black person. The jury rendered a verdict for Edmonson, assessing his total damages at $90,000. It also attributed 80% of the fault to Edmonson's contributory negligence, however, and awarded him the sum of $18,000.

Edmonson appealed, and a divided panel of the Court of Appeals for the Fifth Circuit reversed, holding that our opinion in *Batson* applies to a private attorney representing a private litigant and that peremptory challenges may not be used in a civil trial for the purpose of excluding jurors on the basis of race. The Court of Appeals panel held that private parties become state actors when they exercise peremptory challenges and that to limit *Batson* to criminal cases "would betray *Batson*'s fundamental principle [that] the state's use, toleration, and approval of peremptory challenges based on race violates the equal protection clause." The panel remanded to the trial court to consider whether Edmonson had established a prima facie case of racial discrimination under *Batson*.

The full court then ordered rehearing en banc. A divided en banc panel affirmed the judgment of the District Court, holding that a private litigant in a civil case can exercise peremptory challenges without accountability for alleged racial classifications. The court concluded that the use of peremptories by private litigants does not constitute state action and, as a result, does not implicate constitutional guarantees. The dissent reiterated the arguments of the vacated panel opinion. The courts of appeals have divided on the issue. . . .

II

A

In *Powers* v. *Ohio* (1991), we held that a criminal defendant, regardless of his or her race, may object to a prosecutor's race-based exclusion of persons from the petit jury. Our conclusion rested on a two-part analysis. First, following our opinions in *Batson* and in *Carter* v. *Jury Commission of Greene County,* 396 U.S. 320 (1970), we made clear that a prosecutor's race-based peremptory challenge violates the equal protection rights of those excluded from jury service. Second, we relied on well-established rules of third-party standing to hold that a defendant may raise the excluded juror's equal protection rights.

Powers relied upon over a century of jurisprudence dedicated to the elimination of race prejudice within the jury selection process. . . . While these decisions were for the most part directed at discrimination by a prosecutor or other government officials in the context of criminal proceedings, we have not intimated that race discrimination is permissible in civil proceedings. . . .

That an act violates the Constitution when committed by a government official, however, does not answer the question whether the same act offends constitutional guarantees if committed by a private litigant or his attorney. The Constitution's protections of individual liberty and equal protection apply in general only to action by the government. . . . Thus, the legality of the exclusion at issue here turns on the extent to which a litigant in a civil case may be subject to the Constitution's restrictions. . . .

. . . Peremptory challenges are permitted only when the government, by statute or decisional law, deems it appropriate to allow parties to exclude a given number of persons who otherwise would satisfy the requirements for service on the petit jury.

Legislative authorizations, as well as limitations, for the use of peremptory challenges date as far back as the founding of the Republic; and the common-law origins of peremptories predate that. Today in most jurisdictions, statutes or rules make a limited number of peremptory challenges available to parties in both civil and criminal proceedings. In the case before us, the challenges were exercised under a federal statute that provides, *inter alia:*

> "In civil cases, each party shall be entitled to three peremptory challenges. Several defendants or several plaintiffs may be considered as a single party for the purposes of making challenges, or the court may allow additional peremptory challenges and permit them to be exercised separately or jointly."

Without this authorization, granted by an Act of Congress itself, Leesville would not have been able to engage in the alleged discriminatory acts.

Given that the statutory authorization for the challenges exercised in this case is clear, the remainder of our state action analysis centers around . . . whether a private litigant in all fairness must be deemed a government actor in the use of peremptory challenges. . . . Our precedents establish that, in determining whether a particular action or course of conduct is governmental in character, it is relevant to examine the following: the extent to which the actor relies on governmental assistance and benefits; whether the actor is performing a traditional governmental function; and whether the injury caused is aggravated in a unique way by the incidents of governmental authority.

. . . It cannot be disputed that, without the overt, significant participation of the government, the peremptory challenge system, as well as the jury trial system of which it is a part, simply could not exist. As discussed above, peremptory challenges have no utility outside the jury system, a system which the government alone administers. . . .

. . . [A] private party could not exercise its peremptory challenges absent the overt, significant assistance of the court. The government summons jurors, constrains their freedom of movement, and subjects them to public scrutiny and examination. The party who exercises a challenge invokes the formal authority of the court, which must discharge the prospective juror. . . .

In determining Leesville's state-actor status, we next consider whether the action in question involves the performance of a traditional function of the government. A traditional function of government is evident here. The peremptory challenge is used in selecting an entity that is a quintessential governmental body, having no attributes of a private actor. The jury exercises the power of the court and of the government that confers the court's jurisdiction. . . .

We find respondent's reliance on *Polk County* v. *Dodson,* 454 U.S. 312 (1981), unavailing. In that case, we held that a public defender is not a state actor in his general representation of a criminal defendant, even though he may be in his performance of other official duties. . . .

In the case before us, the parties do not act pursuant to any contractual relation with the government. Here, as in most civil cases, the initial decision whether to sue at all, the selection of counsel, and any number of ensuing tactical choices in the course of discovery and trial may be without the requisite governmental character to be deemed state action. That cannot be said of the exercise of peremptory challenges, however; when private litigants participate in the selection of jurors, they serve an important function within the government and act with its substantial assistance. If peremptory challenges based on race were permitted, persons could be required by summons to be put at risk of open and public discrimination as a condition of their participation in the justice system. The injury to excluded jurors would be the direct result of governmental delegation and participation. . . .

B

Having held that in a civil trial exclusion on account of race violates a prospective juror's equal protection rights, we consider whether an opposing litigant may rise the excluded person's rights on his or her behalf. As we noted in *Powers:* "[I]n the ordinary course, a litigant must assert his or her own legal rights and interests, and cannot rest a claim to relief on the legal rights or interests of third parties." We also noted, however, that this fundamental restriction on judicial authority admits of "certain, limited exceptions," and that a litigant may raise a claim on behalf of a third party if the litigant can demonstrate that he or she has suffered a concrete, redressable injury, that he or she has a close relation with the third party, and that there exists some hindrance to the third party's ability to protect his or her own interests. All three of these requirements for third-party standing were held satisfied in the criminal context, and they are satisfied in the civil context as well. . . .

It may be true that the role of litigants in determining the jury's composition provides one reason for wide acceptance of the jury system and of its verdicts. But if race stereotypes are the price for acceptance of a jury panel as fair, the price is too high to meet the standard of the Constitution. Other means exist for litigants to satisfy themselves of a jury's impartiality without using skin color as a test. . . .

III

It remains to consider whether a prima facie case of racial discrimination has been established in the case before us, requiring Leesville to offer race-neutral explanations for its peremptory challenges. In *Batson,* we held that determining whether a prima facie case has been established requires consideration of all relevant circumstances, including whether there has been a pattern of strikes against members of a particular race. The same approach applies in the civil context, and we leave it to the trial courts in the first instance to develop evidentiary rules for implementing our decision.

The judgment is reversed, and the case is remanded for further proceedings consistent with our opinion.

It is so ordered.

JUSTICE O'CONNOR, with whom THE CHIEF JUSTICE and JUSTICE SCALIA join, dissenting.

The Court concludes that the action of a private attorney exercising a peremptory challenge is attributable to the government and therefore may compose a constitutional violation. This conclusion is based on little more than that the challenge occurs in the course of a trial. Not everything that happens in a courtroom is state action. A trial, particularly a civil trial, is by design largely a stage on which private parties may act; it is a forum through which they can resolve their disputes in a peaceful and ordered manner. The government erects the platform; it does not thereby become responsible for all that occurs upon it. As much as we would like to eliminate completely from the courtroom the specter of racial discrimination, the Constitution does not sweep that broadly. Because I believe that a peremptory strike by a private litigant is fundamentally a matter of private choice and not state action, I dissent.

I

In order to establish a constitutional violation, Edmonson must first demonstrate that Leesville's use of peremptory challenge can fairly be attributed to the government. Unfortunately, our cases deciding when private action might be deemed that of the state have not been a model of consistency. . . . Whatever the reason, and despite the confusion, a coherent principle has emerged. We have stated the rule in various ways, but at base, "constitutional standards are invoked only when it can be said that the [government] is *responsible* for the specific conduct of which the plaintiff complains." [Quoting] *Blum* v. *Yaretsky,* 457 U.S. 991, 1004 (1982). . . .

The court concludes that this standard is met in the present case. It rests this conclusion primarily on two empirical assertions. First, that private parties use peremptory challenges with the "overt, significant participation of the government." Second, that the use of a peremptory challenge by a private party "involves the performance of a traditional function of the government." Neither of these assertions is correct.

A

The Court begins with a perfectly accurate definition of the peremptory challenge. Peremptory challenges "allow parties to exclude a given number of persons who otherwise would satisfy the requirements for service on the petit jury." This description is worth more careful analysis, for it belies the court's later conclusions about the peremptory.

The peremptory challenge "allow[s] parties," in this case *private* parties, to exclude potential jurors. It is the nature of a peremptory that its exercise is left wholly within the discretion of the litigant. The purpose of this longstanding practice is to establish for each party an " 'arbitrary and capricious species of challenge' " whereby the " 'sudden impressions and unaccountable prejudices we are apt to conceive upon the bare looks and gestures of another' " may be acted upon. By allowing the litigant to strike jurors for even the most subtle of discerned biases, the peremptory challenge fosters both the perception and reality of an impartial jury. In both criminal and civil trials, the peremptory challenge is a mechanism for the exercise of *private* choice in the pursuit of fairness. The peremptory is, by design, an enclave of private action in a government-managed proceeding.

The court amasses much ostensible evidence of the Federal Government's "overt, significant participation" in the peremptory process. Most of this evidence is irrelevant to the issue at hand. The bulk of the practices the Court describes—the establishment of qualifications for jury service, the location and summoning of perspective jurors, the jury wheel, the voter lists, the jury qualification forms, the per diem for jury service—are independent of the statutory entitlement to peremptory strikes, or of their use. All of this government action is in furtherance of the Government's distinct obligation to provide a qualified jury; the Government would do these things even if there were no peremptory challenges. All of this activity, as well as the trial judge's control over *voir dire* are merely prerequisites to the use of a peremptory challenge; they do not constitute participation *in* the challenge. . . .

B

The Court errs also when it concludes that the exercise of a peremptory challenge is a traditional government function. . . . Whatever reason a private litigant may have for using a peremptory challenge, it is not the government's reason. The government otherwise establishes its requirements for jury service, leaving to the private litigant the unfettered discretion to use the strike for any reason. This is not part of the government's function in establishing the requirements for jury service. . . .

C

. . . [T]his case is fairy well controlled by *Polk County* v. *Dodson*, 454 U.S. 312 (1981). We there held that a public defender, employed by the State, does not act under color of state law when representing a defendant in a criminal trial. In such a circumstance, government employment is not sufficient to create state action. More important for present purposes, neither is the performance of a lawyer's duties in a courtroom. This is because a lawyer, when representing a private client, cannot at the same time represent the government. . . .

Our conclusion in *Dodson* was that "a public defender does not act under color of state law when performing a lawyer's traditional functions as counsel to a defendant in a criminal proceeding." It cannot be gainsaid that a peremptory strike is a traditional adversarial act; parties use these strikes to further their own perceived interests, not as an aid to the government's process of jury selection. The Court does not challenge the rule of *Dodson,* yet concludes that private attorneys performing this adversarial function are state actors. Where is the distinction?

The Court wishes to limit the scope of *Dodson* to the actions of public defenders in an adversarial relationship with the government. At a minimum then, the Court must concede that *Dodson* stands for the proposition that a criminal defense attorney is not a state actor when using peremptory strikes on behalf of a client, nor is an attorney representing a private litigant in a civil suit against the government. Both of these propositions are true, but the Court's distinction between this case and *Dodson* turns state action doctrine on its head. Attorneys in an adversarial relation to the state are not state actors, but that does not mean that attorneys who are not in such a relation *are* state actors.

The Court is plainly wrong when it asserts that "[i]n the jury-selection process, the government and private litigants work for the same end." In a civil trial, the attorneys for each side are in "an adversarial relation"; they use their peremptory strikes in direct opposition to one another, and for precisely contrary ends. The government cannot "work for the same end" as both parties. In fact, the government is neutral as to private litigants' use of peremptory strikes. That's the point. The government does not encourage or approve these strikes, or direct that they be used in any particular way, or even that they be used at all. The government is simply not "responsible" for the use of peremptory strikes by private litigants.

Constitutional "liability attaches only to those wrongdoers 'who carry a badge of authority of [the government] and represent it in some capacity.' " A government attorney who uses a peremptory challenge on behalf of the client is, by definition, representing the government. The challenge thereby becomes state action. It is antithetical to the nature of our adversarial process, however, to say that a private attorney acting on behalf of a private client represents the government for constitutional purposes.

II

Racism is a terrible thing. It is irrational, destructive, and mean. Arbitrary discrimination based on race is particularly abhorrent when manifest in a courtroom, a forum established by the government for the resolution of disputes through "quiet rationality." But not every opprobrious and inequitable act is a constitutional violation. The Fifth Amendment's Due Process Clause prohibits only actions for which the Government can be held responsible. The Government is not responsible for everything that occurs in a courtroom. The government is not responsible for a peremptory challenge by a private litigant. I respectfully dissent.

JUSTICE SCALIA, dissenting.

I join JUSTICE O'CONNOR's dissent, which demonstrates that today's opinion is wrong in principle. I write to observe that it is also unfortunate in its consequences.

The concrete benefits of the Court's newly discovered constitutional rule are problematic. It will not necessarily be a net help rather than hindrance to minority litigants in obtaining racially diverse juries. In criminal cases, *Batson* v. *Kentucky,* 476 U.S. 79 (1986), already prevents the *prosecution* from using race-biased strikes. The effect of today's decision (which logically must apply to criminal prosecutions) will be to prevent the *defendant* from doing so—so that the minority defendant can no longer seek to prevent an all-white jury, or to seat as many jurors of his own race as possible. . . .

Although today's decision neither follows the law nor produces desirable concrete results, it certainly has great symbolic value. To overhaul the doctrine of state action in this fashion—what a magnificent demonstration of this institution's uncompromising hostility to race-based judgments, even by private actors! The price of the demonstration is, alas, high, and most of it will be paid by the minority litigants who use our courts. I dissent.

□□□

Nos. 90-757 and 90-1032

Ronald Chisom, et al., Petitioners v. Charles E. Roemer, Governor of Louisiana, et al.

United States, Petitioner v. Charles E. Roemer, Governor of Louisiana, et al.

On writs of certiorari to the United States Court of Appeals for the Fifth Circuit

[June 20, 1991]

JUSTICE STEVENS delivered the opinion of the Court.

The preamble to the Voting Rights Act of 1965 establishes that the central purpose of the Act is "[t]o enforce the fifteenth amendment to the

Constitution of the United States." The Fifteenth Amendment provides:

> "The right of citizens of the United States to vote shall not be denied or abridged by the United States or by any State on account of race, color, or previous condition of servitude."

In 1982, Congress amended § 2 of the Voting Rights Act to make clear that certain practices and procedures that *result* in the denial or abridgement of the right to vote are forbidden. even though the absence of proof of discriminatory intent protects them from constitutional challenge. The question presented by this case is whether this "results test" protects the right to vote in state judicial elections. We hold that the coverage provided by the 1982 amendment is coextensive with the coverage provided by the Act prior to 1982 and that judicial elections are embraced within that coverage.

I

Petitioners in No. 90-757 represent a class of approximately 135,000 black registered voters in Orleans Parish, Louisiana. They brought this action against the Governor and other state officials (respondents) to challenge the method of electing justices of the Louisiana Supreme Court from the New Orleans area. The United States, petitioner in No. 90-1032, intervened to support the claims advanced by the plaintiff class.

The Louisiana Supreme Court consists of seven justices, five of whom are elected from five single-member Supreme Court Districts, and two of whom are elected from one multimember Supreme Court district. Each of the seven members of the court must be a resident of the district from which he or she is elected and must have resided there for at least two years prior to election. Each of the justices on the Louisiana Supreme Court serves a term of 10 years. The one multimember district, the First Supreme Court District, consists of the parishes of Orleans, St. Bernard, Plaquemines, and Jefferson. Orleans Parish contains about half of the population of the First Supreme Court District and about half of the registered voters in that district. *Chisom* v. *Edwards*, 839 F. 2d 1056, 1057 (CA5 1988). More than one-half of the registered voters of Orleans Parish are black, whereas more than three-fourths of the registered voters in the other three parishes are white.

Petitioners allege that "the present method of electing two Justices to the Louisiana Supreme Court at-large from the New Orleans area impermissibly dilutes minority voting strength" in violation of § 2 of the Voting Rights Act. Furthermore, petitioners claimed in the courts below that the current electoral system within the First Supreme Court District violates the Fourteenth and Fifteenth Amendments of the Federal

Constitution because the purpose and effect of this election practice "is to dilute, minimize, and cancel the voting strength" of black voters in Orleans Parish. Petitioners seek a remedy that would divide the First District into two districts, one for Orleans Parish and the second for the other three parishes. If this remedy were adopted, the seven members of the Louisiana Supreme court would each represent a separate single-member judicial district, and each of the two new districts would have approximately the same population. According to petitioners, the new Orleans Parish district would also have a majority black population and majority black voter registration.

The District Court granted respondents' motion to dismiss the complaint. It held that the constitutional claims were insufficient because the complaint did not adequately allege a specific intent to discriminate. With respect to the statutory claim, the court held that § 2 is not violated unless there is an abridgement of minority voters' opportunity "to elect representatives of their choice." The court concluded that because judges are not "representatives," judicial elections are not covered by § 2.

The Court of Appeals for the Fifth Circuit reversed. *Chisom* v. *Edwards*. Before beginning its analysis, the court remarked that "[i]t is particularly significant that no black person has ever been elected to the Louisiana Supreme Court, either from the First Supreme Court District or from any one of the other five judicial districts." . . . Consistent with Congress' efforts to broaden coverage under the Act, the court rejected the State's contention that the term "representatives" in the 1982 amendment was used as a word of limitation. Instead, the court concluded that representative " 'denotes anyone selected or chosen by popular election from among a field of candidates to fill an office, including judges.' ". . .

After the case was remanded to the District Court, the United States filed a complaint in intervention in which it alleged that the use of a multimember district to elect two members of the Louisiana Supreme Court is a "standard, practice or procedure" that "results in a denial or abridgment of the right to vote on account of race or color in violation of Section 2 of the Voting Rights Act." After a nonjury trial, however, the District Court concluded that the evidence did not establish a violation of § 2 under the standards set forth in *Thornburg* v. *Gingles,* 478 U.S. 30 (1986). The District Court also dismissed the constitutional claims. Petitioners and the United States appealed. While their appeal was pending, the Fifth Circuit, sitting en banc in another case, held that judicial elections were not covered under § 2 of the Act as amended. *League of United Latin American Citizens Council No. 4434* v. *Clements,* 914 F. 2d 620 (1990) (hereinafter *LULAC*). . . .

II

Our decision today is limited in character, and thus, it is useful to begin by identifying certain matters that are not in dispute. No constitutional claims are before us. . . . [T]his case presents us solely with a question of statutory construction. That question involves only the scope of the coverage of § 2 of the Voting Rights Act as amended in 1982. We therefore do not address any question concerning the elements that must be proved to establish a violation of the Act or the remedy that might be appropriate to redress a violation if proved.

It is also undisputed that § 2 applied to judicial elections prior to the 1982 amendment, and that § 5 of the amended statute continues to apply to judicial elections. Moreover, there is no question that the terms "standard, practice, or procedure" are broad enough to encompass the use of multimember districts to minimize a racial minority's ability to influence the outcome of an election covered by § 2. The only matter in dispute is whether the test for determining the legality of such a practice, which was added to the statute in 1982, applies in judicial elections as well as in other elections.

III

The text of § 2 of the Voting Rights Act as originally enacted read as follows:

> "SEC. 2. No voting qualification or prerequisite to voting, or standard, practice, or procedure shall be imposed or applied by any State or political subdivision to deny or abridge the right of any citizen of the United States to vote on account of race or color."

The terms "vote" and "voting" were defined elsewhere in the Act to include "all action necessary to make a vote effective *in any primary, special, or general election.*" (emphasis added). The statute further defined vote and voting as "votes cast with respect to candidates for public or party office and propositions for which votes are received in an election."

At the time of the passage of the Voting Rights Act of 1965, § 2, unlike other provisions of the Act, did not provoke significant debate in Congress because it was viewed largely as a restatement of the Fifteenth Amendment. . . . This Court took a similar view of § 2 in *Mobile* v. *Bolden*, 446 U.S. 55, 60-61 (1980). There, we recognized that the coverage provided by § 2 was unquestionably coextensive with the coverage provided by the Fifteenth Amendment. . . .

Justice Stewart's opinion for the plurality in *Mobile* . . . served as the impetus for the 1982 amendment. One year after the decision in *Mobile,*

Chairman [Peter W.] Rodino of the House Judiciary Committee introduced a bill . . . to amend § 2 by striking out "to deny or abridge" and substituting "in a manner which *results* in a denial or abridgement of." The "results" test proposed by Chairman Rodino was incorporated into S. 1992, and ultimately into the 1982 amendment to § 2, and is now the focal point of this litigation.

Under the amended statute, proof of intent is no longer required to prove a § 2 violation. Now plaintiffs can prevail under § 2 by demonstrating that a challenged election practice has resulted in the denial or abridgement of the right to vote based on color or race. . . .

The two purposes of the amendment are apparent from its text. Subsection 2(a) adopts a results test, thus providing that proof of discriminatory intent is no longer necessary to establish *any* violation of the section. Subsection 2(b) provides guidance about how the results test is to be applied. . . .

IV

The *LULAC* majority assumed that § 2 provides two distinct types of protection for minority voters—it protects their opportunity "to participate in the political process" and their opportunity "to elect representatives of their choice." Although the majority interpreted "representatives" as a word of limitation, it assumed that the word eliminated judicial elections only from the latter protection, without affecting the former. In other words, a standard, practice, or procedure in a judicial election, such as a limit on the times that polls are open, which has a disparate impact on black voters' opportunity to cast their ballots under § 2, may be challenged even if a different practice that merely affects their opportunity to elect representatives of their choice to a judicial office may not. This reading of § 2, however, is foreclosed by the statutory text and by our prior cases.

. . . The statute does not create two separate and distinct rights. Subsection (a) covers every application of a qualification, standard, practice, or procedure that results in a denial or abridgement of *"the right"* to vote. The singular form is also used in subsection (b) when referring to an injury to members of the protected class who have less "opportunity" than others "to participate in the political process *and* to elect representatives of their choice." (emphasis added). It would distort the plain meaning of the sentence to substitute the word "or" for the word "and." Such radical surgery would be required to separate the opportunity to participate from the opportunity to elect.

The statutory language is patterned after the language used by JUSTICE WHITE in his opinions for the Court in *White* v. *Regester,*

412 U.S. 755 (1973) and *Whitcomb* v. *Chavis,* 403 U.S. 124 (1971). In both opinions, the Court identified the opportunity to participate and the opportunity to elect as inextricably linked. . . .

The results test mandated by the 1982 amendment is applicable to all claims arising under § 2. If the word "representatives" did place a limit on the coverage of the Act for judicial elections, it would exclude all claims involving such elections from the protection of § 2. For all such claims must allege an abridgement of the opportunity to participate in the political process *and* to elect representatives of one's choice. Even if the wisdom of Solomon would support the *LULAC* majority's proposal to preserve claims based on an interference with the right to vote in judicial elections while eschewing claims based on the opportunity to elect judges, we have no authority to divide a unitary claim created by Congress.

V

Both respondent and the *LULAC* majority place their principal reliance on Congress' use of the word "representatives" instead of "legislators" in the phrase "to participate in the political process and to elect representatives of their choice." When Congress borrowed the phrase from *White* v. *Regester,* it replaced "legislators" with "representatives.". . .

The *LULAC* majority was, of course, entirely correct in observing that "judges need not be elected at all," and that ideally public opinion should be irrelevant to the judge's role because the judge is often called upon to disregard, or even to defy, popular sentiment. The Framers of the Constitution had a similar understanding of the judicial role, and as a consequence, they established that Article III judges would be appointed, rather than elected, and would be sheltered from public opinion by receiving life tenure and salary protection. Indeed, these views were generally shared by the States during the early years of the Republic. Louisiana, however, has chosen a different course. It has decided to elect its judges and to compel judicial candidates to vie for popular support just as other political candidates do.

The fundamental tension between the ideal character of the judicial office and the real world of electoral politics cannot be resolved by crediting judges with total indifference to the popular will while simultaneously requiring them to run for elected office. When each of several members of a court must be a resident of a separate district, and must be elected by the voters of that district, it seems both reasonable and realistic to characterize the winners as representatives of that district. Indeed, at one time the Louisiana Bar Association characterized the members of the

Louisiana Supreme Court as representatives for that reason: "Each justice and judge now in office shall be considered as a representative of the judicial district within which is situated the parish of his residence at the time of his election." . . .

VI

Finally, both respondents and the *LULAC* majority suggest that no judicially manageable standards for deciding vote dilution claims can be fashioned unless the standard is based on the one-person, one-vote principle. They reason that because we have held the one-person, one-vote rule inapplicable to judicial elections, see *Wells* v. *Edwards,* 409 U.S. 1095 (1973), it follows that judicial elections are entirely immune from vote dilution claims. The conclusion, however, does not follow from the premise.

The holding in *Wells* rejected a constitutional challenge based on the Equal Protection Clause of the Fourteenth Amendment. It has no more relevance to a correct interpretation of this statute than does our decision in *Mobile* v. *Bolden,* which also rejected a constitutional claim. . . .

VII

The judgment of the Court of Appeals is reversed and the case is remanded for further proceedings consistent with this opinion.

It is so ordered.

JUSTICE SCALIA, with whom THE CHIEF JUSTICE and JUSTICE KENNEDY join, dissenting.

Section 2 of the Voting Rights Act is not some all-purpose weapon for well-intentioned judges to wield as they please in the battle against discrimination. It is a statute. I thought we had adopted a regular method for interpreting the meaning of language in a statute: first, find the ordinary meaning of the language in its textual context; and second, using established canons of construction, ask whether there is any clear indication that some permissible meaning other than the ordinary one applies. If not—and especially if a good reason for the ordinary meaning appears plain—we apply that ordinary meaning. . . .

Today, however, the Court adopts a method quite out of accord with that usual practice. It begins not with what the statute says, but with an expectation about what the statute must mean absent particular phenomena ("*we are convinced* that if Congress had . . . an intent [to exclude judges] Congress would have made it explicit in the statute, or at least some of the Members would have identified or mentioned it at some point in the unusually extensive legislative history"); and the Court then interprets the words of the statute to fulfill its expectation. Finding nothing in the legislative history affirming that judges were excluded from the coverage of § 2, the Court gives the phrase "to elect representatives" the quite extraordinary meaning that covers the election of judges.... In my view, that reading reveals that § 2 extends to vote dilution claims for the elections of representatives only, and judges are not representatives.

I

...I agree with the Court that that original legislation, directed towards intentional discrimination, applied to all elections, for it clearly said so.... The 1982 amendments, however, radically transformed the Act. As currently written, the statute proscribes intentional discrimination only if it has a discriminatory effect, but proscribes practices with discriminatory effect whether or not intentional. This new "results" criterion provides a powerful, albeit sometimes blunt, weapon with which to attack even the most subtle forms of discrimination. The question we confront here is how broadly the new remedy applies. The foundation of the Court's analysis, the itinerary for its journey in the wrong direction, is the following statement: "It is difficult to believe that Congress, in an express effort to broaden the protection afforded by the Voting Rights Act, withdrew, without comment, an important category of elections from that protection." There are two things wrong with this. First is the notion that Congress cannot be credited with having achieved anything of major importance by simply saying it, in ordinary language, in the text of a statute....

The more important error in the Court's starting-point, however, is the assumption that the effect of excluding judges from the revised § 2 would be to "withdr[aw] ... an important category of elections from [the] protection [of the Voting Rights Act]." There is absolutely no question here of *withdrawing* protection. Since the pre-1982 content of § 2 was coextensive with the Fifteenth Amendment, the entirety of that protection subsisted in the Constitution, and could be enforced through the other provisions of the Voting Rights Act. Nothing was lost from the prior coverage; *all* of the new "results" protection was an add-on. The issue is not, therefore, as the Court would have it, whether Congress has cut back on the coverage of the Voting Rights Act; the issue is how far it has extended it....

...It is unclear to me why the rules of English usage require that conclusion here, any more than they do in the case of the First Amendment—which reads "Congress shall make no law ... abridging ...

the right of the people peaceably to assemble, and to petition the Government for a redress of grievances." This has not generally been thought to protect the right peaceably to assemble only when the purpose of the assembly is to petition the Government for a redress of grievances. . . .

There is little doubt that the ordinary meaning of "representatives" does not include judges, see Webster's Second New International Dictionary 2114 (1950). The Court's feeble argument to the contrary is that "representatives" means those who "are chosen by popular election." On that hypothesis, the fan-elected members of the baseball All-Star teams are "representatives"—hardly a common, if even a permissible, usage. Surely the word "representative" connotes one who is not only *elected by* the people, but who also, at a minimum, *acts on behalf of* the people. Judges do that in a sense—but not in the ordinary sense. . . .

As I said at the outset, this case is about method. The Court transforms the meaning of § 2, not because the ordinary meaning is irrational, or inconsistent with other parts of the statute, but because it does not fit the Court's conception of what Congress must have had in mind. When we adopt a method that psychoanalyzes Congress rather than reads its laws, when we employ a tinkerer's toolbox, we do great harm. Not only do we reach the wrong result with respect to the statute at hand, but we poison the well of future legislation, depriving legislators of the assurance that ordinary terms, used in an ordinary context, will be given a predictable meaning. Our highest responsibility in the field of statutory construction is to read the laws in a consistent way, giving Congress a sure means by which it may work the people's will. We have ignored that responsibility today. I respectfully dissent.

□□□

No. 90-26

Michael Barnes, Prosecuting Attorney of St. Joseph County, Indiana, et al. v. Glen Theatre, Inc., et al.

On writ of certiorari to the United States Court of Appeals for the Seventh Circuit

[June 21, 1991]

CHIEF JUSTICE REHNQUIST announced the judgment of the Court and delivered an opinion, in which JUSTICE O'CONNOR and JUSTICE KENNEDY join.

Respondents are two establishments in South Bend, Indiana, that wish to provide totally nude dancing as entertainment, and individual dancers who are employed at these establishments. They claim that the first Amendment's guarantee of freedom of expression prevents the State of Indiana from enforcing its public indecency law to prevent this form of dancing. We reject their claim.

The facts appear from the pleadings and findings of the District Court, and are uncontested here. The Kitty Kat Lounge, Inc. (Kitty Kat) is located in the city of South Bend. It sells alcoholic beverages and presents "go-go dancing." Its proprietor desires to present "totally nude dancing," but an applicable Indiana statute regulating public nudity requires that the dancers wear "pasties" and a "G-string" when they dance. The dancers are not paid an hourly wage, but work on commission. They receive a 100 percent commission on the first $60 in drink sales during their performances. Darlene Miller, one of the respondents in the action, had worked at the Kitty Kat for about two years at the time this action was brought. Miller wishes to dance nude because she believes she would make more money doing so.

Respondent Glen Theatre, Inc., is an Indiana corporation with a place of business in South Bend. Its primary business is supplying so-called adult entertainment through written and printed materials, movie showings, and live entertainment at an enclosed "bookstore." The live entertainment at the "bookstore" consists of nude and seminude performances and showings of the female body through glass panels. Customers sit in a booth and insert coins into a timing mechanism that permits them to observe the live nude and seminude dancers for a period of time. One of Glen Theatre's dancers, Gayle Ann Marie Sutro, has danced, modeled, and acted professionally for more than 15 years, and in addition to her performances at the Glen Theatre, can be seen in a pornographic movie at a nearby theater.

Respondents sued in the United States District Court for the Northern District of Indiana to enjoin the enforcement of the Indiana public indecency statute, asserting that its prohibition against complete nudity in public places violated the First Amendment. The District Court originally granted respondents' prayer for an injunction, finding that the statute was facially overbroad. The Court of Appeals for the Seventh Circuit reversed, deciding that previous litigation with respect to the statute in the Supreme Court of Indiana and this Court precluded the possibility of such a challenge, and remanded to the District Court in order for the plaintiffs to pursue their claim that the statute violated the First Amendment as applied to their dancing. On remand, the District Court concluded that "the type of dancing these plaintiffs wish to perform is not expressive activity protected by the Constitution of the United States," and rendered judgment in favor of the defendants. The case was again appealed to the Seventh Circuit, and a panel of that court reversed the District Court, holding that the nude dancing involved here was expressive conduct protected by the First Amendment. The Court of Appeals then heard the case *en banc,* and the court rendered a series of comprehensive and thoughtful opinions. The majority concluded that non-obscene nude dancing performed for entertainment is expression protected by the First amendment, and that the public indecency statute was an improper infringement of that expressive activity because its purpose was to prevent the message of eroticism and sexuality conveyed by the dancers. . . .

Indiana, of course, has not banned nude dancing as such, but has proscribed public nudity across the board. The Supreme Court of Indiana has construed the Indiana statute to preclude nudity in what are essentially places of public accommodation such as the Glen Theatre and the Kitty Kat Lounge. In such places, respondents point out, minors are excluded and there are no non-consenting viewers. Respondents contend that while the state may license establishments such as the ones involved here, and limit the geographical area in which they do business, it may not in any way limit the performance of the dances within them without violating the First Amendment. The petitioner contends, on the other hand, that Indiana's restriction on nude dancing is a valid "time, place, or manner" restriction under cases such as *Clark* v. *Community for Creative Non-Violence,* 468 U.S. 288 (1984).

The "time, place, or manner" test was developed for evaluating restrictions on expression taking place on public property which had been dedicated as a "public forum." . . . In *Clark* we observed that this test has been interpreted to embody much the same standards as those set forth in *United States* v. *O'Brien,* 391 U.S. 367 (1968), and we turn, therefore, to the rule enunciated in *O'Brien.*

O'Brien burned his draft card on the steps of the South Boston courthouse in the presence of a sizable crowd, and was convicted of violating a statute that prohibited the knowing destruction or mutilation of such a card. He claimed that his conviction was contrary to the First Amendment because his act was "symbolic speech"—expressive conduct. The court rejected his contention that symbolic speech is entitled to full First Amendment protection, saying:

> ". . . [W]e think it clear that a government regulation is sufficiently justified if it is within the constitutional power of the Government; if it furthers an important or substantial governmental interest; if the governmental interest is unrelated to the suppression of free expression; and if the incidental restriction on alleged First Amendment freedoms is no greater than is essential to the furtherance of that interest."

Applying the four-part *O'Brien* test enunciated above, we find that Indiana's public indecency statute is justified despite its incidental limitations on some expressive activity. The public indecency statute is clearly within the constitutional power of the State and furthers substantial governmental interests. It is impossible to discern, other than from the test of the statute, exactly what governmental interest the Indiana legislators had in mind when they enacted this statute, for Indiana does not record legislative history, and the state's highest court has not shed additional light on the statute's purpose. Nonetheless, the statute's purpose of protecting societal order and morality is clear from its text and history. Public indecency statutes of this sort are of ancient origin, and presently exist in at least 47 States. . . .

[P]ublic indecency statutes were designed to protect morals and public order. The traditional police power of the States is defined as the authority to provide for the public health, safety, and morals, and we have upheld such a basis for legislation. . . .

Thus, the public indecency statute furthers a substantial government interest in protecting order and morality.

This interest is unrelated to the suppression of free expression. Some may view restricting nudity on moral grounds as necessarily related to expression. We disagree. It can be argued, of course, that almost limitless types of conduct—including appearing in the nude in public—are "expressive," and in one sense of the word this is true. People who go about in the nude in public may be expressing something about themselves by so doing. But the court rejected this expansive notion of "expressive conduct" in *O'Brien*, saying:

> "We cannot accept the view that an apparently limitless variety of conduct can be labelled 'speech' whenever the person engaging in the conduct intends thereby to express an idea."

. . . Respondents contend that even though prohibiting nudity in public generally may not be related to suppressing expression, prohibiting the performance of nude dancing is related to expression because the state seeks to prevent its erotic message. Therefore, they reason that the application of the Indiana statute to the nude dancing in this case violates the First Amendment, because it fails the third part of the O'Brien test, viz: the governmental interest must be unrelated to the suppression of free expression.

But we do not think that when Indiana applies its statute to the nude dancing in these nightclubs it is proscribing nudity because of the erotic message conveyed by the dancers. Presumably numerous other erotic performances are presented at these establishments and similar clubs without any interference from the state, so long as the performers wear a scant amount of clothing. Likewise, the requirement that the dancers don pasties and a G-string does not deprive the dance of whatever erotic message it conveys; it simply makes the message slightly less graphic. The perceived evil that Indiana seeks to address in not erotic dancing, but public nudity. The appearance of people of all shapes, sizes and ages in the nude at a beach, for example, would convey little if any erotic message, yet the state still seeks to prevent it. . . .

The fourth part of the *O'Brien* test requires that the incidental restriction on First Amendment freedom be no greater than is essential to the furtherance of the governmental interest. As indicated in the discussion above, the governmental interest served by the text of the prohibition is societal disapproval of nudity in public places and among strangers. The statutory prohibition is not a means to come greater end, but an end in itself. It is without cavil that the public indecency statute is "narrowly tailored;" Indiana's requirement that the dancers wear at least pasties and a G-string is modest, and the bare minimum necessary to achieve the state's purpose.

The judgment of the Court of Appeals accordingly is

Reversed.

JUSTICE SCALIA, concurring in the judgment.

I agree that the judgment of the Court of Appeals must be reversed. In my view, however, the challenged regulation must be upheld, not because it survives some lower level of First-Amendment scrutiny, but because, as a general law regulating conduct and not specifically directed at expression, it is not subject to First-Amendment scrutiny at all. . . .

[I omitted]

II

Since the Indiana regulation is a general law not specifically targeted at expressive conduct, its application to such conduct does not in my view implicate the First Amendment.

The First Amendment explicitly protects "the freedom of speech [and] of the press"—oral and written speech—not "expressive conduct." When any law restricts speech, even for a purpose that has nothing to do with the suppression of communication (for instance, to reduce noise, to regulate election campaigns, or to prevent littering), we insist that it meet the high, First-Amendment standard of justification. But virtually *every* law restricts conduct, and virtually *any* prohibited conduct can be performed for an expressive purpose—if only expressive of the fact that the actor disagrees with the prohibition. It cannot reasonably be demanded, therefore, that every restriction of expression incidentally produced by a general law regulating conduct pass normal First-Amendment scrutiny, or even—as some of our cases have suggested—that it be justified by an "important or substantial" government interest. Nor do our holdings require such justification: we have never invalidated the application of a general law simply because the conduct that it reached was being engaged in for expressive purposes and the government could not demonstrate a sufficiently important state interest.

This is not to say that the First Amendment affords no protection to expressive conduct. Where the government prohibits conduct *precisely because of its communicative attributes,* we hold the regulation unconstitutional. See, *e.g., United States* v. *Eichman* (1990) (burning flag); *Texas* v. *Johnson* (1989) (same); *Spence* v. *Washington* (1974) (defacing flag); *Tinker* v. *Des Moines Independent Community School District* (1969) (wearing black arm bands); *Brown* v. *Louisiana* (1966) (participating in silent sit-in); *Stromberg* v. *California* (1931) (flying a red flag). In each of the foregoing cases, we explicitly found that suppressing communication was the object of the regulation of conduct. Where that has not been the case, however—where suppression of communicative use of the conduct was merely the incidental effect of forbidding the conduct for other reasons—we have allowed the regulation to stand. . . .

III

While I do not think the plurality's conclusions differ greatly from my own, I cannot entirely endorse its reasoning. The plurality purports to apply to this general law, insofar as it regulates this allegedly expressive conduct, an intermediate level of First Amendment scrutiny: the government interest in the regulation must be " 'important or substantial,' " quoting *O'Brien*. As I have indicated, I do not believe such a heightened standard exists. I think we should avoid wherever possible, moreover, a method of analysis that requires judicial assessment of the "importance" of government interests—and especially of government interests in various aspects of morality. . . .

Indiana may constitutionally enforce its prohibition of public nudity even against those who choose to use public nudity as a means of communication. The State is regulating conduct, not expression, and those who choose to employ conduct as a means of expression must make sure that the conduct they select is not generally forbidden. For these reasons, I agree that the judgment should be reversed.

JUSTICE SOUTER, concurring in the judgment.

. . . I . . . write separately to rest my concurrence in the judgment, not on the possible sufficiency of society's moral views to justify the limitations at issue, but on the State's substantial interest in combating the secondary effects of adult entertainment establishments of the sort typified by respondents' establishments. . . . In my view, the interest asserted by petitioners in preventing prostitution, sexual assault, and other criminal activity, although presumably not a justification for all applications of the statute, is sufficient under *O'Brien* to justify the State's enforcement of the statute against the type of adult entertainment at issue here. . . .

Because the State's interest in banning nude dancing results from a simple correlation of such dancing with other evils, rather than from a relationship between the other evils and the expressive component of the dancing, the interest is unrelated to the suppression of free expression. . . .

Accordingly, I find *O'Brien* satisfied and concur in the judgment.

JUSTICE WHITE, with whom JUSTICE MARSHALL, JUSTICE BLACKMUN, and JUSTICE STEVENS join, dissenting.

The first question presented to us in this case is whether nonobscene nude dancing performed as entertainment is expressive conduct protected by the First Amendment. The Court of Appeals held that it is, observing that our prior decisions permit no other conclusion. Not surprisingly, then, the Court now concedes that "nude dancing of the kind sought to be performed here is expressive conduct within the outer perimeters of the First Amendment. . . ."

Having arrived at the conclusion that nude dancing performed as entertainment enjoys First Amendment protection, the Court states that it must "determine the level of protection to be afforded to the expressive conduct at issue, and must determine whether the Indiana statute is an impermissible infringement of that protected activity." The Court finds that the Indiana statute satisfies the *O'Brien* test in all respects.

The Court acknowledges that it is impossible to discern the exact state interests which the Indiana legislature had in mind when it enacted the Indiana statute, but the Court nonetheless concludes that it is clear from the statute's text and history that the law's purpose is to protect "societal order and morality." The Court goes on to conclude that Indiana's statute "was enacted as *a general prohibition*" (emphasis added) on people appearing in the nude among strangers in public places. The Court then points to cases in which we upheld legislation based on the State's police power, and ultimately concludes that the Indiana statute "furthers a substantial government interest in protecting order and morality." The Court also holds that the basis for banning nude dancing is unrelated to free expression and that it is narrowly drawn to serve the State's interest.

The Court's analysis is erroneous in several respects. Both the Court and JUSTICE SCALIA in his concurring opinion overlook a fundamental and critical aspect of our cases upholding the States' exercise of their police powers. None of the cases they rely upon, including *O'Brien* and *Bowers* v. *Hardwick*, 478 U.S. 186 (1986), involved anything less than truly *general* proscriptions on individual conduct. In *O'Brien*, for example, individuals were prohibited from destroying their draft cards at any time and in any place, even in completely private places such as the home. Likewise, in

Bowers, the State prohibited sodomy, regardless of where the conduct might occur, including the home as was true in that case.... By contrast, in this case Indiana does not suggest that its statute applies to, or could be applied to, nudity wherever it occurs, including the home. We do not understand the Court or JUSTICE SCALIA to be suggesting that Indiana could constitutionally enact such an intrusive prohibition, nor do we think such a suggestion would be tenable in light of our decision in *Stanley* v. *Georgia,* 394 U.S. 557 (1969), in which we held that States could not punish the mere possession of obscenity in the privacy of one's own home.

...[W]hen the State enacts a law which draws a line between expressive conduct which is regulated and nonexpressive conduct of the same type which is not regulated, *O'Brien* places the burden on the State to justify the distinctions it has made. Closer inquiry as to the purpose of the statute is surely appropriate.

Legislators do not just randomly select certain conduct for proscription; they have reasons for doing so and those reasons illuminate the purpose of the law that is passed. Indeed, a law may have multiple purposes. The purpose of forbidding people from appearing nude in parks, beaches, hot dog stands, and like public places is to protect others from offense. But that could not possible be the purpose of preventing nude dancing in theaters and barrooms since the viewers are exclusively consenting adults who pay money to see these dances. The purpose of the proscription in these contexts is to protect the viewers from what the State believes is the harmful message that nude dancing communicates....

The Court nevertheless holds that the third requirement of the *O'Brien* test, that the governmental interest be unrelated to the suppression of free expression, is satisfied because in applying the statute to nude dancing, the State is not "proscribing nudity because of the erotic message conveyed by the dancers." The Court suggests that this is so because the State does not ban dancing that sends an erotic message; it is only nude erotic dancing that is forbidden. The perceived evil is not erotic dancing but public nudity, which may be prohibited despite any incidental impact on expressive activity. This analysis is transparently erroneous.

In arriving at its conclusion, the Court concedes that nude dancing conveys an erotic message and concedes that the message would be muted if the dancers wore pasties and G-strings. Indeed, the emotional or erotic impact of the dance is intensified by the nudity of the performers.... The nudity is itself an expressive component of the dance, not merely incidental "conduct."...

That the performances in the Kitty Kat Lounge may not be high art, to say the least, and may not appeal to the Court, is hardly an excuse for distorting and ignoring settled doctrine. The Court's assessment of the artistic merits of nude dancing performances should not be the determining factor in deciding this case....

The Court and JUSTICE SOUTER do not go beyond saying that the state interests asserted here are important and substantial. But even if there were compelling interests, the Indiana statute is not narrowly drawn. If the State is genuinely concerned with prostitution and associated evils, as JUSTICE SOUTER seems to think . . . it can adopt restrictions that do not interfere with the expressiveness of nonobscene nude dancing performances. For instance, the State could perhaps require that, while performing, nude performers remain at all times a certain minimum distance from spectators, that nude entertainment be limited to certain hours, or even that establishments providing such entertainment be dispersed throughout the city. Likewise, the State clearly has the authority to criminalize prostitution and obscene behavior. Banning an entire category of expressive activity, however, generally does not satisfy the narrow tailoring requirement of strict First Amendment scrutiny. . . .

As I see it, our cases require us to affirm absent a compelling state interest supporting the statute. Neither the Court nor the State suggest that the statute could withstand scrutiny under that standard. . . .

Accordingly, I would affirm the judgment of the Court of Appeals, and dissent from this Court's judgment.

□□□

No. 90-634

Dan Cohen, Petitioner v. Cowles Media Company, DBA Minneapolis Star and Tribune Company, et al.

On writ of certiorari to the Supreme Court of Minnesota

[June 24, 1991]

JUSTICE WHITE delivered the opinion of the Court.

The question before us is whether the First Amendment prohibits a plaintiff from recovering damages, under state promissory estoppel law, for a newspaper's breach of a promise of confidentiality given to the plaintiff in exchange for information. We hold that it does not.

During the closing days of the 1982 Minnesota gubernatorial race, Dan Cohen, an active Republican associated with Wheelock Whitney's Independent-Republican gubernatorial campaign, approached reporters from the St. Paul Pioneer Press Dispatch (Pioneer Press) and the Minneapolis Star and Tribune (Star Tribune) and offered to provide documents relating to a candidate in the upcoming election. Cohen made clear to the reporters that he would provide the information only if he was given a promise of confidentiality. Reporters from both papers promised to keep Cohen's identity anonymous and Cohen turned over copies of two public court records concerning Marlene Johnson, the Democratic-Farmer-Labor candidate for Lieutenant Governor. The first record indicated that Johnson had been charged in 1969 with three counts of unlawful assembly, and the second that she had been convicted in 1970 of petit theft. Both newspapers interviewed Johnson for her explanation and one reporter tracked down the person who had found the records for Cohen. As it turned out, the unlawful assembly charges arose out of Johnson's participation in a protest of an alleged failure to hire minority workers on municipal construction projects and the charges were eventually dismissed. The petit theft conviction was for leaving a store without paying for $6.00 worth of sewing materials. The incident apparently occurred at a time during which Johnson was emotionally distraught, and the conviction was later vacated.

After consultation and debate, the editorial staffs of the two newspapers independently decided to publish Cohen's name as part of their stories concerning Johnson. In their stories, both papers identified Cohen as the source of the court records, indicated his connection to the Whitney campaign, and included denials by Whitney campaign officials of any role in the matter. The same day the stories appeared, Cohen was fired by his employer.

Cohen sued respondents, the publishers of the Pioneer Press and Star Tribune, in Minnesota state court, alleging fraudulent misrepresentation and breach of contract. The trial court rejected respondents' argument that the First Amendment barred Cohen's lawsuit. A jury returned a verdict in Cohen's favor, awarding him $200,000 in compensatory damages and $500,000 in punitive damages. The Minnesota Court of Appeals, in a split decision, reversed the award of punitive damages after concluding that Cohen had failed to establish a fraud claim, the only claim which would support such an award. However, the court upheld the finding of liability for breach of contract and the $200,000 compensatory damage award.

A divided Minnesota Supreme Court reversed the compensatory damages award....

... [T]he court concluded that "in this case enforcement of the promise of confidentiality under a promissory estoppel theory would violate defendants' First Amendment rights." ...

Respondents initially contend that the Court should dismiss this case without reaching the merits because the promissory estoppel theory was not argued or presented in the courts below and because the Minnesota Supreme Court's decision rests entirely on the interpretation of state law. These contentions do not merit extended discussion. It is irrelevant to this Court's jurisdiction whether a party raised below and argued a federal-law issue that the state supreme court actually considered and decided....

The initial question we face is whether a private cause of action for promissory estoppel involves "state action" within the meaning of the Fourteenth Amendment such that the protections of the First Amendment are triggered. For if it does not, then the First Amendment has no bearing on this case. The rationale of our decision in *New York Times Co.* v. *Sullivan* (1964), and subsequent cases compels the conclusion that there is state action here. Our cases teach that the application of state rules of law in state courts in a manner alleged to restrict First Amendment freedoms constitutes "state action" under the Fourteenth Amendment. In this case, the Minnesota Supreme Court held that if Cohen could recover at all it would be on the theory of promissory estoppel, a state-law doctrine which, in the absence of a contract, creates obligations never explicitly assumed by the parties. These legal obligations would be enforced through the official power of the Minnesota courts. Under our cases, that is enough to constitute "state action" for purposes of the Fourteenth Amendment.

Respondents rely on the proposition that "if a newspaper lawfully obtains truthful information about a matter of public significance then state officials may not constitutionally punish publication of the information, absent a need to further a state interest of the highest order." [quoting] *Smith* v. *Daily Mail Publishing Co.* (1979). . . .

This case, however, is not controlled by this line of cases but rather by the equally well-established line of decisions holding that generally applicable laws do not offend the First Amendment simply because their enforcement against the press has incidental effects on its ability to gather and report the news. As the cases relied on by respondents recognize, the truthful information sought to be published must have been lawfully acquired. . . . It is therefore beyond dispute that "[t]he publisher of a newspaper has no special immunity from the application of general laws. He has no special privilege to invade the rights and liberties of others." [quoting] *Associated Press* v. *NLRB* (1937). Accordingly, enforcement of such general laws against the press is not subject to stricter scrutiny than would be applied to enforcement against other persons or organizations.

There can be little doubt that the Minnesota doctrine of promissory estoppel is a law of general applicability. It does not target or single out the press. Rather, in so far as we are advised, the doctrine is generally applicable to the daily transactions of all the citizens of Minnesota. The First Amendment does not forbid its application to the press. . . .

. . . Moreover, JUSTICE BLACKMUN'S reliance on cases like *The Florida Star* and *Smith* v. *Daily Mail* is misplaced. In those cases, the State itself defined the content of publications that would trigger liability. Here, by contrast, Minnesota law simply requires those making promises to keep them. The parties themselves, as in this case, determine the scope of their legal obligations and any restrictions which may be placed on the publication of truthful information are self-imposed.

Also, it is not at all clear that Respondents obtained Cohen's name "lawfully" in this case, at least for purposes of publishing it. Unlike the situation in *The Florida Star*, where the rape victim's name was obtained through lawful access to a police report, respondents obtained Cohen's name only by making a promise which they did not honor. The dissenting opinions suggest that the press should not be subject to any law, including copyright law for example, which in any fashion or to any degree limits or restricts the press' right to report truthful information. The First Amendment does not grant the press such limitless protection.

Nor is Cohen attempting to use a promissory estoppel cause of action to avoid the strict requirements for establishing a libel or defamation claim. As the Minnesota Supreme Court observed here, "Cohen could not sue for defamation because the information disclosed [his name] was true." Cohen is not seeking damages for injury to his reputation or his state of mind. He sought damages in excess of $50,000 for a breach of a promise that caused him to lose his job and lowered his earning capacity....

Respondents and *amici* [supporting petitioners] argue that permitting Cohen to maintain a cause of action for promissory estoppel will inhibit truthful reporting because news organizations will have legal incentives not to disclose a confidential source's identity even when that person's identity is itself newsworthy. JUSTICE SOUTER makes a similar argument. But if this is the case, it is no more than the incidental, and constitutionally insignificant, consequence of applying to the press a generally applicable law that requires those who make certain kinds of promises to keep them.... Accordingly, the judgment of the Minnesota Supreme Court is reversed, and the case is remanded for further proceedings not inconsistent with this opinion.

So ordered.

JUSTICE BLACKMUN, with whom JUSTICE MARSHALL and JUSTICE SOUTER join, dissenting.

I agree with the Court that the decision of the Supreme Court of Minnesota rested on federal grounds and that the judicial enforcement of petitioner's promissory estoppel claim constitutes state action under the Fourteenth Amendment. I do not agree, however, that the use of that claim to penalize the reporting of truthful information regarding a political campaign does not violate the First Amendment. Accordingly, I dissent.

... In my view, the [Minnesota Supreme] court's decision is premised, not on the identity of the speaker, but on the speech itself. Thus, the court found it to be of "critical significance," that "the promise of anonymity arises in the classic First Amendment context of the quintessential public debate in our democratic society, namely, a political source involved in a political campaign."... The majority's admonition that

" '[t]he publisher of a newspaper has no special immunity from the application of general laws,' " and its reliance on the cases that support that principle, are therefore misplaced. . . .

To the extent that truthful speech may ever be sanctioned consistent with the First Amendment, it must be in furtherance of a state interest "of the highest order." Because the Minnesota Supreme Court's opinion makes clear that the State's interest in enforcing its promissory estoppel doctrine in this case was far from compelling, I would affirm that court's decision.

I respectfully dissent.

JUSTICE SOUTER, with whom JUSTICE MARSHALL, JUSTICE BLACKMUN and JUSTICE O'CONNOR join, dissenting.

I agree with JUSTICE BLACKMUN that this case does not fall within the line of authority holding the press to laws of general applicability where commercial activities and relationships, not the content of publication, are at issue. . . .

. . . There can be no doubt that the fact of Cohen's identity expanded the universe of information relevant to the choice faced by Minnesota voters in that State's 1982 gubernatorial election, the publication of which was thus of the sort quintessentially subject to strict First Amendment protection. The propriety of his leak to respondents could be taken to reflect on his character, which in turn could be taken to reflect on the character of the candidate who had retained him as an adviser. An election could turn on just such a factor; if it should, I am ready to assume that it would be to the greater public good, at least over the long run. . . .

Because I believe the State's interest in enforcing a newspaper's promise of confidentiality insufficient to outweigh the interest in unfettered publication of the information revealed in this case, I respectfully dissent.

□□□

No. 90-5721

Pervis Tyrone Payne, Petitioner v. Tennessee

On writ of certiorari to the Supreme Court of Tennessee, Western Division

[June 27, 1991]

CHIEF JUSTICE REHNQUIST delivered the opinion of the court.

In this case we reconsider our holdings in *Booth* v. *Maryland*, 482 U.S. 496 (1987), and *South Carolina* v. *Gathers*, 490 U.S. 805 (1989), that the Eighth Amendment bars the admission of victim impact evidence during the penalty phase of a capital trial.

The petitioner, Pervis Tyrone Payne, was convicted by a jury on two counts of first-degree murder and one count of assault with intent to commit murder in the first degree. He was sentenced to death for each of the murders, and to 30 years in prison for the assault.

The victims of Payne's offenses were 28-year-old Charisse Christopher, her 2-year-old daughter Lacie, and her 3-year-old son Nicholas. The three lived together in an apartment in Millington, Tennessee, across the hall from Payne's girlfriend, Bobbie Thomas. On Saturday, June 27, 1987, Payne . . . entered the Christophers' apartment, and began making sexual advances towards Charisse. Charisse resisted and Payne became violent. . . .

Inside the apartment, the police encountered a horrifying scene. Blood covered the walls and floor throughout the unit. Charisse and her children were lying on the floor in the kitchen. Nicholas, despite several wounds inflicted by a butcher knife that completely penetrated through his body from front to back, was still breathing. Miraculously, he survived. . . .

During the sentencing phase of the trial . . . [t]he State presented the testimony of Charisse's mother, Mary Zvolanek. When asked how Nicholas had been affected by the murders of his mother and sister, she responded:

> "He cries for his mom. He doesn't seem to understand why she doesn't come home. And he cries for his sister Lacie. He comes to me many times during the week and asks me, Grandmama, do you miss my Lacie. And I tell him yes. He says, I'm worried about my Lacie."

In arguing for the death penalty during closing argument, the prosecutor commented on the continuing effects of Nicholas' experience, stating:

> ". . . There is nothing you can do to ease the pain of any of the families involved in this case. There is nothing you can do to ease the pain of Bernice or Carl Payne, and that's a tragedy. There is nothing you can do basically to ease the pain of Mr. and Mrs. Zvolanek, and that's a tragedy. They will have to live with it the rest of their lives. There is obviously nothing you can do for Charisse and Lacie Jo. But there is something that you can do for Nicholas.
>
> "Somewhere down the road Nicholas is going to grow up, hopefully. He's going to want to know what happened. And he is going to know what happened to his baby sister and his mother. He is going to want to know what type of justice was done. He is going to want to know what happened. With your verdict, you will provide the answer."

In the rebuttal to Payne's closing argument, the prosecutor stated:

> "You saw the videotape this morning. You saw what Nicholas Christopher will carry in his mind forever. When you talk about cruel, when you talk

about atrocious, and when you talk about heinous, that picture will always come into your mind, probably throughout the rest of your lives.

". . . No one will ever know about Lacie Jo because she never had the chance to grow up. Her life was taken from her at the age of two years old. So, no there won't be a high school principal to talk about Lacie Jo Christopher, and there won't be anybody to take her to her high school prom. And there won't be anybody there—there won't be her mother there or Nicholas' mother there to kiss him at night. His mother will never kiss him good night or pat him as he goes off to bed, or hold him and sing him a lullaby.

"[Petitioner's attorney] wants you to think about a good reputation, people who love the defendant and things about him. He doesn't want you to think about the people who love Charisse Christopher, her mother and daddy who loved her. The people who loved little Lacie Jo, the grandparents who are still here. The brother who mourns for her every single day and wants to know where his best little playmate is. He doesn't have anybody to watch cartoons with him, a little one. These are the things that go into why it is especially cruel, heinous, and atrocious, the burden that that child will carry forever."

The jury sentenced Payne to death on each of the murder counts.

The Supreme Court of Tennessee affirmed the conviction and sentence. The court rejected Payne's contention that the admission of the grandmother's testimony and the State's closing argument constituted prejudicial violations of his rights under the Eighth Amendment as applied in *Booth* v. *Maryland* (1987), and *South Carolina* v. *Gathers* (1989). The court characterized the grandmother's testimony as "technically irrelevant," but concluded that it "did not create a constitutionally unacceptable risk of an arbitrary imposition of the death penalty and was harmless beyond a reasonable doubt."

The court determined that the prosecutor's comments during closing argument were "relevant to [Payne's] personal responsibility and moral guilt." The court explained that "[w]hen a person deliberately picks a butcher knife out of a kitchen drawer and proceeds to stab to death a twenty-eight-year-old mother, her two and one-half year old daughter and her three and one-half year old son, in the same room, the physical and mental condition of the boy he left for dead is surely relevant in determining his 'blameworthiness.' " The court concluded that any violation of Payne's rights under *Booth* and *Gathers* "was harmless beyond a reasonable doubt."

We granted certiorari to reconsider in *Booth* and *Gathers* that the Eighth Amendment prohibits a capital sentencing jury from considering "victim impact" evidence relating to the personal characteristics of the victim and the emotional impact of the crimes on the victim's family.

In *Booth*, the defendant robbed and murdered an elderly couple. As required by a state statute, a victim impact statement was prepared based on interviews with the victims' son, daughter, son-in-law, and granddaughter. The statement, which described the personal characteristics of the victims, the emotional impact of the crimes on the family, and set forth the family members' opinions and characterizations of the crimes and the defendant, was submitted to the jury at sentencing. The jury imposed the death penalty. The conviction and sentence were affirmed on appeal by the State's highest court.

This Court held by a 5-to-4 vote that the Eighth Amendment prohibits a jury from considering a victim impact statement at the sentencing phase of a capital trial. The Court made clear that the admissibility of victim impact evidence was not to be determined on a case-by-case basis, but that such evidence was *per se* inadmissible in the sentencing phase of a capital case except to the extent that it "relate[d] directly to the circumstances of the crime." In *Gathers*, decided two years later, the Court extended the rule announced in *Booth* to statements made by a prosecutor to the sentencing jury regarding the personal qualities of the victim.

The *Booth* Court began its analysis with the observation that the capital defendant must be treated as a " 'uniquely individual human bein[g]' " (quoting *Woodson* v. *North Carolina*, 428 U.S. 280, 304 (1976)), and therefore the Constitution requires the jury to make an individualized determination as to whether the defendant should be executed based on the " 'character of the individual and the circumstances of the crime' " (quoting *Zant* v. *Stephens*, 462 U.S. 862, 879 (1983)). The Court concluded that while no prior decision of this Court had mandated that only the defendant's character and immediate characteristics of the crime may constitutionally be considered, other factors are irrelevant to the capital sentencing decision unless they have "some bearing on the defendant's 'personal responsibility and moral guilt.' " (quoting *Enmund* v. *Florida*, 458 U.S. 782, 801 (1982)). To the extent that victim impact evidence presents "factors about which the defendant was unaware, and that were irrelevant to the decision to kill," the Court concluded, it has nothing to do with the "blameworthiness of a particular defendant." Evidence of the victim's character, the Court observed, "could well distract the sentencing jury from its constitutionally required task [of] determining whether the death penalty is appropriate in light of the background and record of the accused and the particular circumstances of the crime." The Court concluded that, except to the extent that victim impact evidence relates "directly to the circumstances of the crime," the prosecution may not introduce such evidence at a capital sentencing hearing because "it creates an impermissible risk that the capital sentencing decision will be made in an arbitrary manner."

Booth and *Gathers* were based on two premises: that evidence relating to a particular victim or to the harm that a capital defendant causes a victim's family do not in general reflect on the defendant's "blameworthiness," and that only evidence relating to "blameworthiness" is relevant to the capital sentencing decision. However, the assessment of harm caused by the defendant as a result of the crime charged has understandably been an important concern of the criminal law, both in determining the elements of the offense and in determining the appropriate punishment. . . .

The principles which have guided criminal sentencing—as opposed to criminal liability—have varied with the times. The book of Exodus prescribes the *Lex talionis*, "An eye for an eye, a tooth for a tooth." In England and on the continent of Europe, as recently as the 18th century, crimes which would be regarded as quite minor today were capital offenses. . . .

Gradually the list of crimes punishable by death diminished, and legislatures began grading the severity of crimes in accordance with the harm done by the criminal. The sentence for a given offense, rather than being precisely fixed by the legislature, was prescribed in terms of a minimum and a maximum, with the actual sentence to be decided by the judge. With the increasing importance of probation, as opposed to imprisonment, as a part of the penological process, some States such as California developed the "indeterminate sentence," where the time of incarceration was left almost entirely to the penological authorities rather than to the courts. But more recently the pendulum has swung back. The Federal Sentencing Guidelines, which went into effect in 1987, provided for very precise calibration of sentences, depending upon a number of factors. These factors relate both to the subjective guilt of the defendant and to the harm caused by his acts.

Wherever judges in recent years have had discretion to impose sentence, the consideration of the harm caused by the crime has been an important factor in the exercise of that discretion. . . . Whatever the prevailing sentencing philosophy, the sentencing authority has always been free to consider a wide range of relevant material. In the federal system, we observed that "a judge may appropriately conduct an inquiry broad in scope, largely unlimited as to the kind of information he may consider, or the source from which it may come." *United States* v. *Tucker*. . . .

The Maryland statute involved in *Booth* required that the presentence report in all felony cases include a "victim impact statement" which would describe the effect of the crime on the victim and his family. Congress and most of the States have, in recent years, enacted similar legislation to enable the sentencing authority to consider information about the harm caused by the crime committed by the defendant. The evidence involved in the present case was not admitted pursuant to any such enactment, but its purpose and effect was much the same as if it had been. . . .

"We have held that a State cannot preclude the sentencer from considering 'any relevant mitigating evidence' that the defendant proffers in support of a sentence less than death." *Eddings* v. *Oklahoma* (1982). Thus we have, as the Court observed in *Booth*, required that the capital defendant be treated as a " 'uniquely individual human bein[g].' " But it was never held or even suggested in any of our cases preceding *Booth* that the defendant, entitled as he was to individualized consideration, was to receive that consideration wholly apart from the crime which he had committed. The language quoted from *Woodson* in the *Booth* opinion was not intended to describe a class of evidence that *could not* be received, but a class of evidence which *must* be received. . . . This misreading of precedent in *Booth* has, we think, unfairly weighted the scales in a capital trial; while virtually no limits are placed on the relevant mitigating evidence a capital defendant may introduce concerning his own circumstances, the State is barred from either offering "a glimpse of the life" which a defendant "chose to extinguish," or demonstrating the loss to the victim's family and to society which have resulted from the defendant's homicide.

Booth reasoned that victim impact evidence must be excluded because it would be difficult, if not impossible, for the defendant to rebut such evidence without shifting the focus of the sentencing hearing away from the defendant, thus creating a " 'mini-trial' on the victim's character." In many cases the evidence relating to the victim is already before the jury at least in part because of its relevance at the guilt phase of the trial. But even as to additional evidence admitted at the sentencing phase, the mere fact that for tactical reasons it might not be prudent for the defense to rebut victim impact evidence makes the case no different than others in which a party is faced with this sort of a dilemma. . . .

Payne echoes the concern voiced in *Booth*'s case that the admission of victim impact evidence permits a jury to find that defendants whose victims were assets to their community are more deserving of punishment than those whose victims are perceived to be less worthy. As a general matter, however, victim impact evidence is not offered to encourage comparative judgments of this kind—for instance, that the killer of a hardworking, devoted parent deserves the death penalty, but that the murderer of a reprobate does not. It is designed to show instead *each* victim's "uniqueness as an individual human being," whatever the jury might think the loss to the community resulting from his death might be. . . .

Under our constitutional system, the primary responsibility for defining crimes against state law, fixing punishments for the commission of these crimes, and establishing procedures for criminal trials rests with the States. The state laws respecting crimes, punishments, and criminal procedure are of course subject to the overriding provisions of the United States Constitution. Where the State imposes the death penalty for a particular crime, we have held that the Eighth Amendment imposes special limitations upon that process. . . . But, as we noted in *California* v. *Ramos* (1983), "[b]eyond these limitations . . . the Court has deferred to the State's choice of substantive factors relevant to the penalty determination." . . . The States remain free, in capital cases, as well as others, to devise new procedures and new remedies to meet felt needs. Victim impact evidence is simply another form or method of informing the sentencing authority about the specific harm caused by the crime in question, evidence of a general type long considered by sentencing authorities. We think the *Booth* Court was wrong in stating that this kind of evidence leads to the arbitrary imposition of the death penalty. In the majority of cases, and in this case, victim impact evidence serves entirely legitimate purposes. In the event that evidence is introduced that is so unduly prejudicial that it renders the trial fundamentally unfair, the Due Process Clause of the Fourteenth Amendment provides a mechanism for relief. . . .

We are now of the view that a State may properly conclude that for the jury to assess meaningfully the defendant's moral culpability and blameworthiness, it should have before it at the sentencing phase evidence of the specific harm caused by the defendant. . . . By turning the victim into a "faceless stranger at the penalty phase of a capital trial," *Booth* deprives the State of the full moral force of its evidence and may prevent the jury from having before it all the information necessary to determine the proper punishment for a first-degree murder.

The present case is an example of the potential for such unfairness. The capital sentencing jury heard testimony from Payne's girlfriend that they met at church, that he was affectionate, caring, kind to her children, that he was not an abuser of drugs or alcohol, and that it was inconsistent with his character to have committed the murders. Payne's parents testified that he was a good son, and a clinical psychologist testified that Payne was an extremely polite prisoner and suffered from a low IQ. None of this testimony was related to the circumstances of Payne's brutal crimes. In contrast, the only evidence of the impact of Payne's offenses during the sentencing phase was Nicholas' grandmother's description—in response to a single question—that the child misses his mother and baby sister. Payne argues that the Eighth Amendment commands that the jury's death sentence must be set aside because the jury heard this testimony. But the testimony illustrated quite poignantly some of the harm that Payne's killing had caused; there is nothing unfair about allowing the jury to bear in mind that harm at the same time as it considers the mitigating evidence introduced by the defendant. . . .

We thus hold that if the State chooses to permit the admission of victim impact evidence and prosecutorial argument on that subject, the Eighth Amendment erects no *per se* bar. A State may legitimately conclude that evidence about the victim and about the impact of the murder on the victim's family is relevant to the jury's decision as to whether or not the death penalty should be imposed. There is no reason to treat such evidence differently than other relevant evidence is treated.

Payne and his *amicus* [friends-of-the-court petitions] argue that despite these numerous infirmities in the rule created by *Booth* and *Gathers*, we should adhere to the doctrine of *stare decisis* and stop short of overruling those cases. *Stare decisis* is the preferred course because it promotes the evenhanded, predictable, and consistent development of legal principles, fosters reliance on judicial decisions, and contributes to the actual and perceived integrity of the judicial process. Adhering to precedent "is usually the wise policy, because in most matters it is more important that the applicable rule of law be settled than it be settled right." [quoting] *Burnet* v. *Coronado Oil & Gas Co.* (1932). Nevertheless, when governing decisions are unworkable or are badly reasoned, "this Court has never felt constrained to follow precedent," [quoting] *Smith* v. *Allwright* (1944). *Stare decisis* is not an inexorable command. . . .

[T]he Court has during the past 20 Terms overruled in whole or in part 33 of its previous constitutional decisions. *Booth* and *Gathers* were decided by the narrowest of margins, over spirited dissents challenging the basic underpinnings of those decisions. They have been questioned by members of the Court in later decisions, and have defied consistent application by the lower courts. . . . Reconsidering these decisions now, we conclude for the reasons heretofore stated, that they were wrongly decided and should be, and now are, overruled. We accordingly affirm the judgment of the Supreme Court of Tennessee.

Affirmed.

JUSTICE O'CONNOR, with whom JUSTICE WHITE and JUSTICE KENNEDY join, concurring.

. . . I agree with the Court that *Booth* v. *Maryland* and *Gathers* were wrongly decided. The Eighth Amendment does not prohibit a State from choosing to admit evidence concerning a murder victim's personal characteristics or the impact of the crime on the victim's family and community. *Booth* also addressed another kind of victim impact evidence—opinions of the victim's family about the crime, the defendant, and the appropriate sentence. As the Court notes in today's decision, we do not reach this issue as no evidence of this kind was introduced at petitioner's trial. Nor do we express an opinion as to other aspects of the prosecutor's conduct. As to the victim impact evidence that was introduced, its admission did not violate the Constitution. Accordingly, I join the Court's opinion.

JUSTICE SCALIA, with whom JUSTICE O'CONNOR and JUSTICE KENNEDY join as to Part II, concurring.

I

The Court correctly observes the injustice of requiring the exclusion of relevant aggravating evidence during capital sentencing, while requiring the admission of all relevant mitigating evidence. . . .

II

. . . It seems to me difficult for those who were in the majority in *Booth* to hold themselves forth as ardent apostles of *stare decisis*. That doctrine, to the extent it rests upon anything more than administrative convenience, is merely the application to judicial precedents of a more general principle that the settled practices and expectations of a democratic society should generally not be disturbed by the courts. It is hard to have a genuine regard for *stare decisis* without honoring that more general principle as well. A decision of this Court which, while not overruling a prior holding, nonetheless announces a novel rule, contrary to long and unchallenged practice, and pronounces it to be the Law of the Land—such a decision, no less than an explicit overruling, should be approached with great caution. It was, I suggest, *Booth*, and not today's decision, that compromised the fundamental values underlying the doctrine of *stare decisis*.

JUSTICE SOUTER, with whom JUSTICE KENNEDY joins, concurring.

. . . I fully agree with the majority's conclusion, and the opinions expressed by the dissenters in *Booth* and *Gathers*, that nothing in the Eighth Amendment's condemnation of cruel and unusual punishment would require that evidence to be excluded. . . .

I do not, however, rest my decision to overrule wholly on the constitutional error that I see in the cases in question. I must rely as well on my further view that *Booth* sets an unworkable standard of constitutional relevance that threatens, on its own terms, to produce such arbitrary consequences and uncertainty of application as virtually to guarantee a result far diminished from the case's promise of appropriately individualized sentencing for capital defendants. These conclusions will be seen to result from the interaction of three facts. First, although *Booth* was prompted by the introduction of a systematically prepared "victim impact statement" at the sentencing phase of the trial, *Booth*'s restriction of relevant facts to what the defendant knew and considered in deciding to kill applies to any evidence, however derived or presented. Second, details of which the defendant was unaware, about the victim and survivors, will customarily be disclosed by the evidence introduced at the guilt phase of the trial. Third, the jury that determines guilt will usually determine, or make recommendations about, the imposition of capital punishment. . . .

. . . If we were to require the rules of guilt-phase evidence to be changed to guarantee the full effect of *Booth*'s promise to exclude consideration of specific facts unknown to the defendant and thus supposedly without significance in morally evaluating his decision to kill, we would seriously reduce the comprehensibility of most trials by depriving jurors of those details of context that allow them to understand what is being described. If, on the other hand, we are to leave the rules of trial evidence alone, *Booth*'s objective will not be attained without requiring a separate sentencing jury to be empaneled. This would be a major imposition on the States, however, and I suppose that no one would seriously consider adding such a further requirement. . . .

Thus, the status quo is unsatisfactory and the question is whether the case that has produced it should be overruled. . . . In prior cases, when this Court has confronted a wrongly decided, unworkable precedent calling for some further action by the Court, we have chosen not to compound the original error, but to overrule the precedent. . . . Following this course here not only has itself the support of precedent but of practical sense as well. Therefore, I join the Court in its partial overruling of *Booth* and *Gathers*.

JUSTICE MARSHALL, with whom JUSTICE BLACKMUN joins, dissenting.

Power, not reason, is the new currency of this Court's decisionmaking. Four Terms ago, a five-Justice majority of this Court held that "victim impact" evidence of the type at issue in this case could not constitutionally be introduced during the penalty phase of a capital trial. *Booth* v. *Maryland* (1987). By another 5-4 vote, a majority of this Court rebuffed an attack upon this ruling just two Terms ago. *South Carolina* v. *Gathers* (1989). Nevertheless, having expressly invited respondent to renew the attack, today's majority overrules *Booth* and *Gathers* and credits the dissenting views expressed in those cases. Neither the law nor the facts supporting *Booth* and *Gathers* underwent any change in the last four years. Only the personnel of this Court did.

In dispatching *Booth* and *Gathers* to their graves, today's majority ominously suggests that an even more extensive upheaval of this Court's precedents may be in store. . . . [T]he majority declares itself free to discard any principle of constitutional liberty which was recognized or reaffirmed over the dissenting votes of four Justices and with which five or more Justices *now* disagree. The implications of this radical new exception to the doctrine of *stare decisis* are staggering. The majority today sends a clear signal that scores of established constitutional liberties are now ripe for reconsideration, thereby inviting the very type of open defiance of our precedents that the majority rewards in this case. Because I believe that this Court owes more to its constitutional precedents in general and to *Booth* and *Gathers* in particular, I dissent.

I

Speaking for the Court as then constituted, Justice Powell and Justice Brennan set out the rationale for excluding victim-impact evidence from the sentencing proceedings in a capital case. . . . As Justice [Lewis] Powell explained in *Booth*, the probative value of such evidence is always outweighed by its prejudicial effect because of its inherent capacity to draw the jury's attention away from the character of the defendant and the circumstances of the crime to such illicit considerations as the eloquence with which family members express their grief and the status of the victim in the community. I continue to find these considerations wholly persuasive. . . .

There is nothing new in the majority's discussion of the supposed deficiencies in *Booth* and *Gathers*. Every one of the arguments made by the majority can be found in the dissenting opinions filed in those two cases, and . . . each argument was convincingly answered by Justice Powell and Justice Brennan.

But contrary to the impression that one might receive from reading the majority's lengthy rehearsing of the issues addressed in *Booth* and *Gathers*, the outcome of this case does not turn simply on who—the *Booth* and *Gathers* dissenters—had the better of the argument. Justice Powell and Justice Brennan's position carried the day in those cases and became the law of the land. The real question, then, is whether today's majority has come forward with the type of extraordinary showing that this Court has historically demanded before overruling one of its precedents. In my view, the majority clearly has not made any such showing. Indeed, the striking feature of the majority's opinion is its radical assertion that it need not even try.

II

The overruling of one of this Court's precedents ought to be a matter of great moment and consequence. Although the doctrine of *stare decisis* is not an "inexorable command," this Court has repeatedly stressed that fidelity to precedent is fundamental to "a society governed by the rule of law." . . . Consequently, this Court has never departed from precedent without "special justification." *Arizona* v. *Rumsey* (1984). Such justifications include the advent of "subsequent changes or development in the law" that undermine a decision's rationale; the need "to bring [a decision] into agreement with experience and with facts newly ascertained"; and a showing that a particular precedent has become a "detriment to coherence and consistency in the law."

The majority cannot seriously claim that *any* of these traditional bases for overruling a precedent applies to *Booth* or *Gathers*. . . . The majority does assert that *Booth* and *Gathers* "have defied consistent application by the lower courts," but the evidence that the majority proffers is so feeble that the majority cannot sincerely expect anyone to believe this claim. . . .

This truncation of the Court's duty to stand by its own precedents is astonishing. By limiting full protection of the doctrine of *stare decisis* to "cases involving property and contract rights," the majority sends a clear signal that essentially *all* decisions implementing the personal liberties protected by the Bill of Rights and the Fourteenth Amendment are open to reexamination. . . .

III

Today's decision charts an unmistakable course. If the majority's radical reconstruction of the rules for overturning this Court's decisions is to be taken at face value—and the majority offers us no reason why it should not—then the overruling of *Booth* and *Gathers* is but a preview of an even broader and more far-reaching assault upon this Court's precedents. Cast aside today are those condemned to face society's ultimate penalty. Tomorrow's victims may be minorities, women, or the indigent. Inevitably, this campaign to resurrect yesterday's "spirited dissents" will squander the authority and the legitimacy of this Court as a protector of the powerless.

I dissent.

JUSTICE STEVENS, with whom JUSTICE BLACKMUN joins, dissenting.

The novel rule that the Court announces today represents a dramatic departure from the principles that have governed our capital sentencing jurisprudence for decades. JUSTICE MARSHALL is properly concerned about the majority's trivialization of the doctrine of *stare decisis*. But even if *Booth* and *Gathers* had not been decided, today's decision would represent a sharp break with past decisions. Our cases provide no support whatsoever for the majority's conclusion that the prosecutor may introduce evidence that sheds no light on the defendant's guilt or moral culpability, and thus serves no purpose other than to encourage jurors to decide in favor of death rather than life on the basis of their emotions rather than their reason.

Until today our capital punishment jurisprudence has required that any decision to impose the death penalty be based solely on evidence that tends to inform the jury about the character of the offense and the character of the defendant. Evidence that serves no purpose other than to appeal to the sympathies or emotions of the jurors has never been considered admissible. Thus, if a defendant, who had murdered a convenience store clerk in cold blood in the course of an armed robbery, offered evidence unknown to him at the time of the crime about the immoral character of his victim, all would recognize immediately that the evidence was irrelevant and inadmissible. Evenhanded justice requires that the same constraint be imposed on the advocate of the death penalty.

[I omitted]

II

Today's majority has obviously been moved by an argument that has strong political appeal but no proper place in a reasoned judicial opinion. Because our decision in *Lockett* recognizes the defendant's right to introduce all mitigating evidence that may inform the jury about his character, the Court suggests that fairness requires that the State be allowed to respond with similar evidence about the *victim*. This argument is a classic non sequitur: The victim is not on trial; her character, whether good or bad, cannot therefore constitute either an aggravating or mitigating circumstance.

. . . Just as the defendant is entitled to introduce any relevant mitigating evidence, so the State may rebut that evidence and may designate any relevant conduct to be an aggravating factor provided that the factor is sufficiently well defined and consistently applied to cabin the sentencer's discretion.

The premise that a criminal prosecution requires an evenhanded balance between the State and the defendant is also incorrect. The Constitution grants certain rights to the criminal defendant and imposes special limitations on the State designed to protect the individual from overreaching by the disproportionately powerful State. Thus, the State must prove a defendant's guilt beyond a reasonable doubt. Rules of evidence are also weighted in the defendant's favor. For example, the prosecution generally cannot introduce evidence of the defendant's character to prove his propensity to commit a crime, but the defendant can introduce such reputation evidence to show his law-abiding nature. Even if balance were required or desirable, today's decision, by permitting both the defendant and the State to introduce irrelevant evidence for the sentencer's consideration without any guidance, surely does nothing to enhance parity in the sentencing process.

III

Victim impact evidence, as used in this case, has two flaws, both related to the Eighth Amendment's command that the punishment of death may not be meted out arbitrarily or capriciously. First, aspects of the character of the victim unforeseeable to the defendant at the time of his crime are irrelevant to the defendant's "personal responsibility and moral guilt" and therefore cannot justify a death sentence....

Second, the quantity and quality of victim impact evidence sufficient to turn a verdict of life in prison into a verdict of death is not defined until after the crime has been committed and therefore cannot possibly be applied consistently in different cases. The sentencer's unguided consideration of victim impact evidence thus conflicts with the principle central to our capital punishment jurisprudence that, "where discretion is afforded a sentencing body on a matter so grave as the determination of whether a human life should be taken or spared, that discretion must be suitably directed and limited so as to minimize the risk of wholly arbitrary and capricious action." *Gregg* v. *Georgia* (1976)....

IV

... In the case before us today, much of what might be characterized as victim impact evidence was properly admitted during the guilt phase of the trial and, given the horrible character of this crime, may have been sufficient to justify the Tennessee Supreme Court's conclusion that the error was harmless because the jury would necessarily have imposed the death sentence even absent the error....

In reaching our decision today, however, we should not be concerned with the cases in which victim impact evidence will not make a difference. We should be concerned instead with the cases in which it will make a difference. In those cases, defendants will be sentenced arbitrarily to death on the basis of evidence that would not otherwise be admissible because it is irrelevant to the defendants' moral culpability. The Constitution's proscription against the arbitrary imposition of the death penalty must necessarily proscribe the admission of evidence that serves no purpose other than to result in such arbitrary sentences.

V

The notion that the inability to produce an ideal system of justice in which every punishment is precisely married to the defendant's blameworthiness somehow justifies a rule that completely divorces some capital sentencing determinations from moral culpability is incomprehensible to me. Also incomprehensible is the argument that such a rule is required for the jury to take into account that each murder victim is a "unique" human being. The fact that each of us is unique is a proposition so obvious that it surely requires no evidentiary support. What is not obvious, however, is the way in which the character or reputation in one case may differ from that of other possible victims. Evidence offered to prove such differences can only be intended to identify some victims as more worthy of protection than others. . . .

Given the current popularity of capital punishment in a crime-ridden society, the political appeal of arguments that assume that increasing the severity of sentences is the best cure for the cancer of crime, and the political strength of the "victims' rights" movement, I recognize that today's decision will be greeted with enthusiasm by a large number of concerned and thoughtful citizens. The great tragedy of the decision, however, is the danger that the "hydraulic pressure" of public opinion that Justice Holmes once described . . . has played a role not only in the Court's decision to hear this case, and in its decision to reach the constitutional question without pausing to consider affirming on the basis of the Tennessee Supreme Court's rationale, but even in its resolution of the constitutional issue involved. Today is a sad day for a great institution.

5 *Preview of the 1991-1992 Term*

As the Supreme Court's 1991-1992 term was set to begin, Massachusetts Democrat Barney Frank had a two-word warning for his colleagues in the House of Representatives. They were suggesting to resolve a legislative dispute by putting compromise language into a committee report, which would accompany the bill to the floor. "Justice Scalia," said Frank, urging them to make clear in the bill itself what they wanted the law to be.

Antonin Scalia's name evoked new fear on Capitol Hill, where the traditional way to resolve conflicts and garner votes is to keep bill language vague. Congressional committees issue reports to explain what they have done in plain English rather than legalese, and they often use these reports to make subtle distinctions about what the bill would do. Report language is a negotiation tool that helps pass legislation but also leaves to bureaucrats—and the courts—the job of deciphering from such "legislative history" exactly what Congress intended.

As the Court's term began October 7, 1991, members of Congress, lawyers, and other justices were paying new attention to Scalia, who for his five years on the Supreme Court had declared in opinions that he pays little heed to what legislators say they mean and relies instead on what they write into law. "We are a government of laws, not of committee reports," he maintained in a concurring opinion in the 1991 case of *Wisconsin Public Intervenor v. Mortier.*

A majority of the Supreme Court justices did not subscribe to his view, but Scalia was winning increasing support for his resistance to analyzing legislative history, particularly from Chief Justice William H. Rehnquist and Anthony M. Kennedy. Furthermore, Scalia's philosophy clearly was changing the way lawyers, administration officials, and legislators did business with the high Court.

The Court's 1991-1992 term could bring more support for the Scalia analysis, which departs from decades of Court reliance on legislative history. Clarence Thomas showed a similar conservative bent and skepticism of the congressional process before joining the Court in October 1991.

The Court's docket even as the term opened held a number of cases that could turn on what Congress meant in a statute. The approach the Court takes, for example, could determine whether a civil rights law stops abortion protesters from blocking clinics and whether a federal cigarette labeling law preempts a state claim arising from a woman's death from smoking.

The Scalia approach is an offshoot of the conservativism that dominates the Court, which since the late 1980s has forced the Democratic Congress to try to write legislation on civil rights, abortion, and religious freedom, among other topics, undoing Court rulings. In 1989, the Court reversed longstanding interpretations of federal laws barring job discrimination. The next year, the Court abandoned precedent in an important religious liberty case and held that states do not have to prove a "compelling interest" in enforcing a general statute that infringed on religion. In the term that ended in June of 1991, the Court allowed a Bush administration prohibition on abortion counseling at public clinics to stand and, separately, overruled five criminal law precedents.

That conservative bent also could affect rulings in a number of high-profile cases that were on the Court's docket as its 1991-1992 term began. Among the controversies before the Court were prayer in schools, the constitutionality of "hate crime" laws, when a school is free of segregation, and the reach of environmental laws, including a case over the spotted owl and timber harvesting that considers congressional limits on federal court jurisdiction.

Congress now realizes that when courts rely only on the words of a statute, judges have greater latitude to make their own interpretations or to defer to the regulatory framework of the executive branch. And conservatives, who dominate the Supreme Court, are likely to interpret the law from that ideological viewpoint. "By taking a persistently narrow view of congressional statutes, by tilting toward the president and his exercise of executive branch authority, the Supreme Court can dramatically shift the balance of power in government and diminish the constitutional role of Congress," said Sen. Edward M. Kennedy, D-Mass.

Frank warned his colleagues that ambiguous bill language would invite deference to an administration viewpoint. That is what happened in *Rust v. Sullivan* (1991), in which the Court adopted an administration interpretation of a 1970 law and allowed its ban on abortion counseling at public clinics to remain in force. The law, Title X of the Public Health Service Act, said, "None of the funds appropriated under this title shall be used in programs where abortion is a method of family planning." Members of Congress who opposed the administration's extension of the provision to abortion counseling argued that if Congress had wanted to ban abortion counseling, it would have done so explicitly. Members also pointed to subsequent statements by the bill's drafters that counseling should not be prohibited, noting further that between 1981 and 1988 the administration itself had required public clinics to mention abortion as an option for women with unplanned pregnancies.

Since the 1984 ruling in *Chevron v. Natural Resources Defense Council*, the Court generally has given special consideration to agency interpretations of statutes in the absence of clear evidence of contrary congressional intention. The question is where the court should look for congressional intent. Scalia, whose "textualist" approach is shared by a handful of other conservative jurists throughout the federal court system, reasons that a congressional majority votes on a bill, not a committee report. So when a court is construing a statute at the heart of a dispute, it should stick to the text. He lectured his colleagues on that point in a number of cases in the 1990-1991 term.

Wisconsin Public Intervenor v. Mortier involved a small Wisconsin town's effort to impose pesticide regulations that were tougher than federal law. The court ruled 9-0 that the town could do so, but, while Scalia voted with the majority, he wrote a separate opinion admonishing the state court's reliance on legislative history. Scalia wrote that the "only mistake" of the Wisconsin Supreme Court, which was reversed, "was

The Court in its 1991-1992 term was to decide when a school district has complied with a court desegregation order.

failing to recognize how unreliable committee reports are—not only as a genuine indicator of congressional intent but as a safe predictor of judicial construction."

Scalia's rejection of legislative history won the majority in another case, *West Virginia University Hospitals v. Casey*. The Court ruled that Congress, in a 1976 attorneys' fees statute, did not intend to allow winning civil rights plaintiffs to get compensation for expert witness fees. The dissenting justices argued that the majority was ignoring the legislative history, which spoke to the contrary. "We needlessly ignore persuasive evidence of Congress' actual purpose," John Paul Stevens wrote in objection to the majority's literalism.

While a narrow approach to statutory interpretation does not track along liberal-conservative lines, conservatives are its most ardent proponents. In the conservative camp were Rehnquist, Scalia, Kennedy, and David H. Souter. Byron R. White and Sandra Day O'Connor usually have joined the conservatives, but they have been swing votes on a number of controversial cases and typically reject narrow statutory interpretation.

On the liberal side were Thurgood Marshall (now retired), Harry A. Blackmun, and, usually, Stevens, who on many occasions has written separately to criticize Scalia's approach.

New justice Thomas's views on the issue remain unclear. During his confirmation hearings he divorced himself from earlier statements scoffing at the congressional process and said he could not envision interpreting a statute without looking at legislative history.

Whether members of Congress agreed with individual rulings or not, the fact that legislative history might be getting short shrift made many of them nervous, even some Republicans. Sen. Arlen Specter, R-Pa., said, "Justice Scalia doubts that there is any such thing as congressional intent." Specter insisted the narrow statutory construction is a byproduct of the Court's "revisionist" tendencies.

Like members of Congress, lawyers who press their cases before the Supreme Court showed signs of tailoring their arguments to a stricter reading of statutes. For example, in an abortion-related case, the Bush administration's brief appealed in part to a narrow view of congressional intent. At the heart of *Bray v. Alexandria Women's Health Clinic* was a claim that Congress, in passing an 1871 Ku Klux Klan law, intended to protect women and other groups, not just blacks, from conspiracies to deprive people of equal protection under the law. The abortion clinic and the women who sued the anti-abortion group Operation Rescue under the law said the protesters interfered with the rights of women to obtain abortions and to travel interstate.

But U.S. Solicitor General Kenneth W. Starr, in support of the anti-abortion protesters, contended that the 1871 law does not extend to women seeking access to abortion clinics. "Nothing in the text of [the statute] indicates an affirmative intention to reach conspiracies based on gender, and it would be fanciful to ascribe such an intent to the 1871 Congress," Starr stated in his brief. Congress's only purpose, he said, was to prevent attacks on blacks and their supporters. In the next breath, Starr acknowledged that the statute could be read to cover women as a class. But he discouraged the Court from resolving whether the legislative history indicated that the statute should go that far.

The NOW Legal Defense and Education Fund, which represented the abortion clinic, said that, while the Supreme Court has never given women protection under the Klan law, earlier Court interpretations of the statute and its legislative history demand that result. NOW lawyers urged the Court to look at the statute's basic purpose: to provide protections to persons who may be victims of conspiracies against their rights. "On its face, the statute is not limited to protecting blacks, or blacks and the champions of their cause, though it was clearly the lawless treatment of the former slaves and their Republican allies in the Reconstruction Era South that inspired the legislation," their brief stated. "Congress could have limited the reach of the statute to the evil that immediately inspired it, but it did not."

The Supreme Court in recent years had narrowly construed related Reconstruction-era statutes. In *Patterson v. McLean Credit Union* (1989), a 5-4 majority ruled that an 1866 law forbidding discrimination in contracts applied only to hiring agreements, not to on-the-job bias.

Another important case before the Court was likely to come down to a debate over congressional intent. In *Cipollone v. Liggett Group*, the question was whether a federal cigarette labeling and advertising law that requires tobacco firms to print warning labels on cigarette packages effectively preempts state penalties for failure to warn smokers about health hazards. The brief for the estate of a woman who died of lung cancer argued that Congress intended to allow smoking victims to sue for damages under state laws. Lawyers for the cigarette manufacturers said Congress sought to supersede state laws because the statute speaks of imposing uniform federal standards.

Some business groups predicted this would be their most important case this term, not only because it seriously could affect the tobacco industry but also because it could determine whether federal law preempts tougher state actions in a host of regulatory areas. Under the Constitution's Supremacy Clause, the laws of Congress supersede those of the states. But the Supreme Court generally has held that any attempts to preempt state law need to be clearly expressed. An exception arises when federal regulation is "so pervasive as to make reasonable the inference that Congress left no room for the states to supplement it," according to Court rulings.

The Federal Cigarette Labeling and Advertising Act says that states may not require tobacco companies to provide additional warnings. It also

Several cases involving restrictive abortion laws were on a path to the Court in fall 1991. When the term opened, the justices meanwhile were set to decide whether anti-abortion protesters could be sued for blocking medical clinics.

says states may not prohibit or restrict tobacco advertising or promotion as long as cigarette package labeling conforms to federal law. Tobacco industry lawyers contended that the statutory language and "background of the act" show that Congress established a "comprehensive federal program to deal with cigarette labeling and advertising with respect to any relationship between smoking and health." They urged the Court to look beyond the statute to its purpose, and they quote freely from committee reports and members' floor debates in the *Congressional Record*.

The brief for the woman's family urged the justices to narrow their search for congressional intent. It said because Congress did not write preemptive language "with drastic clarity" into the law, it did not want to supersede state injury claims. The woman's lawyers referred to the Scalia opinion in *West Virginia University Hospitals*, the expert witness fees case, and implored: "Where the statute's language is plain, the function of the court is to enforce it according to its terms, without resorting to evidence beyond the words of the statute." Even then, the plaintiffs' lawyers went on to refer to legislative history to back up their claim. As is usually the case, parties before the high Court want to provide justices with as many tools as possible to rule for their side.

Following were some of the major cases on the Supreme Court's docket as it began its 1991-1992 term:

Free Speech

R.A.V. v. St. Paul. Does a local government's "hate crime" ordinance, which includes prohibitions on cross burnings and the display of Nazi swastikas, deny free expression under the First Amendment? The ordinance is intended to punish offensive acts against race, color, creed, religion, or gender. The case could cause the Court to reconsider its recent decisions that flag-burning laws infringed upon the expression of political protest.

Simon & Schuster v. Members of the New York State Crime Victims Board. Does a state "Son of Sam" law, barring publishers from paying criminals for their stories, violate free speech and press protections? New York law directs money earned by authors recounting their crimes to a victims' compensation fund. The Bush administration entered the case because of a similar federal law, urging the Court to uphold the restrictions so criminals do not profit from their exploits.

Church-State Separation

Lee v. Weisman. Does a school violate the Establishment Clause when it allows a prayer to be given at a public junior high school or high school graduation ceremony? The administration urged the Court to use this Providence, Rhode Island, case to discard a 1971 test for determining whether government has established religion. *Lemon v. Kurtzman* (1971) requires a state to show that a challenged action has a secular purpose, that its primary effect neither advances nor inhibits religion, and that it does not foster excessive church-state entanglement.

Abortion Clinic Blockades

Bray v. Alexandria Women's Health Clinic. Are women seeking abortions a protected "class" under an 1871 civil rights law, allowing them to sue protesters blocking access to abortion clinics? *(Details, above)*

State Preemption

Cipollone v. Liggett Group. Does a federal cigarette labeling law preempt a state law claim by a woman who died of lung cancer? The

The Court in 1991-1992 Again Faces . . .

The Supreme Court's 1973 ruling in *Roe v. Wade* made abortion legal nationwide. Since the conservative majority began coalescing in 1989, however, the votes no longer existed to uphold the belief that a woman has a fundamental right to end a pregnancy.

Although no case challenging the legality of abortion was on the 1991-1992 docket at the start of the term, cases calling *Roe v. Wade* into question were on a path to the high Court. The justices, meanwhile, were set to decide whether anti-abortion protesters could be sued under a civil rights law for blocking medical clinics.

Several cases involving restrictive abortion laws were pending in the federal courts in October 1991, and three of them—from Pennsylvania, Louisiana, and Guam—were before appeals courts. The Pennsylvania law required husband notification and parental consent, put in place a waiting period for abortions, and banned them after twenty-four weeks of pregnancy except to save the life of the woman or spare her other serious impairment. The law, the furthest along in the appeals process, was partially upheld by a panel of the U.S. Court of Appeals for the Third Circuit on October 20, 1991. By late November it was not clear whether the Supreme Court would hear a challenge to the Pennsylvania law in this term.

In the 1991-1992 term, the Court would hear *Bray v. Alexandria Women's Health Clinic*. The case arose after women were blocked by the anti-abortion protest group Operation Rescue from entering a Northern Virginia abortion clinic. The clinic and the women seeking abortions sued under an 1871 civil rights law. The protest group, which said it tried to "rescue" fetuses, blockaded clinics throughout the country, most visibly in Wichita, Kansas, during the summer of 1991.

woman's estate alleges that the cigarette manufacturer failed to warn her of the hazards of filtered cigarettes it produced. *(Details, above)*

Environmental

Robertson v. Seattle Audubon Society. Did Congress's temporary suspension of environmental laws that were subject to dispute in pending court cases violate constitutional separation of powers? At the heart of the case is a conflict between loggers in Oregon and Washington and their impact on the northern spotted owl. A 1989

. . . the Perennial Issue of Abortion

The legal dispute centered on whether the women could use the 1871 law, written to rein in the Ku Klux Klan, to win an injunction or money damages for interference by the protesters. The statute was intended to provide relief for conspiracies to deprive individuals and classes of people of equal protections and privileges under the law. The women said the protesters interfered with their rights to obtain abortions and to travel interstate.

Agreeing, a federal district judge issued an injunction barring Operation Rescue and some of its members from obstructing the facilities. Critical to the case, the district court ruled that those trying to obtain abortions were part of a protected class of women. Under the 1871 law, plaintiffs must show a "class-based animus" on the part of their antagonists, and the district court found the women met that key test. An appeals court affirmed.

In its appeal to the Supreme Court, the protesters argued that no class-based animus existed on the part of the protesters. " 'Women seeking abortions' cannot be a proper class under [the law] because it is not really a class at all; rather, it is an *activity* dressed up to look like a class," according to the anti-abortion protesters' brief. The protesters were backed by the Bush administration, which added in an amicus curiae brief that the protesters did not target women but anyone involved in the abortion process.

The NOW Legal Defense and Education Fund, which represented the clinic, countered that Operation Rescue singled out women. "It is women, and only women, who can exercise the federally-guaranteed rights at issue in this case," the group argued in its brief.

congressional mandate temporarily freed timber sales from most court-ordered bans.

Arkansas v. Oklahoma; Environmental Protection Agency v. Oklahoma. Must a state that wants to discharge treated sewage into a river comply with the water quality standards of a downstream state? How much discretion does the Environmental Protection Agency (EPA) have to decide the water quality standards under the Clean Water Act? Oklahoma says EPA ignored congressional intent in the act when it granted a permit for a Fayetteville, Arkansas, sewerage plant. The administration urges the Court to defer to the EPA interpretation.

School Desegregation

Freeman v. Pitts. When has a school district demonstrated compliance with a court desegregation order? A lower court ruled in this case involving Georgia public schools that a district could not be found "unitary," or desegregated, until it had achieved racial equality in student assignments, faculty, staff, transportation, extracurricular activities, and facilities for at least three years. In *Board of Education of Oklahoma City Public Schools v. Dowell* (1991), the Court said a school district can be freed of a desegregation order if it has eliminated the vestiges of discrimination as much as practicable. The Court did not define that standard.

United States v. Mabus; Ayers v. Mabus. When does a higher education system satisfy its obligation to dismantle its racially divided system? The administration argued that Mississippi steers whites and blacks into separate programs.

How the Court Works

The Constitution makes the Supreme Court the final arbiter in "cases" and "controversies" arising under the Constitution or the laws of the United States. As the interpreter of the law, the Court often is viewed as the least mutable and most tradition-bound of the three branches of the federal government.

The Court has undergone innumerable changes in its history, some of which have been mandated by law. Almost all of the changes, however, were made because the justices thought they would provide a more efficient or a more equitable way of dealing with the Court's responsibilities. Some of the changes are embodied in Court rules; others are informal adaptations to needs and circumstances.

The Schedule of the Term

The Court's annual schedule reflects both continuity and change. During its formal annual sessions, certain times are set aside for oral argument, for conferences, for the writing of opinions, and for the announcement of decisions. Given the number of cases they face each year, the justices are confronted with a tremendous amount of work during the regular term, which now lasts nine months. Their work does not end when the session is finished, however. During the summer recess, the justices receive new cases to consider. About a fourth of the applications for review filed during the term are read by the justices and their law clerks during the summer interim.

Annual Terms

By law, the Supreme Court begins its regular annual term on the first Monday in October and may hold a special term whenever necessary. The regular session, known as the October term, lasts nine months. The summer recess, which is not determined by statute or Court rules, generally begins in late June or early July of the following year.

In the past the Court adjourned when the summer recess began. The chief justice would announce in open court, "All cases submitted and all business before the Court at this term in readiness for disposition having been disposed of, it is ordered by this Court that all cases on the docket be, and they are hereby, continued to the next term." Since 1979, however, the Court has been in continuous session throughout the year, marked by periodic recesses. This system makes it unnecessary to convene a special term to deal with matters arising in the summer.

Opening Day

Opening day ceremonies of the new term have changed considerably since the Court first met on February 1, 1790. Chief Justice John Jay was forced to postpone the first formal session for a day because some of the justices were unable to reach New York City—at that time the nation's capital and home of the Court. Proceedings began the next day in a crowded courtroom and with an empty docket.

Beginning in 1917 and until 1975, the opening day and week were spent in conference. The justices discussed cases that had not been disposed of during the previous term and some of the petitions that had reached the Court during the summer recess. The decisions arrived at during this initial conference on which cases to accept for oral argument were announced on the second Monday of October.

At the beginning of the October 1975 term, this practice was changed. The justices reassembled for the initial conference during the last week in September. When the justices formally convened on the first Monday in October, oral arguments began.

Arguments and Conferences

At least four justices must request that a case be argued before it can be accepted. Arguments are heard on Monday, Tuesday, and Wednesday for seven two-week sessions, beginning in the first week in October and ending in the last week of April or the first week of May. Two-week or longer recesses are held between the sessions of oral arguments during which the justices consider the cases and deal with other Court business.

The schedule for oral arguments—10:00 a.m. to noon and 1 p.m. to 3 p.m.—began during the 1969 term. Since most cases receive one hour apiece for argument, the Court can hear twelve cases a week.

The Court holds conferences on the Friday just before the two-week oral argument periods and on Wednesday and Friday during the weeks when oral arguments are scheduled. The conferences are designed for consideration of cases heard in oral argument during the preceding week, and to resolve other business.

Prior to each of the Friday conferences, the chief justice circulates a "discuss" list—a list of cases deemed important enough for discussion and a vote. Appeals (of which there now are only a small number) are placed on the discuss list almost automatically, but as many as three-quarters of the petitions for certiorari are summarily denied a place on the list and simply

Visiting the Supreme Court

The Supreme Court building comprises six levels, only two of which are accessible to the public. The basement contains a parking garage, a printing press, and offices for security guards and maintenance personnel. A public information office is on the ground floor, while the courtroom itself is on the main floor. The second floor contains the justices' offices, dining rooms, and library as well as various other offices; the third floor, the Court library; and the fourth floor, the gym and storage areas.

From October to the end of April or early May, the Court hears oral arguments Monday through Wednesday for about two weeks a month. These sessions begin at 10 a.m. and continue until 3 p.m., with a one-hour recess starting at noon. They are open to the public on a first-come, first-served basis.

Visitors may inspect the Supreme Court chamber any time the Court is not in session. Historical exhibits and a free motion picture on how the Court works also are available throughout the year. The Supreme Court building is open from 9 a.m. to 4:30 p.m. Monday through Friday, except for legal holidays. When the Court is not in session, lectures are given in the courtroom every hour on the half hour between 9:30 a.m. and 3:30 p.m.

disappear. No case is denied review during conference, however, without an initial examination by the justices and their law clerks. Any one of the justices can have a case placed on the Court's conference agenda for review. Most of the cases scheduled for the discuss list also are denied review in the end, but only after discussion by the justices during the conference.

Although the last oral arguments have been heard by late April or early May of each year, the conferences of the justices continue until the end of the term to consider cases remaining on the Court's agenda.

All conferences are held in secrecy, with no legal assistants or other staff present. The attendance of six justices constitutes a quorum. Conferences begin with handshakes all around. In discussing a case, the chief justice speaks first, followed by each justice in order of seniority.

Decision Days

In the Court's early years, conferences were held whenever the justices decided one was necessary—sometimes in the evening or on weekends. Similarly, decisions were announced whenever they were ready. No formal or informal schedule existed for conferences or for the announcement of decisions.

The tradition of releasing decisions on Monday—"Decision Monday"—began in 1857. This practice continued until the Court said on April 5, 1965, that "commencing the week of April 26, 1965, it will no longer adhere to the practice of reporting its decisions only at Monday sessions and that in the future they will be reported as they become ready for decision at any session of the Court." At present, opinions are released on Tuesdays and Wednesdays only during the weeks that the Court is hearing oral arguments; during other weeks, they are released on Mondays.

In addition to opinions, the Court also releases an "orders" list—the summary of the Court's action granting or denying review. The orders list is posted at the beginning of the Monday session. It is not announced orally but can be obtained from the clerk and the public information officer. When urgent or important matters arise, the Court's summary orders may be made available on a day other than Monday.

Unlike its orders, decisions of the Court are announced orally in open Court. The justice who wrote the opinion announces the Court's decision, and justices writing concurring or dissenting opinions may state their views as well. When more than one decision is to be rendered, the justices who wrote the opinion make their announcements in reverse order of seniority. Rarely, all or a large portion of the opinion is read aloud. More often, the author will summarize the opinion or simply announce the result and state that a written opinion has been filed.

Reviewing Cases

In determining whether to accept a case for review, the Court has considerable discretion, subject only to the restraints imposed by the Constitution and Congress. Article III, Section 2, of the Constitution provides that "In all Cases affecting Ambassadors, other public Ministers and Consuls, and those in which a State shall be Party, the supreme Court shall have original Jurisdiction. In all the other Cases ... the supreme Court shall have appellate Jurisdiction, both as to Law and Fact, with such Exceptions, and under such Regulations as the Congress shall make."

Original jurisdiction refers to the right of the Supreme Court to hear a case before any other court does. Appellate jurisdiction is the right to review the decision of a lower court. The vast majority of cases reaching the Supreme Court are appeals from rulings of the lower courts; generally only a handful of original jurisdiction cases are filed each term.

After enactment of the Judiciary Act of 1925, the Supreme Court had broad discretion to decide for itself what cases it would hear. Since

Congress in 1988 virtually eliminated the Court's mandatory jurisdiction through which it was obliged to hear most appeals, that discretion has been virtually unlimited.

Methods of Appeal

Cases come to the Supreme Court in several ways: through petitions for writs of certiorari, appeals, and requests for certification.

In petitioning for a writ of certiorari, a litigant who has lost a case in a lower court sets out the reasons why the Supreme Court should review the case. If it is granted, the Court requests a certified record of the case from the lower court.

Supreme Court rules state:

> Whenever a petition for writ of certiorari to review a decision of any court is granted, the clerk shall enter an order to that effect and shall forthwith notify the court below and counsel of record. The case will then be scheduled for briefing and oral argument. If the record has not previously been filed, the Clerk of this Court shall request the clerk of the court possessed of the record to certify it and transmit it to this Court. A formal writ shall not issue unless specially directed.

The main difference between the certiorari and appeal routes is that the Court has complete discretion to grant a request for a writ of certiorari but is under more obligation to accept and decide a case that comes to it on appeal.

Most cases reach the Supreme Court by means of the writ of certiorari. In the relatively few cases to reach the Court by means of appeal, the appellant must file a jurisdictional statement explaining why the case qualifies for review and why the Court should grant it a hearing. Often the justices dispose of these cases by deciding them summarily, without oral argument or formal opinion.

Those whose petitions for certiorari have been granted must pay the Court's standard $300 fee for docketing the case. The U.S. government does not have to pay these fees, nor do persons too poor to afford them. The latter may file in forma pauperis (in the character or manner of a pauper) petitions. Another, seldom used, method of appeal is certification, the request by a lower court—usually a court of appeals—for a final answer to questions of law in a particular case. The Supreme Court, after examining the certificate, may order the case argued before it.

Process of Review

Each year the Court is asked to review some 5,000 cases. All petitions are examined by the staff of the clerk of the Court; those found to be in reasonably proper form are placed on the docket and given a number. All cases, except those falling within the Court's original jurisdiction, are placed on a single docket, known simply as "the docket." Only in the numbering of the cases is a distinction made between prepaid and in forma pauperis cases on the docket. Beginning with the 1971 term, prepaid cases were labeled with the year and the number. The first case filed in 1991, for example, would be designated 91-1. In forma pauperis cases contain the year and begin with the number 5001. The second in forma pauperis case filed in 1991 would thus be number 91-5002.

Each justice, aided by law clerks, is responsible for reviewing all cases on the docket. In recent years a number of justices have used a "cert pool" system in this review. Their clerks work together to examine cases, writing a pool memo on several petitions. The memo then is given to the justices who determine if more research is needed. (Other justices prefer to use a system in which they or their clerks review each petition themselves.)

Justice William O. Douglas (1939-1975) called the review of cases on the docket "in many respects the most important and interesting of all our functions." Others have found it time-consuming and tedious and support the cert pool as a mechanism to reduce the burden on the justices and their staffs.

Petitions on the docket vary from elegantly printed and bound documents, of which multiple copies are submitted to the Court, to single sheets of prison stationery scribbled in pencil. All are considered by the justices, however, in the process of deciding which merit review. The decisions to grant or deny review of cases are made in conferences, which are held in the conference room adjacent to the chief justice's chambers. Justices are summoned to the conference room by a buzzer, usually between 9:30 and 10:00 a.m. They shake hands with each other, take their appointed seats, and the chief justice begins the discussion.

Discuss and Orders Lists

A few days before the conference convenes, the chief justice compiles the discuss list of cases deemed important enough for discussion and a vote. As many as three-quarters of the petitions for certiorari are denied a place on the list and thus rejected without further consideration. Any justice can have a case placed on the discuss list simply by requesting that it be placed there.

Only the justices attend conferences, and no legal assistants or staff are present. The junior associate justice acts as doorkeeper and messenger, sending for reference material and receiving messages and data. Unlike other parts of the federal government, few leaks have occurred about what transpires during the conferences.

At the start of the conference, the chief justice makes a brief statement outlining the facts of each case. Then each justice, beginning

The Supreme Court library maintains a collection of Court documents, available for public use, dating from the mid-1800s.

with the senior associate justice, comments on the case, usually indicating in the course of the comments how he intends to vote. A traditional but unwritten rule specifies that it takes four affirmative votes to have a case scheduled for oral argument.

Petitions for certiorari, appeal, and in forma pauperis that are approved for review or denied review during conference are placed on a certified orders list to be released the following Monday in open court.

Arguments

Once the Court announces it will hear a case, the clerk of the Court arranges the schedule for oral argument. Cases are argued roughly in the order in which they were granted review, subject to modification if more time is needed to acquire all the necessary documents. Cases generally are heard not sooner than three months after the Court has agreed to review them. Under special circumstances, the date scheduled for oral argument can be advanced or postponed.

Well before oral argument takes place, the justices receive the briefs and records from counsel in the case. The measure of attention the brief receives—from a thorough and exhaustive study to a cursory glance—depends both on the nature of the case and the work habits of the justice.

As one of the two public functions of the Court, oral arguments are viewed by some as very important. Others dispute their significance, contending that by the time a case is heard most of the justices already have made up their minds. Justice William J. Brennan, Jr., (1956-1990) said, "Oral argument is the absolute indispensable ingredient of appellate advocacy. . . . Often my whole notion of what a case is about crystallizes at oral argument. This happens even though I read the briefs before oral argument."

Time Limits

The time allowed each side for oral argument is thirty minutes. Since the time allotted must accommodate any questions the justices may wish to ask, the actual time for presentation may be considerably shorter than thirty minutes. Under the current rules of the Court, effective January 1, 1990, one counsel only will be heard for each side, except by special permission.

An exception is made for an amicus curiae—a person who volunteers or is invited to take part in matters before a court but is not a party in the case. Counsel for an amicus curiae may participate in oral argument if the party supported by the amicus allows use of part of its argument time or the Court grants a motion permitting argument by counsel for the "friend of the court." The motion must show, the rules state, that the amicus's argument "is thought to provide assistance to the Court not otherwise available."

Because the Court is reluctant to extend the time that each side is given for oral argument and because amicus curiae participation in oral argument often would necessitate such an extension, the Court generally is unreceptive to such motions. And counsel in a case usually is equally unreceptive to a request to give an amicus counsel any of the precious minutes allotted to argue the case.

Court rules provide advice to counsel presenting oral arguments before the Court: "Oral argument should emphasize and clarify the written arguments appearing in the briefs on the merits." That same rule warns—with italicized emphasis—that the Court "looks with disfavor on oral argument read from a prepared text." Most attorneys appearing before the Court use an outline or notes to make sure they cover the important points.

Circulating the Argument

The Supreme Court has tape-recorded oral arguments since 1955. In 1968 the Court, in addition to its own recording, began contracting with private firms to tape and transcribe all oral arguments. The contract stipulates that the transcript "shall include everything spoken in argument, by Court, counsel, or others, and nothing shall be omitted from the transcript unless the Chief Justice or Presiding Justice so directs." But "the names of Justices asking questions shall not be recorded or transcribed; questions shall be indicated by the letter 'Q.' "

The marshal of the Court keeps the Court's tapes during the term when oral arguments are presented. During that time use of these tapes usually is limited to the justices and their law clerks. At the end of the term, the tapes are sent to the National Archives. Persons wishing to listen to the tapes or buy a copy of a transcript can apply to the Archives for permission to do so.

Transcripts made by the private firm can be acquired more quickly. These transcripts usually are available a week after arguments are heard. Those who purchase the transcripts from the firm must agree that they will not be photographically reproduced. Transcripts usually run from forty to fifty pages for one hour of oral argument.

Proposals have been made to tape arguments for television and radio use. To date, the Court has shown little enthusiasm for these proposals.

Use of Briefs

Supreme Court Rule 28 states, "Counsel should assume that all Justices of the Court have read the briefs in advance of oral argument."

Nonetheless, justices vary considerably in the attention they personally give to an attorney's briefs. If the brief has been thoroughly digested by the justices, the attorney can use his arguments to highlight certain elements. But if it merely has been scanned—and perhaps largely forgotten—in the interval between the reading and the oral argument, the attorney will want to go into considerable detail about the nature of the case and the facts involved. Most lawyers therefore prepare their argument on the assumption that the justices know relatively little about their particular case but are well-acquainted with the general principles of relevant law.

The brief of the petitioner or appellant must be filed within forty-five days of the Court's announced decision to hear the case. Except for in forma pauperis cases, forty copies of the brief must be filed with the Court. For in forma pauperis proceedings, the Court requires only that documents be legible. The opposing brief from the respondent or appellee is to be filed within thirty days of receipt of the brief of the petitioner or appellant. Either party may appeal to the clerk for an extension of time in filing the brief.

Court Rules 24 sets forth the elements that a brief should contain. These are: the questions presented for review; a list of all parties to the proceeding; a table of contents and table of authorities; citations of the opinions and judgments delivered in the lower courts; "a concise statement of the grounds on which the jurisdiction of this Court is invoked"; constitutional provisions, treaties, statutes, ordinances, and regulations involved; "a concise statement of the case containing all that is material to the consideration of the questions presented"; a summary of argument; the argument, which exhibits "clearly the points of fact and of law being presented and citing the authorities and statutes relied upon"; and a conclusion "specifying with particularity the relief which the party seeks."

The form and organization of the brief are covered by rules 33 and 34 of the Court. The rules limit the number of pages in various types of briefs. The rules also set out a color code for the covers of different kinds of briefs. Petitions are white; motions opposing them are orange. Petitioner's briefs on the merits are light blue, while those of respondents are red. Reply briefs are yellow; amicus curiae, green; and documents filed by the United States, gray.

Questioning

During oral argument the justices may interrupt with questions or remarks as often as they wish. On the average, questions consume about a third of counsel's allotted half-hour of argument. Unless counsel has been granted special permission extending the thirty-minute limit, he can continue talking after the time has expired only to complete a sentence.

The frequency of questioning, as well as the manner in which questions are asked, depends on the style of the justices and their interest in a particular case. Chief Justice Warren E. Burger (1969-1986) asked very few questions. Justice Antonin Scalia has from his first day on the bench peppered attorneys with questions, sparking more active interrogation from a number of his colleagues.

Questions from the justices may upset and unnerve counsel by interrupting a well-rehearsed argument and introducing an unexpected element. Nevertheless, questioning has several advantages. It serves to alert counsel about what aspects of the case need further elaboration or more information. For the Court, questions can bring out weak points in an argument—and sometimes strengthen it.

Conferences

Cases for which oral arguments have been heard then are dealt with in conference. During the Wednesday afternoon conference, the four cases that were argued the previous Monday are discussed and decided. At the all-day Friday conference, the eight cases argued on the preceding Tuesday and Wednesday are discussed and decided. Justices also consider new motions, appeals, and petitions while in conference.

Conferences are conducted in complete secrecy. No secretaries, clerks, stenographers, or messengers are allowed into the room. This practice began many years ago when the justices became convinced that decisions were being disclosed prematurely.

The justices meet in an oak-paneled, book-lined conference room adjacent to the chief justice's suite. Nine chairs surround the large rectangular table, each chair bearing the nameplate of the justice who sits there. The chief justice sits at the east end of the table, and the senior associate justice at the west end. The other justices take their places in order of seniority. The junior justice is charged with sending for and receiving documents or other information the Court needs.

On entering the conference room the justices shake hands with each other, a symbol of harmony that began in the 1880s. The chief justice begins the conference by calling the first case to be decided and discussing it. When the chief justice is finished, the senior associate justice speaks, followed by the other justices in order of seniority.

The justices can speak for as long as they wish, but they practice restraint because of the amount of business to be completed. By custom each justice speaks without interruption. Other than these procedural arrangements, little is known about what transpires in conference. Although discussions generally are said to be polite and orderly, occasionally they can be acrimonious. Likewise, consideration of the issues in a particular case may be full and probing, or perfunctory, leaving the real debate on the question to go on in the written drafts of opinions circulating up and down the Court's corridors between chambers.

Generally the discussion of the case clearly indicates how a justice plans to vote on it. A majority vote is needed to decide a case—five votes if all nine justices are participating.

Opinions

After the justices have voted on a case, the writing of the opinion or opinions begins. An opinion is a reasoned argument explaining the legal issues in the case and the precedents on which the opinion is based. Soon after a case is decided in conference, the task of writing the majority opinion is assigned. When in the majority, the chief justice designates the writer. When the chief justice is in the minority, the senior associate justice voting with the majority assigns the job of writing the majority opinion.

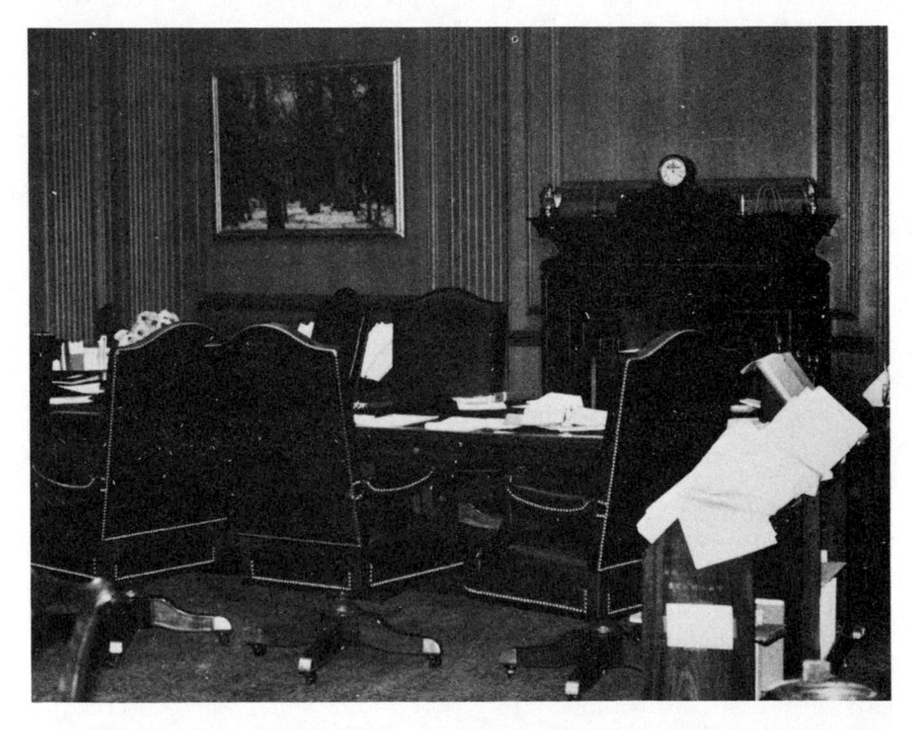

The Court holds conferences to consider cases heard in oral argument and to resolve other business. No secretaries, clerks, stenographers, or messengers are allowed into the conference room when the justices are meeting.

Any justice may write a separate opinion. If in agreement with the Court's decision but not with some of the reasoning in the majority opinion, the justice writes a concurring opinion giving his reasoning. If in disagreement with the majority, the justice writes a dissenting opinion or simply goes on record as a dissenter without an opinion. More than one justice can sign a concurring opinion or a dissenting opinion.

The amount of time consumed between the vote on a case and the announcement of the decision varies from case to case. In simple cases where few points of law are at issue, the opinion sometimes can be written and cleared by the other justices in a week or less. In more complex cases, especially those with several dissenting or concurring opinions, the process can take six months or more. Some cases may have to be reargued or the initial decision reversed after the drafts of opinions have been circulated.

The assigning justice may consider the points made by majority justices during the conference discussion, the workload of the other justices, the need to avoid the more extreme opinions within the majority, and expertise in the particular area of law involved in a case.

The style of writing a Court opinion—majority, concurring, or dissenting—depends primarily on the individual justice. In some cases, the justice may prefer to write a restricted and limited opinion; in others, a broader approach to the subject. The decision likely is to be influenced by the need to satisfy the other justices in the majority.

When a justice is satisfied that the written opinion is conclusive or "unanswerable," it goes into print. In the past this process occurred at a print shop in the Court's basement, where the draft was printed under rigid security, with each copy numbered to prevent the removal of copies from the premises. In the 1980s, however, high technology arrived at the Court; draft opinions are circulated, revised, and printed on a computerized typesetting system.

The circulation of the drafts—whether computer-to-computer or on paper—provokes further discussion in many cases. Often the suggestions and criticisms require the writer to juggle opposing views. To retain a majority, the author of the draft opinion frequently feels obliged to make major emendations to satisfy justices who are unhappy with the initial draft. Some opinions have to be rewritten several times.

One reason for the secrecy surrounding the circulation of drafts is that some of the justices who voted with the majority may find the majority draft opinion so unpersuasive—or one or more of the dissenting drafts so convincing—that they change their vote. If enough justices alter their votes, the majority may shift, so that a former dissent becomes the majority opinion. When a new majority emerges from this process, the task of writing, printing, and circulating a new majority draft begins all over again.

In the past few decades considerable concern has arisen about the lack of unanimity in Court decisions and the frequent use of dissenting and concurring opinions. The chief argument in favor of greater unanimity is that it increases the authority of—and hence the respect for—the Court's decisions. A dissenting justice, however, may hope that the dissent will convince a majority of the other justices that his opinion is the correct one or that a later Court will adopt the view. Moreover, the dissenter generally has only himself to please, a fact that makes many well-reasoned and well-written dissents more memorable or more enjoyable to read than the majority opinion. A concurring opinion indicates that the justice who wrote it agrees in general with the majority opinion but has reservations about the way it was written, the reasoning behind it, or specific points in it. When the drafts of an opinion—including dissents and concurring views—have been written, circulated, discussed, and revised, if necessary, the final versions then are printed. Before the opinion is produced the reporter of decisions adds a "headnote" or syllabus summarizing the decision and a "lineup" at the end showing how the justices voted.

One hundred seventy-five copies of the "bench opinion" are made. As the decision is announced in Court, the bench opinion is distributed to journalists and others in the public information office. Another copy, with any necessary corrections noted on it, is sent to the U.S. Government Printing Office, which prints 4,444 "slip" opinions, which are distributed to federal and state courts and agencies. The Court receives 400 of these, and they are available to the public free through the Public Information Office as long as supplies last. The Government Printing Office also prints the opinion for inclusion in *United States Reports,* the official record of Supreme Court opinions.

The public announcement of opinions in Court probably is the Court's most dramatic function. It also may be the most expendable. Depending on who delivers the opinion and how, announcements can take a considerable amount of the Court's time. Opinions are given simultaneously to the public information officer for distribution. Nevertheless, those who are in the courtroom to hear the announcement of a ruling are participating in a very old tradition. The actual delivery may be tedious or exciting, depending on the nature of the case and the eloquence of the opinion and the style of its oral delivery.

In the twentieth century, the Court has reduced the amount of time spent in delivering opinions. Before 1930 the Court generally read long opinions word for word; some opinions took days to announce. As the workload increased, this practice came to be regarded as a waste of the Court's time. The justice who has written the majority opinion now generally delivers only a summary, and dissenting justices often do the same with their opinions.

Appendix

Brief Biographies

William Hubbs Rehnquist

President Ronald Reagan's appointment of William H. Rehnquist as chief justice of the United States in 1986 clearly indicated that the president was hoping to shift the Court to the right. Since his early years as an associate justice in the 1970s, Rehnquist has been one of the Court's most conservative justices.

Rehnquist, the fourth associate justice to become chief, argues that the original intent of the framers of the Constitution and the Bill of Rights is the proper standard for interpreting those documents today. He also takes a literal approach to individual rights. These beliefs have led him to dissent from the Court's rulings protecting a woman's privacy-based right to abortion, to argue that no constitutional barrier exists to school prayer, and to side with police and prosecutors on questions of criminal law. In 1991, he wrote the Court's decision upholding an administration ban on abortion counseling at publicly financed clinics.

Born in Milwaukee, Wisconsin, October 1, 1924, Rehnquist went west to college. At Stanford University, where he received both his undergraduate and law degrees, classmates recalled him as an intelligent student whose already well-entrenched conservative views set him apart from his more liberal classmates.

After graduating from law school in 1952, Rehnquist came to Washington, D.C., to serve as a law clerk to Supreme Court justice Robert H. Jackson. There, he wrote a memorandum that later would come back to haunt him during his Senate confirmation hearings. In the memo, Rehnquist favored separate but equal schools for blacks and whites. Asked about those views by the Senate Judiciary Committee in 1971, Rehnquist repudiated them, declaring that they were Justice Jackson's—not his own.

Following his clerkship, Rehnquist decided to practice law in the Southwest. He moved to Phoenix and immediately became immersed in Arizona Republican politics. From his earliest days in the state, he was associated with the party's conservative wing. A 1957 speech denouncing the liberalism of the Warren Court typified his views at the time.

During the 1964 presidential race, Rehnquist campaigned ardently for Barry Goldwater. It was then that Rehnquist met and worked with Richard G. Kleindienst, who later, as President Richard Nixon's deputy attorney general, would appoint Rehnquist to head the Justice Department's Office of Legal Counsel as an assistant attorney general. In 1971 the once-obscure Phoenix lawyer was nominated by President Nixon to the Supreme Court.

Controversy surrounded Rehnquist's 1986 nomination as chief justice. He was accused of harassing voters and challenging their right to vote years earlier when he was a GOP poll watcher in Phoenix. Accusations of racial bias also were raised against him. His views on civil rights were questioned, and he was found to have accepted anti-Semitic restrictions in a property deed to a Vermont home.

Before Clarence Thomas's 1991 nomination battle, more votes were cast against Rehnquist for chief justice (thirty-three nays to sixty-five ayes) than against any other successful Supreme Court nominee in the twentieth century. In 1971 Rehnquist had tied for the second-highest number of negative votes (twenty-six nays to sixty-eight ayes) when he was confirmed as an associate justice.

Rehnquist was married to Natalie Cornell, who died in 1991. They had two daughters and a son.

Born October 1, 1924, Milwaukee, Wisconsin; Stanford University B.A. (1948); Phi Beta Kappa; Harvard University M.A. (1949); Stanford University Law School LL.B. (1952); law clerk to Justice Robert H. Jackson, U.S. Supreme Court 1952-1953; married Natalie Cornell 1953; two daughters, one son; practiced law 1953-1969; assistant U.S. attorney general, Office of Legal Counsel 1969-1971; nominated as associate justice of the U.S. Supreme Court by President Nixon October 21, 1971; confirmed December 10, 1971; nominated as chief justice of the United States by President Reagan June 17, 1986; confirmed September 17, 1986.

Byron Raymond White

In 1991, Byron R. White was the most senior justice. After spending years ensconced on the conservative side of the Court, he began emerging as a swing vote as Reagan and Bush justices stepped in far to his right. White is noted for his quick and precise legal mind and his incisive questioning during oral argument. He was born June 8, 1917, in Fort Collins, Colorado, and grew up in Wellington, a small town in a sugar beet growing area of the state. Ranking first in his high school class,

White won a scholarship to the University of Colorado, which he entered in 1934.

At the university White earned a reputation as an outstanding scholar-athlete. He was first in his class, a member of Phi Beta Kappa, and the winner of three varsity letters in football, four in basketball, and three in baseball. By the end of his college career in 1938 he had been nicknamed "Whizzer" for his outstanding performance as a football player, a performance that earned him not only a national reputation but also a one-year contract with the Pittsburgh Pirates (now the Steelers). White already had accepted a coveted Rhodes Scholarship for study at Oxford but decided to postpone his year in England.

Despite his success as a professional player, at the end of the football season White sailed for England to attend Oxford. When the European war broke out in September 1939, White returned to the United States and entered Yale Law School. But during 1940 and 1941 he alternated law study with playing football for the Detroit Lions.

After the United States entered the war, White served in the Navy in the South Pacific. There he renewed an old acquaintance with John F. Kennedy, whom he had met in England and who later would nominate White to the Supreme Court. After the war, White returned to Yale, earning his law degree magna cum laude in 1946. Following graduation, White served as law clerk to U.S. Chief Justice Fred M. Vinson. In 1947 White returned to his native Colorado, where for the next fourteen years he practiced law with the Denver law firm of Lewis, Grant, and Davis.

White renewed his contact with Kennedy during the 1960 presidential campaign, leading the nationwide volunteer group Citizens for Kennedy. After the election, Kennedy named White to the post of deputy attorney general, a position he held until his Supreme Court appointment in 1962.

White has been married since 1946 to Marion Stearns. They have one son and one daughter.

Born June 8, 1917, Fort Collins, Colorado; University of Colorado B.A. (1938); Phi Beta Kappa; Rhodes scholar, Oxford University; Yale University Law School LL.B. magna cum laude (1946); married Marion Stearns 1946; one son, one daughter; law clerk to Chief Justice Fred M. Vinson, U.S. Supreme Court 1946-1947; practiced law, Denver, 1947-1960; U.S. deputy attorney general 1961-1962; nominated as associate justice of the U.S. Supreme Court by President Kennedy March 30, 1962; confirmed April 11, 1962.

Harry Andrew Blackmun

During his first years on the Court, Harry A. Blackmun frequently was described as one of the "Minnesota Twins" along with the Court's other Minnesota native, Chief Justice Warren E. Burger. Blackmun and Burger, who retired in 1986, are lifelong friends who initially voted together on important decisions.

However, Blackmun, who originally impressed observers as a modest, even meek, addition to the Court's conservative bloc, has written some of the Court's most controversial decisions, among them its 1973 ruling upholding a woman's right to an abortion. He since has become the liberal pole.

Blackmun was born in Nashville, Illinois, November 12, 1908, but spent most of his early years in Minneapolis-St. Paul, where his father was an official of the Twin Cities Savings and Loan Company. His lifelong friendship with Burger began in grade school.

Blackmun went east after high school to attend Harvard College on a scholarship. He majored in mathematics and toyed briefly with the idea of becoming a physician.

But he chose the law instead. After graduating from Harvard in 1929, Phi Beta Kappa, Blackmun entered Harvard Law School, from which he graduated in 1932. During his law school years Blackmun supported himself with a variety of odd jobs, including tutoring in math and driving the launch for the college crew team.

Following law school Blackmun returned to St. Paul, where he served for a year and a half as a law clerk to United States Circuit Court judge John B. Sanborn, whom Blackmun succeeded twenty years later. He left the clerkship at the end of 1933 and joined the Minneapolis law firm of Dorsey, Colman, Barker, Scott, and Barber. At the same time he taught for a year at William Mitchell College of Law in St. Paul, the alma mater of former chief justice Burger. In addition to his practice, Blackmun taught for two years during the 1940s at the University of Minnesota Law School.

In 1950 he accepted a post as "house counsel" for the world-famous Mayo Clinic in Rochester, Minnesota. Among his colleagues at the clinic, Blackmun quickly developed a reputation as a serious man, totally engrossed in his profession. The reputation followed him to the bench of the U.S. Court of Appeals for the Eighth Circuit, to which Blackmun was appointed by President Dwight D. Eisenhower in 1959. As a judge, Blackmun was known for his scholarly and thorough opinions.

Blackmun's total devotion to the law leaves little time for outside activities. He is an avid reader, delving primarily into judicial tomes. Over the years he also has been active in Methodist church affairs. Before he developed knee problems, Blackmun was a proficient squash and tennis player. It was on the tennis court that Blackmun met his future wife, Dorothy E. Clark. They were married in 1941 and have three daughters.

Born November 12, 1908, Nashville, Illinois; Harvard College B.A. (1929); Phi Beta Kappa; Harvard University Law School LL.B. (1932); law clerk to John Sanborn, U.S. Court of Appeals for the Eighth Circuit, St. Paul, 1932-1933; practiced law, Minneapolis, 1934-1950; married Dorothy E. Clark 1941; three daughters; resident counsel, Mayo Clinic, Rochester, Minnesota, 1950-1959; judge, U.S. Court of Appeals for the Eighth Circuit 1959-1970; nominated as associate justice of the U.S. Supreme Court by President Nixon April 14, 1970; confirmed May 12, 1970.

John Paul Stevens

When President Gerald R. Ford nominated federal appeals court judge John Paul Stevens to the Supreme Court seat vacated by veteran liberal William O. Douglas in 1975, Court watchers and other observers struggled to pin an ideological label on the new nominee. The consensus that finally emerged was that Stevens was neither a doctrinaire liberal nor conservative, but a judicial centrist. His subsequent opinions bear out this description, although in recent years he has leaned more toward the liberal side.

A soft-spoken, mild-mannered man who occasionally sports a bow tie under his judicial robes, Stevens had a long record of excellence in scholarship. A member of a prominent Chicago family, Stevens graduated Phi Beta Kappa from the University of Chicago in 1941. After a wartime stint in the Navy, during which he earned the Bronze Star, he returned to Chicago to enter Northwestern University Law School, from which he graduated magna cum laude in 1947. From there, Stevens left for Washington, where he served as a law clerk to Supreme Court justice Wiley Rutledge. He returned to Chicago to join the prominent law firm of Poppenhusen, Johnston, Thompson, and Raymond, which specialized in antitrust law. Stevens developed a reputation as a preeminent antitrust lawyer, and after three years with Poppenhusen he left in 1952 to form his own firm, Rothschild, Stevens, Barry, and Myers. He remained there, engaging in private practice and teaching part time at Northwestern and the University of Chicago law schools, until his appointment by President Richard Nixon in 1970 to the U.S. Court of Appeals for the Seventh Circuit.

Stevens developed a reputation as a political moderate during his undergraduate days at the University of Chicago, then an overwhelmingly liberal campus. Although he is a registered Republican, he has never been active in partisan politics.

Nevertheless, Stevens did serve as Republican counsel in 1951 to the House Judiciary Subcommittee on the Study of Monopoly Power. He also served from 1953 to 1955, during the Eisenhower administration, as a member of the Attorney General's National Committee to Study the Antitrust Laws.

An enthusiastic pilot, Stevens flies his own small plane. He gave up playing squash following open heart surgery, from which he is said to have recovered fully. In 1942 Stevens married Elizabeth Jane Sheeren. They have four children. They were divorced in 1979. Stevens subsequently married Maryan Mulholland Simon, a longtime neighbor in Chicago.

Born April 20, 1920, Chicago, Illinois; University of Chicago B.A. (1941); Phi Beta Kappa; Northwestern University School of Law J.D. magna cum laude (1947); married Elizabeth Jane Sheeren 1942; three daughters, one son; divorced 1979; married Maryan Mulholland Simon 1980; law clerk to Justice Wiley Rutledge, U.S. Supreme Court 1947-1948; practiced law, Chicago, 1949-1970; judge, U.S. Court of Appeals for the Seventh Circuit 1970-1975; nominated as associate justice of the U.S. Supreme Court by President Ford November 28, 1975; confirmed December 17, 1975.

Sandra Day O'Connor

Pioneering came naturally to Sandra Day O'Connor. Her grandfather left Kansas in 1880 to take up ranching in the desert land that eventually would become the state of Arizona. O'Connor, born in El Paso, Texas, where her mother's parents lived, was raised on the Lazy B Ranch, the 162,000-acre spread that her grandfather founded in southeastern Arizona near Duncan. She spent her school years in El Paso, living with her grandmother. She graduated from high school at age sixteen and then entered Stanford University.

Six years later, in 1952, Sandra Day had won degrees, with great distinction, both from the university, in economics, and from Stanford

Law School. At Stanford, she met John J. O'Connor III, her future husband, and William H. Rehnquist, a future colleague on the Supreme Court. While in law school, Sandra Day was an editor of the *Stanford Law Review* and a member of Order of the Coif, both reflecting her academic leadership.

But despite her outstanding law school record, she found it difficult to secure a job as an attorney in 1952 when relatively few women were practicing law. She applied, among other places, to the firm in which William French Smith—first attorney general in the Reagan administration—was a partner, only to be offered a job as a secretary.

After she completed a short stint as deputy county attorney for San Mateo County (California) while her new husband completed law school at Stanford, the O'Connors moved with the U.S. Army to Frankfurt, Germany. There Sandra O'Connor worked as a civilian attorney for the Army, while John O'Connor served his tour of duty.

In 1957 they returned to Phoenix. In the next eight years their three sons were born, and O'Connor's life was a mix of mothering, homemaking, volunteer work, and some "miscellaneous legal tasks" on the side.

In 1965 she resumed her legal career full time, taking a job as an assistant attorney general for Arizona. After four years in that post she was appointed to fill a vacancy in the state Senate, where she served on the judiciary committee. In 1970 she was elected to the same body and two years later was chosen its majority leader, the first woman in the nation to hold such a post.

O'Connor was active in Republican party politics and was co-chairman of the Arizona Committee for the Re-election of the President in 1972.

In 1974 she was elected to the Superior Court for Maricopa County, where she served for five years. Then in 1979 Gov. Bruce Babbitt—acting, some said, to remove a potential rival for the governorship—appointed O'Connor to the Arizona Court of Appeals. It was from that seat that President Ronald Reagan chose her as his first nominee to the Supreme Court, succeeding Potter Stewart, who had retired. Reagan described her as "a person for all seasons."

By a vote of 99-0 the Senate confirmed O'Connor September 21, 1981, as the first woman associate justice of the U.S. Supreme Court.

Born March 26, 1930, El Paso, Texas; Stanford University B.A. magna cum laude (1950); Stanford University Law School LL.B. with high honors (1952); married John J. O'Connor III 1952; three sons;

deputy county attorney, San Mateo, California, 1952-1953; assistant attorney general, Arizona, 1965-1969; Arizona state senator 1969-1975; Arizona Senate majority leader 1972-1975; judge, Maricopa County Superior Court 1974-1979; judge, Arizona Court of Appeals 1979-1981; nominated as associate justice of the U.S. Supreme Court by President Reagan August 19, 1981; confirmed September 21, 1981.

Antonin Scalia

After Warren E. Burger resigned from the Court and Ronald Reagan named William H. Rehnquist to succeed him as chief justice, the president's next move—appointing Antonin Scalia as associate justice—was not surprising. On issues dear to Reagan, Scalia clearly met the president's tests for conservatism. Scalia, whom Reagan had named to theU.S. Court of Appeals for the District of Columbia in 1982, became the first Supreme Court justice of Italian ancestry. A Roman Catholic, he has nine children and opposes abortion. He also has expressed opposition to "affirmative action" preferences for minorities.

Deregulation, which Reagan pushed as president, was a subject of considerable interest to Scalia, a specialist in administrative law. From 1977 to 1982 he was editor of the magazine *Regulation*, published by the American Enterprise Institute for Public Policy Research.

In sharp contrast to the hours of floor debate over Rehnquist's nomination as chief justice, only a few moments of speeches were given in opposition to the equally conservative Scalia before he was confirmed, 98-0. He has since become the scourge of some members of Congress because of his suspicion of committee reports, floor speeches, and other artifacts of legislative history that courts traditionally relied on in interpreting a statute.

Born in Trenton, New Jersey, March 11, 1936, Scalia grew up in Queens, New York. He graduated from Georgetown University in 1957 and from Harvard Law School in 1960. He worked for six years for the firm of Jones, Day in Cleveland and then taught contract, commercial, and comparative law at the University of Virginia Law School.

Scalia served as general counsel of the White House Office of Telecommunications Policy from 1971 to 1972. He then headed the Administrative Conference of the United States, a group that advises the government on questions of administrative law and procedure. From 1974 through the Ford administration he headed the Justice Department's Office of Legal Counsel, a post Rehnquist had held three years earlier. Scalia then returned to academia, to teach at the University of Chicago Law School.

Scalia showed himself to be a hard worker, an aggressive interrogator, and an articulate advocate. On the appeals court he was impatient with what he saw as regulatory or judicial overreaching. In 1983 he dissented from a ruling requiring the Food and Drug Administration (FDA) to consider whether drugs used for legal injections met FDA standards as safe and effective. The Supreme Court agreed, reversing the appeals court in 1985.

Scalia was thought to be the principal author of an unsigned decision in 1986 that declared major portions of the Gramm-Rudman-Hollings budget-balancing act unconstitutional. The Supreme Court upheld the decision later in the year.

Born March 11, 1936, Trenton, New Jersey; Georgetown University A.B. (1957); Harvard University Law School LL.B. (1960); practiced law, Cleveland, 1960-1967; married Maureen McCarthy 1960; five sons, four daughters; taught at the University of Virginia 1967-1971; general counsel, White House Office of Telecommunications Policy 1971-1972; chairman, Administrative Conference of the United States 1972-1974; head, Office of Legal Counsel 1974-1977; taught at the University of Chicago Law School 1977-1982; judge, U.S. Court of Appeals for the District of Columbia 1982-1986; nominated as associate justice of the U.S. Supreme Court by President Reagan June 17, 1986; confirmed September 17, 1986.

Anthony McLeod Kennedy

Quiet, scholarly Anthony M. Kennedy, President Reagan's third choice for his third appointment to the Supreme Court, made all the difference when the Court's conservative majority began coalescing in 1989.

Kennedy proved to be a crucial fifth vote for the Court's conservative wing in civil rights cases, a firm supporter of state authority over defendants' rights in criminal cases, and a strict constructionist in the mode of Chief Justice William H. Rehnquist in most cases. Kennedy's presence effectively ushered in a new era on the Court. Both of Reagan's earlier appointees, Sandra Day O'Connor and Antonin Scalia, were somewhat more conservative than the men they replaced, Potter Stewart and Warren E. Burger, but they did not shift the balance on the Court. That role fell to Kennedy, who succeeded Lewis F. Powell, Jr., a moderate conservative and a critical swing vote. On a range of issues where Powell often joined the Court's four liberals, Kennedy has gone the other way.

Kennedy, who has voted close to 90 percent of the time with Rehnquist, broke with the chief justice in the controversial flag-burning cases of the 1988-1989 and 1989-1990 terms. Kennedy was the reluctant fifth vote to declare flag-desecration laws unconstitutional. Saying his decision exacted a "personal toll," Kennedy wrote in a concurring opinion, "The hard fact is that sometimes we must make decisions we do not like. We make them because they are right, right in the sense that the law and the Constitution, as we see them, compel the result."

Before Kennedy's nomination in November 1987, the Senate and the country agonized through Reagan's two unsuccessful attempts to replace Powell, first with Robert H. Bork and then with Douglas H. Ginsburg. The Senate rejected Bork's nomination after contentious hearings, and Ginsburg withdrew his name amid controversy about his qualifications and admitted past use of marijuana.

A quiet sense of relief came to pass when Reagan finally selected a nominee who could be confirmed without another wrenching confrontation. Later, Republicans would note the irony in that the man who anti-Bork Democrats so willingly called a moderate conservative tipped the balance on the Court.

Kennedy spent twelve years as a judge on the U.S. Court of Appeals for the Ninth Circuit. But unlike Bork, who wrote and spoke extensively for twenty years, Kennedy's record was confined mostly to his approximately 500 judicial opinions. His views thus were based in large part on issues that were distilled at the trial level and further refined by legal and oral arguments. Furthermore, Kennedy sought to decide issues narrowly instead of using his opinions as a testing ground for constitutional theories. He continued this approach in the decisions he has written on the high Court.

Confirmed by the Senate 97-0 February 3, 1988, Kennedy was sworn in February 18.

A native Californian, Kennedy attended Stanford University from 1954 to 1957 and the London School of Economics from 1957 to 1958. He received an A.B. from Stanford in 1958 and an LL.B. from Harvard Law School in 1961. Admitted to the California bar in 1962, he was in private law practice until 1975, when President Gerald R. Ford appointed him to the appeals court. From 1965 to 1988 he taught constitutional law at McGeorge School of Law, University of the Pacific.

He and his wife, Mary Davis, have three children.

Born July 23, 1936, Sacramento, California; Stanford University A.B. (1958); Phi Beta Kappa; Harvard University Law School LL.B. (1961); California Army National Guard 1961; married Mary Davis 1963; two sons, one daughter; associate, Thelen, Marrin, John & Bridges, San Francisco, 1961-1963; sole practitioner, Sacramento, 1963-1967; partner, Evans, Jackson & Kennedy, Sacramento, 1967-1975; professor of constitutional law, McGeorge School of Law, University of the Pacific 1965-1988; judge, U.S. Court of Appeals for the Ninth Circuit 1975-1988; nominated as associate justice of the U.S. Supreme Court by President Reagan November 11, 1987; confirmed February 3, 1988.

David Hackett Souter

At first, the Senate did not know what to make of David H. Souter, a cerebral, button-down nominee who was President Bush's first appointment to the Court. Souter was little known outside of his home state of New Hampshire, where he had been attorney general (1976-1978), a trial judge (1978-1983), and a state supreme court justice (1983-1990).

Unlike Antonin Scalia and Anthony M. Kennedy, his immediate predecessors on the Court, Souter had virtually no scholarly writings to dissect and little federal court experience to scrutinize. Only three months earlier Bush had appointed him to the U.S. Court of Appeals for the First Circuit. Souter had yet to write a legal opinion on the appeals court.

And during Souter's first year on the Supreme Court he remained a mystery. He was a tenacious questioner during oral argument but was reserved in the opinions he authored. He wrote eight opinions, the fewest of any justice, and the majority of those cases were decided by unanimous votes.

He, however, could be counted on to side with the conservative wing of the Court. In the 1989-1990 term, before Souter replaced Justice William J. Brennan, Jr., one-third of the Court's decisions were 5-4 rulings. In 1990-1991, only one-fifth were so narrowly decided, and many controversial disputes were settled by 6-3 votes.

Further, Souter provided Chief Justice William H. Rehnquist with a majority when the more centrist conservatives, Sandra Day O'Connor and Byron R. White, went to the opposing side. Without Souter's vote, the

Court would have neither upheld the abortion counseling ban in *Rust v. Sullivan* nor ruled that states may outlaw nude dancing in adult clubs in *Barnes v. Glen Theatre*.

During his confirmation hearings, the Harvard graduate and former Rhodes scholar demonstrated intellectual rigor and a masterly approach to constitutional law. Souter was able to recognize where a particular questioner was headed and to deflect most tough inquiries. He took refuge in the history of legal principles.

His earlier work as state attorney general and as a New Hampshire Supreme Court justice had a conservative bent, but Souter came across as more moderate in the hearings, winning over both Democrats and Republicans with his knowledge of judicial precedent. Senators predicted he would be a swing vote, but in his first year that was not the case.

Souter was approved by the Senate 90-9; dissenting senators cited his reluctance to take a stand on abortion. During his confirmation hearings, Souter refused to say how he would vote if the question of overruling *Roe v. Wade* arose.

Souter is known for his intensely private, ascetic life. He was born September 17, 1939, in Melrose, Massachusetts. An only child, he moved with his parents to Weare, New Hampshire, at age eleven. Except for college, he had lived in Weare since.

Souter graduated from Harvard College in 1961. He attended Oxford University on a Rhodes Scholarship from 1961 to 1963, then returned to Cambridge for Harvard Law School. Graduating in 1966, he worked for two years in a Concord law firm. In 1968 he became an assistant attorney general, rose to deputy attorney general in 1971, and in 1976 was appointed attorney general. Under conservative governor Meldrim Thomson, Jr., Attorney General Souter defended a number of controversial orders, including the lowering of state flags to half-staff on Good Friday to observe the death of Jesus. He prosecuted Jehovah's Witnesses who obscured the state motto "Live Free or Die" on their license plates.

Souter served as attorney general until 1978, when he was named to the state's trial court. Five years later, Gov. John H. Sununu appointed Souter to the state Supreme Court. Sununu was Bush's chief of staff when Souter was named to the U.S. Supreme Court.

Souter, a bachelor, is a nature enthusiast and avid hiker.

Born September 17, 1939, Melrose, Massachusetts; Harvard College B.A. (1961); Rhodes scholar, Oxford University 1961-1963; Harvard University Law School LL.B. (1966); private law practice, Concord, New Hampshire, 1966-1968; assistant attorney general, New Hampshire, 1968-1971; deputy attorney general, New Hampshire, 1971-1976; attorney general, New Hampshire, 1976-1978; associate justice, New Hampshire Superior Court 1978-1983; associate justice, New Hampshire

Supreme Court 1983-1990; judge, U.S. Court of Appeals for the First Circuit 1990; nominated as associate justice of the U.S. Supreme Court by President Bush July 23, 1990; confirmed October 2, 1990.

Clarence Thomas

The Senate's 52-48 vote on Clarence Thomas was the closest Supreme Court confirmation vote in more than a century and followed a tumultuous nomination process that culminated in accusations against Thomas of sexual harassment. The charges, brought out in nationally televised hearings, were never proved and led the black nominee to accuse the Senate of a "high-tech lynching."

Thomas, who took his judicial oath on October 23, 1991, succeeded Thurgood Marshall, the Court's last consistent liberal and a man whose six-decade legal career shaped the country's civil rights struggle. Marshall was the first black justice and Thomas became the second.

Thomas also was the fifth conservative appointment by a Republican president in ten years, a historic record that raised the stakes for the Democratically controlled Senate and led in part to the politics surrounding the confirmation. Thomas was a forty-three-year-old federal appeals court judge when named by President Bush, and senators noted that Thomas likely would be affecting the outcome of major constitutional rulings well into the twenty-first century. His confirmation also solidified the conservative majority on the Court that began asserting itself in the late 1980s.

Most difficult for Thomas were the eleventh-hour allegations from a former employee that he had sexually harassed her when he was assistant secretary of education for civil rights and then chairman of the Equal Employment Opportunity Commission (EEOC). In an unprecedented move, senators abruptly postponed a scheduled confirmation vote and reconvened hearings to take testimony from accuser Anita F. Hill, a University of Oklahoma law professor; Thomas; and witnesses for both.

In the end, most senators said Hill's charges and Thomas's defense—a categorical denial—were inconclusive. Senators fell back on their previous positions based on Thomas's judicial philosophy or his determined character and rise from poverty in rural Georgia.

Thomas's first round of hearings were controversial, although not as sensational. He publicly backed off from the opinions that he proclaimed while serving for eight years in the Reagan and Bush administrations. Whether by his design or that of the White House advisers who sat behind him as he testified, Thomas distanced himself from his earlier hard-line conservatism, hints that he might oppose abortion, and an attraction for natural law, which holds that some human rights are beyond the reach of any government restriction. He described his interest in natural law not as a constitutional philosophy but as an off-hours interest in political theory.

Instead, Thomas sounded other themes, mostly his but vigorously adopted by the White House, too. He referred often to his impoverished youth in Pin Point, Georgia, and what he said was his constant quest in a conservative administration to bring civil rights to the fore. Thomas recounted how his grandfather, who raised him after his parents broke up, fostered in him hard work and independence. He also expressed gratitude to the white nuns who were the only other people to believe in him in segregated Georgia schools.

After Thomas graduated from Yale Law School in 1974, he worked as an assistant attorney general of Missouri and later was a staff attorney for Monsanto Co. He worked for Sen. John C. Danforth, R-Mo., as a legislative assistant and served in the Department of Education as assistant secretary for civil rights for one year before being named to the EEOC.

Born June 23, 1948, Savannah, Georgia; Immaculate Conception Seminary 1967-1968; Holy Cross College B.A. cum laude 1971; Yale University Law School J.D. 1974; assistant attorney general, Missouri, 1974-1977; one son from first marriage; attorney, Monsanto Co. 1977-1979; legislative assistant to Sen. John C. Danforth, R-Mo., 1979-1981; assistant secretary of education for the civil rights division 1981-1982; chairman, Equal Employment Opportunity Commission 1982-1990; married Virginia Bess Lamp 1987; judge, U.S. Court of Appeals for the District of Columbia 1990-1991; nominated as associate justice of the U.S. Supreme Court by President Bush July 1, 1991; confirmed October 15, 1991.

Thurgood Marshall (Retired)

Unlike jurists who undergo striking philosophical changes once elevated to the Supreme Court, Thurgood Marshall deviated little from his earlier convictions. For more than a quarter of a century, Marshall exemplified, through his work with the National Association for the Advancement of Colored People (NAACP), the part of the civil rights movement that sought change through legal processes. Once on the Court Marshall continued to champion the rights of minorities. And as a member of the Court's minority liberal wing, Marshall persisted in his defense of individual rights. He resigned on October 1, 1991.

Thurgood Marshall was born July 2, 1908, in Baltimore, Maryland, the son of a primary school teacher and a club steward. In 1926, he began studies at all-black Lincoln University in Chester, Pennsylvania, where he developed a reputation as an outstanding debater. After graduating cum laude in 1930, Marshall decided to study law. He entered Howard University in Washington, D.C., in 1931.

During his law school years, Marshall began to develop an interest in civil rights. After graduating first in his law school class in 1933, Marshall began a long and historic involvement with the NAACP. In 1940 Marshall became the head of the newly formed NAACP Legal Defense and Educational Fund, a position he held for more than twenty years.

Over the next two and one-half decades, Marshall coordinated the fund's attack on segregation in voting, housing, public accommodations, and education. The culmination of his career as a civil rights attorney came in 1954 as chief counsel in a series of cases grouped under the title *Brown v. Board of Education.* In that historic dispute, which Marshall argued before the Supreme Court, civil rights advocates convinced the Court to declare that segregation in public schools was unconstitutional.

In 1961 President John F. Kennedy appointed Marshall to the U.S. Court of Appeals for the Second Circuit, but because of heated opposition from Southern Democratic senators Marshall was not confirmed until a year later.

Four years after he was named to the circuit court, Marshall was chosen by President Lyndon B. Johnson to be the nation's first black solicitor general. During his years as the government's chief advocate before the Supreme Court, Marshall scored impressive victories in the areas of civil and constitutional rights. He won Court approval of the 1965 Voting Rights Act, voluntarily informed the Court that the government had used electronic eavesdropping devices in two cases, and joined in a suit that successfully overturned a California constitutional amendment prohibiting open housing legislation.

On June 13, 1967, Marshall became the first black appointed to be a justice of the Supreme Court, chosen by President Johnson.

Marshall was married in 1955 to Cecelia A. Suyat. He has two sons.

Born July 2, 1908, Baltimore, Maryland; Lincoln University B.A. (1930); Howard University LL.B. (1933); practiced law 1933-1937; assistant special counsel, NAACP 1936-1938; special counsel, NAACP 1938-1950; married Vivian Burey 1929; married Cecelia A. Suyat 1955;

two sons; director-counsel, NAACP Legal Defense and Educational Fund 1940-1961; judge, U.S. Court of Appeals for the Second Circuit 1961-1965; U.S. solicitor general 1965-1967; nominated as associate justice of the U.S. Supreme Court by President Johnson June 13, 1967; confirmed August 30, 1967.

Glossary of Legal Terms

Accessory. In criminal law, a person not present at the commission of an offense who commands, advises, instigates, or conceals the offense.

Acquittal. A person is acquitted when a jury returns a verdict of not guilty. A person also may be acquitted when a judge determines that insufficient evidence exists to convict him or that a violation of due process precludes a fair trial.

Adjudicate. To determine finally by the exercise of judicial authority, to decide a case.

Affidavit. A voluntary written statement of facts or charges affirmed under oath.

A fortiori. With stronger force, with more reason.

Amicus curiae. A friend of the court, a person, not a party to litigation, who volunteers or is invited by the court to give his views on a case.

Appeal. To take a case to a higher court for review. Generally, a party losing in a trial court may appeal once to an appellate court as a matter of right. If the party loses in the appellate court, appeal to a higher court is within the discretion of the higher court. Most appeals to the U.S. Supreme Court are within its discretion.

However, when the highest court in a state rules that a U.S. statute is unconstitutional or upholds a state statute against the claim that it is unconstitutional, appeal to the Supreme Court is a matter of right.

Appellant. The party who appeals a lower court decision to a higher court.

Appellee. One who has an interest in upholding the decision of a lower court and is compelled to respond when the case is appealed to a higher court by the appellant.

Arraignment. The formal process of charging a person with a crime, reading that person the charge, asking whether he pleads guilty or not guilty, and entering the plea.

Attainder, Bill of. A legislative act pronouncing a particular individual guilty of a crime without trial or conviction and imposing a sentence.

Bail. The security, usually money, given as assurance of a prisoner's due appearance at a designated time and place (as in court) to procure in the interim the prisoner's release from jail.

Bailiff. A minor officer of a court usually serving as an usher or a messenger.

Brief. A document prepared by counsel to serve as the basis for an argument in court, setting out the facts of and the legal arguments in support of the case.

Burden of proof. The need or duty of affirmatively providing a fact or facts that are disputed.

Case law. The law as defined by previously decided cases, distinct from statutes and other sources of law.

Cause. A case, suit, litigation, or action, civil or criminal.

Certiorari, Writ of. A writ issued from the Supreme Court, at its discretion, to order a lower court to prepare the record of a case and send it to the Supreme Court for review.

Civil law. Body of law dealing with the private rights of individuals, as distinguished from criminal law.

Class action. A lawsuit brought by one person or group on behalf of all persons similarly situated.

Code. A collection of laws, arranged systematically.

Comity. Courtesy, respect; usually used in the legal sense to refer to the proper relationship between state and federal courts.

Common law. Collection of principles and rules of action, particularly from unwritten English law, that derive their authority from longstanding usage and custom or from courts recognizing and enforcing these customs. Sometimes used synonymously with case law.

Consent decree. A court-sanctioned agreement settling a legal dispute and entered into by the consent of the parties.

Contempt (civil and criminal). Civil contempt arises from a failure to follow a court order for the benefit of another party. Criminal contempt occurs when a person willfully exhibits disrespect for the court or obstructs the administration of justice.

Conviction. Final judgment or sentence that the defendant is guilty as charged.

Criminal law. The branch of law that deals with the enforcement of laws and the punishment of persons who, by breaking laws, commit crimes.

Declaratory judgment. A court pronouncement declaring a legal right or interpretation but not ordering a specific action.

De facto. In fact, in reality.

Defendant. In a civil action, the party denying or defending itself against charges brought by a plaintiff. In a criminal action, the person indicted for commission of an offense.

De jure. As a result of law, as a result of official action.

De novo. Anew; afresh; a second time.

Deposition. Oral testimony from a witness taken out of court in response to written or oral questions, committed to writing, and intended to be used in the preparation of a case.

Dicta. *See* Obiter dictum.

Dismissal. Order disposing of a case without a trial.

Docket. A calendar prepared by the clerks of the court listing the cases set to be tried.

Due process. Fair and regular procedure. The Fifth and Fourteenth Amendments guarantee persons that they will not be deprived of life, liberty, or property by the government until fair and usual procedures have been followed.

Error, Writ of. A writ issued from an appeals court to a lower court requiring it to send to the appeals court the record of a case in which it has entered a final judgment and which the appeals court will review for error.

Ex parte. Only from, or on, one side. Application to a court for some ruling or action on behalf of only one party.

Ex post facto. After the fact; an ex post facto law makes an action a crime after it already has been committed, or otherwise changes the legal consequences of some past action.

Ex rel. Upon information from; usually used to describe legal proceedings begun by an official in the name of the state, but at the instigation of, and with information from, a private individual interested in the matter.

Grand jury. Group of twelve to twenty-three persons impanelled to hear, in private, evidence presented by the state against an individual or persons accused of a criminal act and to issue indictments when a majority of the jurors find probable cause to believe that the accused has committed a crime. Called a "grand" jury because it comprises a greater number of persons than a "petit" jury.

Grand jury report. A public report, often called "presentments," released by a grand jury after an investigation into activities of public officials that fall short of criminal actions.

Guilty. A word used by a defendant in entering a plea or by a jury in returning a verdict, indicating that the defendant is legally responsible as charged for a crime or other wrongdoing.

Habeas corpus. Literally, "you have the body"; a writ issued to inquire whether a person is lawfully imprisoned or detained. The writ demands that the persons holding the prisoner justify the detention or release the prisoner.

Immunity. A grant of exemption from prosecution in return for evidence or testimony.

In camera. In chambers. Refers to court hearings in private without spectators.

In forma pauperis. In the manner of a pauper, without liability for court costs.

In personam. Done or directed against a particular person.

In re. In the affair of, concerning. Frequent title of judicial proceedings in which there are no adversaries, but instead where the matter itself—such as a bankrupt's estate—requires judicial action.

In rem. Done or directed against the thing, not the person.

Indictment. A formal written statement, based on evidence presented by the prosecutor, from a grand jury. Decided by a majority vote, an indictment charges one or more persons with specified offenses.

Information. A written set of accusations, similar to an indictment, but filed directly by a prosecutor.

Injunction. A court order prohibiting the person to whom it is directed from performing a particular act.

Interlocutory decree. A provisional decision of the court before completion of a legal action that temporarily settles an intervening matter.

Judgment. Official decision of a court based on the rights and claims of the parties to a case that was submitted for determination.

Jurisdiction. The power of a court to hear a case in question, which exists when the proper parties are present and when the point to be decided is within the issues authorized to be handled by the particular court.

Juries. *See* Grand jury; Petit jury.

Magistrate. A judicial officer having jurisdiction to try minor criminal cases and conduct preliminary examinations of persons charged with serious crimes.

Mandamus. "We command." An order issued from a superior court directing a lower court or other authority to perform a particular act.

Moot. Unsettled, undecided. A moot question also is one that no longer is material; a moot case is one that has become hypothetical.

Motion. Written or oral application to a court or a judge to obtain a rule or an order.

Nolo contendere. "I will not contest it." A plea entered by a defendant at the discretion of the judge with the same legal effect as a plea of guilty, but it may not be cited in other proceedings as an admission of guilt.

Obiter dictum. Statements by a judge or justice expressing an opinion and included with, but not essential to, an opinion resolving a case before the court. Dicta are not necessarily binding in future cases.

Parole. A conditional release from imprisonment under conditions that, if the prisoner abides by the law and other restrictions that may be imposed, the prisoner will not have to serve the remainder of the sentence.

Per curiam. "By the court." An unsigned opinion of the court, or an opinion written by the whole court.

Petit jury. A trial jury, originally a panel of twelve persons who tried to reach a unanimous verdict on questions of fact in criminal and civil proceedings. Since 1970 the Supreme Court has upheld the legality of state juries with fewer than twelve persons. Fewer persons serve on a "petit" jury than on a "grand" jury.

Petitioner. One who files a petition with a court seeking action or relief, including a plaintiff or an appellant. But a petitioner also is a person who files for other court action where charges are not necessarily made; for example, a party may petition the court for an order requiring another person or party to produce documents. The opposite party is called the respondent.

When a writ of certiorari is granted by the Supreme Court, the parties to the case are called petitioner and respondent in contrast to the appellant and appellee terms used in an appeal.

Plaintiff. A party who brings a civil action or sues to obtain a remedy for injury to his rights. The party against whom action is brought is termed the defendant.

Plea bargaining. Negotiations between a prosecutor and the defendant aimed at exchanging a plea of guilty from the defendant for concessions by the prosecutor, such as reduction of charges or a request for leniency.

Pleas. *See* Guilty; Nolo contendere.

Presentment. *See* Grand jury report.

Prima facie. At first sight; referring to a fact or other evidence presumably sufficient to establish a defense or a claim unless otherwise contradicted.

Probation. Process under which a person convicted of an offense, usually a first offense, receives a suspended sentence and is given freedom, usually under the guardianship of a probation officer.

Quash. To overthrow, annul, or vacate; as to quash a subpoena.

Recognizance. An obligation entered into before a court or magistrate requiring the performance of a specified act—usually to appear in court at a later date. It is an alternative to bail for pretrial release.

Remand. To send back. When a decision is remanded, it is sent back by a higher court to the court from which it came for further action.

Respondent. One who is compelled to answer the claims or questions posed in court by a petitioner. A defendant and an appellee may be called respondents, but the term also includes those parties who answer in court during actions where charges are not necessarily brought or where the Supreme Court has granted a writ of certiorari.

Seriatim. Separately, individually, one by one.

Stare decisis. "Let the decision stand." The principle of adherence to settled cases, the doctrine that principles of law established in earlier judicial decisions should be accepted as authoritative in similar subsequent cases.

Statute. A written law enacted by a legislature. A collection of statutes for a particular governmental division is called a code.

Stay. To halt or suspend further judicial proceedings.

Subpoena. An order to present oneself before a grand jury, court, or legislative hearing.

Subpoena duces tecum. An order to produce specified documents or papers.

Tort. An injury or wrong to the person or property of another.

Transactional immunity. Protects a witness from prosecution for any offense mentioned in or related to his testimony, regardless of independent evidence against the witness.

Use immunity. Protects a witness from the use of his testimony against the witness in prosecution.

Vacate. To make void, annul, or rescind.

Writ. A written court order commanding the designated recipient to perform or not perform specified acts.

Constitution of the United States

We the People of the United States, in Order to form a more perfect Union, establish Justice, insure domestic Tranquility, provide for the common defence, promote the general Welfare, and secure the Blessings of Liberty to ourselves and our Posterity, do ordain and establish this Constitution for the United States of America.

Article I

Section 1. All legislative Powers herein granted shall be vested in a Congress of the United States, which shall consist of a Senate and House of Representatives.

Section 2. The House of Representatives shall be composed of Members chosen every second Year by the People of the several States, and the Electors in each State shall have the Qualifications requisite for Electors of the most numerous Branch of the State Legislature.

No Person shall be a Representative who shall not have attained to the age of twenty five Years, and been seven Years a Citizen of the United States, and who shall not, when elected, be an Inhabitant of that State in which he shall be chosen.

[Representatives and direct Taxes shall be apportioned among the several States which may be included within this Union, according to their respective Numbers, which shall be determined by adding to the whole Number of free Persons, including those bound to Service for a Term of Years, and excluding Indians not taxed, three fifths of all other Persons.][1] The actual Enumeration shall be made within three Years after the first Meeting of the Congress of the United States, and within every subsequent Term of ten Years, in such Manner as they shall by Law direct. The Number of Representatives shall not exceed one for every thirty Thousand, but each State shall have at Least one Representative; and until such enumeration shall be made, the State of New Hampshire shall be entitled to chuse three, Massachusetts eight, Rhode-Island and Providence Plantations one, Connecticut five, New-York six, New Jersey four, Pennsylvania eight, Delaware one, Maryland six, Virginia ten, North Carolina five, South Carolina five, and Georgia three.

When vacancies happen in the Representation from any State, the Executive Authority thereof shall issue Writs of Election to fill such Vacancies.

The House of Representatives shall chuse their Speaker and other Officers; and shall have the sole Power of Impeachment.

Section 3. The Senate of the United States shall be composed of two Senators from each State, [chosen by the Legislature thereof,][2] for six Years; and each Senator shall have one Vote.

Immediately after they shall be assembled in Consequence of the first Election, they shall be divided as equally as may be into three Classes. The Seats of the Senators of the first Class shall be vacated at the Expiration of the second Year, of the second Class at the Expiration of the fourth Year, and of the third Class at the Expiration of the sixth Year, so that one third may be chosen every second Year; [and if Vacancies happen by Resignation, or otherwise, during the Recess of the Legislature of any State, the Executive thereof may make temporary Appointments until the next Meeting of the Legislature, which shall then fill such Vacancies.][3]

No Person shall be a Senator who shall not have attained to the Age of thirty Years, and been nine Years a Citizen of the United States, and who shall not, when elected, be an Inhabitant of that State for which he shall be chosen.

The Vice President of the United States shall be President of the Senate, but shall have no Vote, unless they be equally divided.

The Senate shall chuse their other Officers, and also a President pro tempore, in the Absence of the Vice President, or when he shall exercise the Office of President of the United States.

The Senate shall have the sole Power to try all Impeachments. When sitting for that Purpose, they shall be on Oath or Affirmation. When the President of the United States is tried, the Chief Justice shall preside: And no Person shall be convicted without the Concurrence of two thirds of the Members present.

Judgment in Cases of Impeachment shall not extend further than to removal from Office, and disqualification to hold and enjoy any Office of honor, Trust or Profit under the United States: but the Party convicted shall nevertheless be liable and subject to Indictment, Trial, Judgment and Punishment, according to Law.

Section 4. The Times, Places and Manner of holding Elections for Senators and Representatives, shall be prescribed in each State by the Legislature thereof; but the Congress may at any time by Law make or alter such Regulations, except as to the Places of chusing Senators.

The Congress shall assemble at least once in every Year, and such Meeting shall [be on the first Monday in December],[4] unless they shall by Law appoint a different Day.

Section 5. Each House shall be the Judge of the Elections, Returns and Qualifications of its own Members, and a Majority of each shall constitute a Quorum to do Business; but a smaller Number may adjourn from day to day, and may be authorized to compel the Attendance of absent Members, in such Manner, and under such Penalties as each House may provide.

Each House may determine the Rules of its Proceedings, punish its Members for disorderly Behaviour, and, with the Concurrence of two thirds, expel a Member.

Each House shall keep a Journal of its Proceedings, and from time to time publish the same, excepting such Parts as may in their Judgment require Secrecy; and the Yeas and Nays of the Members of either House on any question shall, at the Desire of one fifth of those Present, be entered on the Journal.

Neither House, during the Session of Congress, shall, without the Consent of the other, adjourn for more than three days, nor to any other Place than that in which the two Houses shall be sitting.

Section 6. The Senators and Representatives shall receive a Compensation for their Services, to be ascertained by Law, and paid out of the Treasury of the United States. They shall in all Cases, except Treason, Felony and Breach of the Peace, be privileged from Arrest during their Attendance at the Session of their respective Houses, and in going to and returning from the same; and for any Speech or Debate in either House, they shall not be questioned in any other Place.

No Senator or Representative shall, during the Time for which he was elected, be appointed to any civil Office under the Authority of the United States, which shall have been created, or the Emoluments whereof shall have been encreased during such time; and no Person holding any Office under the United States, shall be a Member of either House during his Continuance in Office.

Section 7. All Bills for raising Revenue shall originate in the House of Representatives; but the Senate may propose or concur with Amendments as on other Bills.

Every Bill which shall have passed the House of Representatives and the Senate, shall, before it become a Law, be presented to the President of the United States; If he approve he shall sign it, but if not he shall return it, with his Objections to that House in which it shall have originated, who shall enter the Objections at large on their Journal, and proceed to reconsider it. If after such Reconsideration two thirds of that House shall agree to pass the Bill, it shall be sent, together with the Objections, to the other House, by which it shall likewise be reconsidered, and if approved by two thirds of that House, it shall become a Law. But in all such Cases the Votes of both Houses shall be determined by yeas and Nays, and the

Names of the Persons voting for and against the Bill shall be entered on the Journal of each House respectively. If any Bill shall not be returned by the President within ten Days (Sundays excepted) after it shall have been presented to him, the Same shall be a Law, in like Manner as if he had signed it, unless the Congress by their Adjournment prevent its Return, in which Case it shall not be a Law.

Every Order, Resolution, or Vote to which the Concurrence of the Senate and House of Representatives may be necessary (except on a question of Adjournment) shall be presented to the President of the United States; and before the Same shall take Effect, shall be approved by him, or being disapproved by him, shall be repassed by two thirds of the Senate and House of Representatives, according to the Rules and Limitations prescribed in the Case of a Bill.

Section 8. The Congress shall have Power To lay and collect Taxes, Duties, Imposts and Excises, to pay the Debts and provide for the common Defence and general Welfare of the United States; but all Duties, Imposts and Excises shall be uniform throughout the United States;

To borrow Money on the credit of the United States;

To regulate Commerce with foreign Nations, and among the several States, and with the Indian Tribes;

To establish an uniform Rule of Naturalization, and uniform Laws on the subject of Bankruptcies throughout the United States;

To coin Money, regulate the Value thereof, and of foreign Coin, and fix the Standard of Weights and Measures;

To provide for the Punishment of counterfeiting the Securities and current Coin of the United States;

To establish Post Offices and post Roads;

To promote the Progress of Science and useful Arts, by securing for limited Times to Authors and Inventors the exclusive Right to their respective Writings and Discoveries;

To constitute Tribunals inferior to the supreme Court;

To define and punish Piracies and Felonies committed on the high Seas, and Offences against the Law of Nations;

To declare War, grant Letters of Marque and Reprisal, and make Rules concerning Captures on Land and Water;

To raise and support Armies, but no Appropriation of Money to that Use shall be for a longer Term than two Years;

To provide and maintain a Navy;

To make Rules for the Government and Regulation of the land and naval Forces;

To provide for calling forth the Militia to execute the Laws of the Union, suppress Insurrections and repel Invasions;

To provide for organizing, arming, and disciplining, the Militia, and for governing such Part of them as may be employed in the Service of the United States, reserving to the States respectively, the Appointment of the Officers, and the Authority of training the Militia according to the discipline prescribed by Congress;

To exercise exclusive Legislation in all Cases whatsoever, over such District (not exceeding ten Miles square) as may, by Cession of particular States, and the Acceptance of Congress, become the Seat of the Government of the United States, and to exercise like Authority over all Places purchased by the Consent of the Legislature of the State in which the Same shall be, for the Erection of Forts, Magazines, Arsenals, dock-Yards, and other needful Buildings; —And

To make all Laws which shall be necessary and proper for carrying into Execution the foregoing Powers, and all other Powers vested by this Constitution in the Government of the United States, or in any Department or Officer thereof.

Section 9. The Migration or Importation of such Persons as any of the States now existing shall think proper to admit, shall not be prohibited by the Congress prior to the Year one thousand eight hundred and eight, but a Tax or duty may be imposed on such Importation, not exceeding ten dollars for each Person.

The Privilege of the Writ of Habeas Corpus shall not be suspended, unless when in Cases of Rebellion or Invasion the public Safety may require it.

No Bill of Attainder or ex post facto Law shall be passed.

No Capitation, or other direct, Tax shall be laid, unless in Proportion to the Census or Enumeration herein before directed to be taken.[5]

No Tax or Duty shall be laid on Articles exported from any State.

No Preference shall be given by any Regulation of Commerce or Revenue to the Ports of one State over those of another; nor shall Vessels bound to, or from, one State, be obliged to enter, clear, or pay Duties in another.

No Money shall be drawn from the Treasury, but in Consequence of Appropriations made by Law; and a regular Statement and Account of the Receipts and Expenditures of all public Money shall be published from time to time.

No Title of Nobility shall be granted by the United States: And no Person holding any Office of Profit or Trust under them, shall, without the Consent of the Congress, accept of any present, Emolument, Office, or Title, of any kind whatever, from any King, Prince, or foreign State.

Section 10. No State shall enter into any Treaty, Alliance, or Confederation; grant Letters of Marque and Reprisal; coin Money; emit

Bills of Credit; make any Thing but gold and silver Coin a Tender in Payment of Debts; pass any Bill of Attainder, ex post facto Law, or Law impairing the Obligation of Contracts, or grant any Title of Nobility.

No State shall, without the Consent of the Congress, lay any Imposts or Duties on Imports or Exports, except what may be absolutely necessary for executing it's inspection Laws: and the net Produce of all Duties and Imposts, laid by any State on Imports or Exports, shall be for the Use of the Treasury of the United States; and all such Laws shall be subject to the Revision and Controul of the Congress.

No State shall, without the Consent of Congress, lay any Duty of Tonnage, keep Troops, or Ships of War in time of Peace, enter into any Agreement or Compact with another State, or with a foreign Power, or engage in War, unless actually invaded, or in such imminent Danger as will not admit of delay.

Article II

Section 1. The executive Power shall be vested in a President of the United States of America. He shall hold his Office during the Term of four Years, and, together with the Vice President, chosen for the same Term, be elected, as follows

Each State shall appoint, in such Manner as the Legislature thereof may direct, a Number of Electors, equal to the whole Number of Senators and Representatives to which the State may be entitled in the Congress: but no Senator or Representative, or Person holding an Office of Trust or Profit under the United States, shall be appointed an Elector.

[The Electors shall meet in their respective States, and vote by Ballot for two Persons, of whom one at least shall not be an Inhabitant of the same State with themselves. And they shall make a List of all the Persons voted for, and of the Number of Votes for each; which List they shall sign and certify, and transmit sealed to the Seat of the Government of the United States, directed to the President of the Senate. The President of the Senate shall, in the Presence of the Senate and House of Representatives, open all the Certificates, and the Votes shall then be counted. The Person having the greatest Number of Votes shall be the President, if such Number be a Majority of the whole Number of Electors appointed; and if there be more than one who have such Majority, and have an equal Number of Votes, then the House of Representatives shall immediately chuse by Ballot one of them for President; and if no Person have a Majority, then from the five highest on the list the said House shall in like Manner chuse the President. But in chusing the President, the Votes shall be taken by States, the Representation from each State having one Vote; A quorum for this Purpose shall consist of a Member or Members from two thirds of the States, and a Majority of all the States shall be necessary to a

Choice. In every Case, after the Choice of the President, the Person having the greatest Number of Votes of the Electors shall be the Vice President. But if there should remain two or more who have equal Votes, the Senate shall chuse from them by Ballot the Vice President.][6]

The Congress may determine the Time of chusing the Electors, and the Day on which they shall give their Votes; which Day shall be the same throughout the United States.

No Person except a natural born Citizen, or a Citizen of the United States, at the time of the Adoption of this Constitution, shall be eligible to the Office of President; neither shall any Person be eligible to that Office who shall not have attained to the Age of thirty five Years, and been fourteen Years a Resident within the United States.

In Case of the Removal of the President from Office, or of his Death, Resignation, or Inability to discharge the Powers and Duties of the said Office,[7] the Same shall devolve on the Vice President, and the Congress may by Law provide for the Case of Removal, Death, Resignation or Inability, both of the President and Vice President, declaring what Officer shall then act as President, and such Officer shall act accordingly, until the Disability be removed, or a President shall be elected.

The President shall, at stated Times, receive for his Services, a Compensation, which shall neither be encreased nor diminished during the Period for which he shall have been elected, and he shall not receive within that Period any other Emolument from the United States, or any of them.

Before he enter on the Execution of his Office, he shall take the following Oath or Affirmation:—"I do solemnly swear (or affirm) that I will faithfully execute the Office of President of the United States, and will to the best of my Ability, preserve, protect and defend the Constitution of the United States."

Section 2. The President shall be Commander in Chief of the Army and Navy of the United States, and of the Militia of the several States, when called into the actual Service of the United States; he may require the Opinion, in writing, of the principal Officer in each of the executive Departments, upon any Subject relating to the Duties of their respective Offices, and he shall have Power to grant Reprieves and Pardons for Offences against the United States, except in Cases of Impeachment.

He shall have Power, by and with the Advice and Consent of the Senate, to make Treaties, provided two thirds of the Senators present concur; and he shall nominate, and by and with the Advice and Consent of the Senate, shall appoint Ambassadors, other public Ministers and Consuls, Judges of the supreme Court, and all other Officers of the United States, whose Appointments are not herein otherwise provided for, and which shall be established by Law: but the Congress may by Law vest the Appointment of such inferior Officers, as they think proper, in the President alone, in the Courts of Law, or in the Heads of Departments.

The President shall have Power to fill up all Vacancies that may happen during the Recess of the Senate, by granting Commissions which shall expire at the End of their next Session.

Section 3. He shall from time to time give to the Congress Information of the State of the Union, and recommend to their Consideration such Measures as he shall judge necessary and expedient; he may, on extraordinary Occasions, convene both Houses, or either of them, and in Case of Disagreement between them, with Respect to the Time of Adjournment, he may adjourn them to such Time as he shall think proper; he shall receive Ambassadors and other public Ministers; he shall take Care that the Laws be faithfully executed, and shall Commission all the Officers of the United States.

Section 4. The President, Vice President and all civil Officers of the United States, shall be removed from Office on Impeachment for, and Conviction of, Treason, Bribery, or other high Crimes and Misdemeanors.

Article III

Section 1. The judicial Power of the United States, shall be vested in one supreme Court, and in such inferior Courts as the Congress may from time to time ordain and establish. The Judges, both of the supreme and inferior Courts, shall hold their Offices during good Behaviour, and shall, at stated Times, receive for their Services, a Compensation, which shall not be diminished during their Continuance in Office.

Section 2. The judicial Power shall extend to all Cases, in Law and Equity, arising under this Constitution, the Laws of the United States, and Treaties made, or which shall be made, under their Authority; — to all Cases affecting Ambassadors, other public Ministers and Consuls; — to all Cases of admiralty and maritime Jurisdiction; — to Controversies to which the United States shall be a Party; — to Controversies between two or more States; — between a State and Citizens of another State;[8] — between Citizens of different States; — between Citizens of the same State claiming Lands under Grants of different States, and between a State, or the Citizens thereof, and foreign States, Citizens or Subjects.[8]

In all Cases affecting Ambassadors, other public Ministers and Consuls, and those in which a State shall be Party, the supreme Court shall have original Jurisdiction. In all the other Cases before mentioned, the supreme Court shall have appellate Jurisdiction, both as to Law and Fact, with such Exceptions, and under such Regulations as the Congress shall make.

The Trial of all Crimes, except in Cases of Impeachment, shall be by Jury; and such Trial shall be held in the State where the said Crimes shall have been committed; but when not committed within any State, the Trial shall be at such Place or Places as the Congress may by Law have directed.

Section 3. Treason against the United States, shall consist only in levying War against them, or in adhering to their Enemies, giving them Aid and Comfort. No Person shall be convicted of Treason unless on the Testimony of two Witnesses to the same overt Act, or on Confession in open Court.

The Congress shall have Power to declare the Punishment of Treason, but no Attainder of Treason shall work Corruption of Blood, or Forfeiture except during the Life of the Person attainted.

Article IV

Section 1. Full Faith and Credit shall be given in each State to the public Acts, Records, and judicial Proceedings of every other State. And the Congress may by general Laws prescribe the Manner in which such Acts, Records and Proceedings shall be proved, and the Effect thereof.

Section 2. The Citizens of each State shall be entitled to all Privileges and Immunities of Citizens in the several States.

A Person charged in any State with Treason, Felony, or other Crime, who shall flee from Justice, and be found in another State, shall on Demand of the executive Authority of the State from which he fled, be delivered up, to be removed to the State having Jurisdiction of the Crime.

[No Person held to Service or Labour in one State, under the Laws thereof, escaping into another, shall, in Consequence of any Law or Regulation therein, be discharged from such Service or Labour, but shall be delivered up on Claim of the Party to whom such Service or Labour may be due.][9]

Section 3. New States may be admitted by the Congress into this Union; but no new State shall be formed or erected within the Jurisdiction of any other State; nor any State be formed by the Junction of two or more States, or Parts of States, without the Consent of the Legislatures of the States concerned as well as of the Congress.

The Congress shall have Power to dispose of and make all needful Rules and Regulations respecting the Territory or other Property belonging to the United States; and nothing in this Constitution shall be so construed as to Prejudice any Claims of the United States, or of any particular State.

Section 4. The United States shall guarantee to every State in this Union a Republican Form of Government, and shall protect each of them against Invasion; and on Application of the Legislature, or of the Executive (when the Legislature cannot be convened) against domestic Violence.

Article V

The Congress, whenever two thirds of both Houses shall deem it necessary, shall propose Amendments to this Constitution, or, on the Application of the Legislatures of two thirds of the several States, shall call a Convention for proposing Amendments, which, in either Case, shall be valid to all Intents and Purposes, as Part of this Constitution, when ratified by the Legislatures of three fourths of the several States, or by Conventions in three fourths thereof, as the one or the other Mode of Ratification may be proposed by the Congress; Provided [that no Amendment which may be made prior to the Year One thousand eight hundred and eight shall in any Manner affect the first and fourth Clauses in the Ninth Section of the first Article; and][10] that no State, without its Consent, shall be deprived of its equal Suffrage in the Senate.

Article VI

All Debts contracted and Engagements entered into, before the Adoption of this Constitution, shall be as valid against the United States under this Constitution, as under the Confederation.

This Constitution, and the Laws of the United States which shall be made in Pursuance thereof; and all Treaties made, or which shall be made, under the Authority of the United States, shall be the supreme Law of the Land; and the Judges in every State shall be bound thereby, any Thing in the Constitution or Laws of any State to the Contrary notwithstanding.

The Senators and Representatives before mentioned, and the Members of the several State Legislatures, and all executive and judicial Officers, both of the United States and of the several States, shall be bound by Oath or Affirmation, to support this Constitution; but no religious Test shall ever be required as a Qualification to any Office or public Trust under the United States.

Article VII

The Ratification of the Conventions of nine States, shall be sufficient for the Establishment of this Constitution between the States so ratifying the Same.

Done in Convention by the Unanimous Consent of the States present the Seventeenth Day of September in the Year of our Lord one thousand seven hundred and Eighty seven and of the Independence of the United States of America the Twelfth. IN WITNESS whereof We have hereunto subscribed our Names,

George Washington,
President and
deputy from Virginia.

New Hampshire: John Langdon,
Nicholas Gilman.

Massachusetts: Nathaniel Gorham,
Rufus King.

Connecticut: William Samuel Johnson,
Roger Sherman.

New York: Alexander Hamilton.

New Jersey: William Livingston,
David Brearley,
William Paterson,
Jonathan Dayton.

Pennsylvania: Benjamin Franklin,
Thomas Mifflin,
Robert Morris,
George Clymer,
Thomas FitzSimons,
Jared Ingersoll,
James Wilson,
Gouverneur Morris.

Delaware: George Read,
Gunning Bedford Jr.,
John Dickinson,
Richard Bassett,
Jacob Broom.

Maryland: James McHenry,
Daniel of St. Thomas Jenifer,
Daniel Carroll.

Virginia: John Blair,
James Madison Jr.

North Carolina: William Blount,
Richard Dobbs Spaight,
Hugh Williamson.

South Carolina: John Rutledge,
Charles Cotesworth Pinckney,
Charles Pinckney,
Pierce Butler.

Georgia: William Few,
Abraham Baldwin.

[The language of the original Constitution, not including the Amendments, was adopted by a convention of the states on September 17, 1787, and was subsequently ratified by the states on the following dates: Delaware, December 7, 1787; Pennsylvania, December 12, 1787; New Jersey, December 18, 1787; Georgia, January 2, 1788; Connecticut, January 9, 1788; Massachusetts, February 6, 1788; Maryland, April 28, 1788; South Carolina, May 23, 1788; New Hampshire, June 21, 1788.

Ratification was completed on June 21, 1788.

The Constitution subsequently was ratified by Virginia, June 25, 1788; New York, July 26, 1788; North Carolina, November 21, 1789; Rhode Island, May 29, 1790; and Vermont, January 10, 1791.]

Amendments

Amendment I

(First ten amendments ratified December 15, 1791.)

Congress shall make no law respecting an establishment of religion, or prohibiting the free exercise thereof; or abridging the freedom of speech, or of the press; or the right of the people peaceably to assemble, and to petition the Government for a redress of grievances.

Amendment II

A well regulated Militia, being necessary to the security of a free State, the right of the people to keep and bear Arms, shall not be infringed.

Amendment III

No Soldier shall, in time of peace be quartered in any house, without the consent of the Owner, nor in time of war, but in a manner to be prescribed by law.

Amendment IV

The right of the people to be secure in their persons, houses, papers, and effects, against unreasonable searches and seizures, shall not be violated, and no Warrants shall issue, but upon probable cause, supported by Oath or affirmation, and particularly describing the place to be searched, and the persons or things to be seized.

Amendment V

No person shall be held to answer for a capital, or otherwise infamous crime, unless on a presentment or indictment of a Grand Jury, except in cases arising in the land or naval forces, or in the Militia, when in actual service in time of War or public danger; nor shall any person be subject for the same offence to be twice put in jeopardy of life or limb; nor shall be compelled in any criminal case to be a witness against himself, nor be deprived of life, liberty, or property, without due process of law; nor shall private property be taken for public use, without just compensation.

Amendment VI

In all criminal prosecutions, the accused shall enjoy the right to a speedy and public trial, by an impartial jury of the State and district wherein the crime shall have been committed, which district shall have been previously ascertained by law, and to be informed of the nature and cause of the accusation; to be confronted with the witnesses against him; to have compulsory process for obtaining witnesses in his favor, and to have the Assistance of Counsel for his defence.

Amendment VII

In Suits at common law, where the value in controversy shall exceed twenty dollars, the right of trial by jury shall be preserved, and no fact tried by a jury, shall be otherwise re-examined in any Court of the United States, than according to the rules of the common law.

Amendment VIII

Excessive bail shall not be required, nor excessive fines imposed, nor cruel and unusual punishments inflicted.

Amendment IX

The enumeration in the Constitution, of certain rights, shall not be construed to deny or disparage others retained by the people.

Amendment X

The powers not delegated to the United States by the Constitution, nor prohibited by it to the States, are reserved to the States respectively, or to the people.

Amendment XI

(Ratified February 7, 1795)

The Judicial power of the United States shall not be construed to extend to any suit in law or equity, commenced or prosecuted against one of the United States by Citizens of another State, or by Citizens or Subjects of any Foreign State.

Amendment XII

(Ratified June 15, 1804)

The Electors shall meet in their respective states and vote by ballot for President and Vice-President, one of whom, at least, shall not be an inhabitant of the same state with themselves; they shall name in their ballots the person voted for as President, and in distinct ballots the person voted for as Vice-President, and they shall make distinct lists of all persons voted for as President, and of all persons voted for as Vice-President, and of the number of votes for each, which lists they shall sign and certify, and transmit sealed to the seat of the government of the United States, directed to the President of the Senate; — The President of the Senate shall, in the presence of the Senate and House of Representatives, open all the certificates and the votes shall then be counted; — The person having the greatest number of votes for President, shall be the President, if such number be a majority of the whole number of Electors appointed; and if no person have such majority, then from the persons having the highest numbers not exceeding three on the list of those voted for as President, the House of Representatives shall choose immediately, by ballot, the President. But in choosing the President, the votes shall be taken by states, the representation from each state having one vote; a quorum for this purpose shall consist of a member or members from two-thirds of the states, and a majority of all the states shall be necessary to a choice. [And if the House of Representatives shall not choose a President whenever the right of choice shall devolve upon them, before the fourth day of March next following, then the Vice-President shall act as President, as in the case of the death or other constitutional disability of the President. —][11] The person having the greatest number of votes as Vice-President, shall be the Vice-President, if such number be a majority of the whole number of Electors appointed, and if no person have a majority, then from the two highest numbers on the list, the Senate shall choose the Vice-President; a quorum for the purpose shall consist of two-thirds of the whole number of Senators, and a majority of the whole number shall be necessary to a choice. But no person constitutionally ineligible to the office of President shall be eligible to that of Vice-President of the United States.

Amendment XIII

(Ratified December 6, 1865)

Section 1. Neither slavery nor involuntary servitude, except as a punishment for crime whereof the party shall have been duly convicted, shall exist within the United States, or any place subject to their jurisdiction.

Section 2. Congress shall have power to enforce this article by appropriate legislation.

Amendment XIV

(Ratified July 9, 1868)

Section 1. All persons born or naturalized in the United States, and subject to the jurisdiction thereof, are citizens of the United States and of the State wherein they reside. No State shall make or enforce any law which shall abridge the privileges or immunities of citizens of the United States; nor shall any State deprive any person of life, liberty, or property, without due process of law; nor deny to any person within its jurisdiction the equal protection of the laws.

Section 2. Representatives shall be apportioned among the several States according to their respective numbers, counting the whole number of persons in each State, excluding Indians not taxed. But when the right to vote at any election for the choice of electors for President and Vice President of the United States, Representatives in Congress, the Executive and Judicial officers of a State, or the members of the Legislature thereof, is denied to any of the male inhabitants of such State, being twenty-one years of age,[12] and citizens of the United States, or in any way abridged, except for participation in rebellion, or other crime, the basis of representation therein shall be reduced in the proportion which the number of such male citizens shall bear to the whole number of male citizens twenty-one years of age in such State.

Section 3. No person shall be a Senator or Representative in Congress, or elector of President and Vice President, or hold any office, civil or military, under the United States, or under any State, who, having previously taken an oath, as a member of Congress, or as an officer of the United States, or as a member of any State legislature, or as an executive or judicial officer of any State, to support the Constitution of the United States, shall have engaged in insurrection or rebellion against the same, or given aid or comfort to the enemies thereof. But Congress may by a vote of two-thirds of each House, remove such disability.

Section 4. The validity of the public debt of the United States, authorized by law, including debts incurred for payment of pensions and bounties for services in suppressing insurrection or rebellion, shall not be questioned. But neither the United States nor any State shall assume or pay any debt or obligation incurred in aid of insurrection or rebellion against the United States, or any claim for the loss or emancipation of any slave; but all such debts, obligations and claims shall be held illegal and void.

Section 5. The Congress shall have power to enforce, by appropriate legislation, the provisions of this article.

Amendment XV

(Ratified February 3, 1870)

Section 1. The right of citizens of the United States to vote shall not be denied or abridged by the United States or by any State on account of race, color, or previous condition of servitude.

Section 2. The Congress shall have power to enforce this article by appropriate legislation.

Amendment XVI

(Ratified February 3, 1913)

The Congress shall have power to lay and collect taxes on incomes, from whatever source derived, without apportionment among the several States, and without regard to any census or enumeration.

Amendment XVII

(Ratified April 8, 1913)

The Senate of the United States shall be composed of two Senators from each State, elected by the people thereof, for six years; and each Senator shall have one vote. The electors in each State shall have the qualifications requisite for electors of the most numerous branch of the State legislatures.

When vacancies happen in the representation of any State in the Senate, the executive authority of such State shall issue writs of election to fill such vacancies: *Provided,* That the legislature of any State may empower the executive thereof to make temporary appointments until the people fill the vacancies by election as the legislature may direct.

This amendment shall not be so construed as to affect the election or term of any Senator chosen before it becomes valid as part of the Constitution.

[Amendment XVIII

(Ratified January 16, 1919)

Section 1. After one year from the ratification of this article the manufacture, sale, or transportation of intoxicating liquors within, the importation thereof into, or the exportation thereof from the United States and all territory subject to the jurisdiction thereof for beverage purposes is hereby prohibited.

Section 2. The Congress and the several States shall have concurrent power to enforce this article by appropriate legislation.

Section 3. This article shall be inoperative unless it shall have been ratified as an amendment to the Constitution by the legislatures of the several States, as provided in the Constitution, within seven years from the date of the submission hereof to the States by the Congress.][13]

Amendment XIX

(Ratified August 18, 1920)

The right of citizens of the United States to vote shall not be denied or abridged by the United States or by any State on account of sex.

Congress shall have power to enforce this article by appropriate legislation.

Amendment XX

(Ratified January 23, 1933)

Section 1. The terms of the President and Vice President shall end at noon on the 20th day of January, and the terms of Senators and Representatives at noon on the 3d day of January, of the years in which such terms would have ended if this article had not been ratified; and the terms of their successors shall then begin.

Section 2. The Congress shall assemble at least once in every year, and such meeting shall begin at noon on the 3d day of January, unless they shall by law appoint a different day.

Section 3.[14] If, at the time fixed for the beginning of the term of the President, the President elect shall have died, the Vice President elect shall become President. If a President shall not have been chosen before the time fixed for the beginning of his term, or if the President elect shall have failed to qualify, then the Vice President elect shall act as President until a President shall have qualified; and the Congress may by law provide for the case wherein neither a President elect nor a Vice President elect shall have qualified, declaring who shall then act as President, or the manner in which one who is to act shall be selected, and such person shall act accordingly until a President or Vice President shall have qualified.

Section 4. The Congress may by law provide for the case of the death of any of the persons from whom the House of Representatives may choose a President whenever the right of choice shall have devolved upon them, and for the case of the death of any of the persons from whom the Senate may choose a Vice President whenever the right of choice shall have devolved upon them.

Section 5. Sections 1 and 2 shall take effect on the 15th day of October following the ratification of this article.

Section 6. This article shall be inoperative unless it shall have been ratified as an amendment to the Constitution by the legislatures of three-fourths of the several States within seven years from the date of its submission.

Amendment XXI

(Ratified December 5, 1933)

Section 1. The eighteenth article of amendment to the Constitution of the United States is hereby repealed.

Section 2. The transportation or importation into any State, Territory, or possession of the United States for delivery or use therein of intoxicating liquors, in violation of the laws thereof, is hereby prohibited.

Section 3. This article shall be inoperative unless it shall have been ratified as an amendment to the Constitution by conventions in the several States, as provided in the Constitution, within seven years from the date of the submission hereof to the States by the Congress.

Amendment XXII

(Ratified February 27, 1951)

Section 1. No person shall be elected to the office of the President more than twice, and no person who has held the office of President, or acted as President, for more than two years of a term to which some other person was elected President shall be elected to the office of the President more than once. But this Article shall not apply to any person holding the office of President when this Article was proposed by the Congress, and shall not prevent any person who may be holding the office of President, or acting as President, during the term within which this Article become operative from holding the office of President or acting as President during the remainder of such term.

Section 2. This article shall be inoperative unless it shall have been ratified as an amendment to the Constitution by the legislatures of three-fourths of the several States within seven years from the date of its submission to the States by the Congress.

Amendment XXIII

(Ratified March 29, 1961)

Section 1. The District constituting the seat of Government of the United States shall appoint in such manner as the Congress may direct:

A number of electors of President and Vice President equal to the whole number of Senators and Representatives in Congress to which the District would be entitled if it were a State, but in no event more than the least populous State; they shall be in addition to those appointed by the States, but they shall be considered, for the purposes of the election of President and Vice President, to be electors appointed by a State; and they shall meet in the District and perform such duties as provided by the twelfth article of amendment.

Section 2. The Congress shall have power to enforce this article by appropriate legislation.

Amendment XXIV

(Ratified January 23, 1964)

Section 1. The right of citizens of the United States to vote in any primary or other election for President or Vice President, for electors for President or Vice President, or for Senator or Representative in Congress, shall not be denied or abridged by the United States or any State by reason of failure to pay any poll tax or other tax.

Section 2. The Congress shall have power to enforce this article by appropriate legislation.

Amendment XXV

(Ratified February 10, 1967)

Section 1. In case of the removal of the President from office or of his death or resignation, the Vice President shall become President.

Section 2. Whenever there is a vacancy in the office of the Vice President, the President shall nominate a Vice President who shall take office upon confirmation by a majority vote of both Houses of Congress.

Section 3. Whenever the President transmits to the President pro tempore of the Senate and the Speaker of the House of Representatives his written declaration that he is unable to discharge the powers and duties of his office, and until he transmits to them a written declaration to the contrary, such powers and duties shall be discharged by the Vice President as Acting President.

Section 4. Whenever the Vice President and a majority of either the principal officers of the executive departments or of such other body as Congress may by law provide, transmit to the President pro tempore of the Senate and the Speaker of the House of Representatives their written declaration that the President is unable to discharge the powers and duties of his office, the Vice President shall immediately assume the powers and duties of the office as Acting President.

Thereafter, when the President transmits to the President pro tempore of the Senate and the Speaker of the House of Representatives his written declaration that no inability exists, he shall resume the powers and duties of his office unless the Vice President and a majority of either the principal officers of the executive department or of such other body as Congress may by law provide, transmit within four days to the President pro tempore of the Senate and the Speaker of the House of Representatives their written declaration that the President is unable to discharge the powers and duties of his office. Thereupon Congress shall decide the issue, assembling within forty-eight hours for that purpose if not in session. If the Congress, within twenty-one days after receipt of the latter written declaration, or, if Congress is not in session, within twenty-one days after Congress is required to assemble, determines by two-thirds vote of both Houses that the President is unable to discharge the powers and duties of his office, the Vice President shall continue to discharge the same as Acting President; otherwise, the President shall resume the powers and duties of his office.

Amendment XXVI

(Ratified July 1, 1971)

Section 1. The right of citizens of the United States, who are eighteen years of age or older, to vote shall not be denied or abridged by the United States or by any State on account of age.

Section 2. The Congress shall have power to enforce this article by appropriate legislation.

Notes

1. The part in brackets was changed by section 2 of the Fourteenth Amendment.
2. The part in brackets was changed by the first paragraph of the Seventeenth Amendment.
3. The part in brackets was changed by the second paragraph of the Seventeenth Amendment.
4. The part in brackets was changed by section 2 of the Twentieth Amendment.
5. The Sixteenth Amendment gave Congress the power to tax incomes.
6. The material in brackets has been superseded by the Twelfth Amendment.
7. This provision has been affected by the Twenty-fifth Amendment.
8. These clauses were affected by the Eleventh Amendment.
9. This paragraph has been superseded by the Thirteenth Amendment.
10. Obsolete.
11. The part in brackets has been superseded by section 3 of the Twentieth Amendment.
12. See the Nineteenth and Twenty-sixth Amendments.
13. This Amendment was repealed by section 1 of the Twenty-first Amendment.
14. See the Twenty-fifth Amendment.

Source: House Committee on the Judiciary, *The Constitution of the United States of America, as Amended,* H. Doc. 100-94, 100th Cong., 1st sess., 1987.

Index